Photoshop®

om® 2

IES®

an

WILEY

Wiley Publishing, Inc.

Photoshop® Lightroom® 2 For Dummies®

Published by
Wiley Publishing, Inc.
111 River Street
Hoboken, NJ 07030-5774
www.wiley.com

Copyright © 2008 by Wiley Publishing, Inc., Indianapolis, Indiana

Published by Wiley Publishing, Inc., Indianapolis, Indiana

Published simultaneously in Canada

For general information on our other products and services, please contact our Customer Care Department within the U.S. at 800-762-2974, outside the U.S. at 317-572-3993, or fax 317-572-4002.

For technical support, please visit www.wiley.com/techsupport.

Wiley also publishes its books in a variety of electronic formats. Some content that appears in print may not be available in electronic books.

Library of Congress Control Number: 2008930829

ISBN: 978-0-470-34539-9

Manufactured in the United States of America

10 9 8 7 6 5 4 3 2 1

About the Author

Rob Sylvan is a photographer, trainer, writer, and Web developer. In addition to being the National Association of Photoshop Professional's Lightroom Help Desk Specialist, he also serves as the site director for iStockphoto. Rob writes the "Under the Loupe" column for *Photoshop User* magazine and blogs about Lightroom at `Lightroomers.com`.

Dedication

To my beloved life partner, Paloma, without whom none of this would be possible (and not nearly as much fun), and my number one son, Quinn, through whose eyes I see the world anew each day.

Author's Acknowledgments

The fact that you're holding this book right now is more a testament to the multitude of people who made it possible than just the person who put the words to paper.

My deepest thanks go to Pete Bauer, for not only taking me on to the NAPP Help Desk, mentoring me over the years, and providing support during the writing of this book, but for opening doors to new worlds. I owe a special debt of gratitude to my Help Desk counterpart Jeanne Rubbo, who undoubtedly picked up my slack over the last few months! Of course, without NAPP I would not be where I am today, and so I would also like to extend my thanks to Scott and Kalebra Kelby, Jim Workman, Jean Kendra, Larry Becker, Jeff Kelby, and Dave Moser for creating and maintaining the most amazing professional resource I have had the pleasure of being associated with. I am also grateful to all the NAPP members who have sent in their Photoshop and Lightroom questions over the years; you served as the voice in the back of my mind as I wrote.

My undying gratitude goes to the awesome team at Wiley. To the folks I worked with directly, Bob Woerner, Paul Levesque, Brian Walls, and Steve Holmes, as well as all those behind the scenes, many thanks for your patience, support, professionalism, and most of all, for making this all come together!

Thanks to the Lightroom team at Adobe for mixing your passion and brilliance into this fantastic tool for digital photographers.

To all my friends at iStockphoto for starting me down a path so many years ago that has led me to this point in time. There are too many to name, but extra special thanks to Bruce Livingstone, Pete Rockwell, Pat Lor, and everyone who has ever made me "lol" in the forums.

All my love to my wife, Paloma, my son Quinn, and the rest of my family and friends for keeping the coffee flowing, putting up with late nights, making me get out of my chair at regular intervals, and generally taking such good care of me. We did it!

Publisher's Acknowledgments

We're proud of this book; please send us your comments through our online registration form located at www.dummies.com/register/.

Some of the people who helped bring this book to market include the following:

Acquisitions and Editorial

Senior Project Editor: Paul Levesque

Acquisitions Editor: Bob Woerner

Copy Editor: Brian Walls

Technical Editor: Steven Holmes

Editorial Manager: Leah Cameron

Editorial Assistant: Amanda Foxworth

Senior Editorial Assistant: Cherie Case

Cartoons: Rich Tennant (www.the5thwave.com)

Composition Services

Project Coordinator: Katherine Key

Layout and Graphics: Ana Carrillo, Carrie A. Cesavice, Reuben W. Davis

Proofreaders: Laura Albert, Melissa D. Buddendeck

Indexer: Ty Koontz

Special Help: Jen Riggs

Publishing and Editorial for Technology Dummies

Richard Swadley, Vice President and Executive Group Publisher

Andy Cummings, Vice President and Publisher

Mary Bednarek, Executive Acquisitions Director

Mary C. Corder, Editorial Director

Publishing for Consumer Dummies

Diane Graves Steele, Vice President and Publisher

Joyce Pepple, Acquisitions Director

Composition Services

Gerry Fahey, Vice President of Production Services

Debbie Stailey, Director of Composition Services

Contents at a Glance

Table of Contents

Introduction

*A*dobe Photoshop Lightroom — more commonly referred to simply as Lightroom — has made an incredible impact on the digital photography world in a very short time. The reason it has made such a splash is due in large part to the fact that the folks behind Lightroom started out by taking a step back and looking at all the tasks today's photographers are required to perform with their digital photos. The Lightroom team wanted to know how they could make the process of taking a photo from camera to finished output as efficient as possible while still holding to a level of quality that professionals demand. They also wanted a means to equally accommodate the surge in photographers turning to shooting in *raw* mode (where the camera saves the photo data to the memory card, but stops short of processing that data to make it look better), as well as all the photographers who still rely on working with photos in *JPEG* format (where the camera captures the data and processes it based on the in-camera settings).

What the Lightroom team found was that (unsurprisingly) photographers wanted to spend more time shooting and less time in front of their computers. Photographers wanted to have a great deal of control over how their photos were managed, edited, and prepared for output, but they wanted the process to be intuitive and visual. Photographers wanted tools that would help them make the most of the photo data that was captured by their cameras, and they wanted consistent output across display mediums (computer screen and prints). Like any group of people they wanted the best of all worlds, and who could blame them!

In rising to meet this challenge, a new way of thinking about how we photographers work with our photos emerged. The old model of having one program for downloading photos, another for managing them, one program for editing raw photos and another for JPG was just growing too cumbersome to meet today's (and tomorrow's) demands. The result of this new way of thinking was Lightroom — a single application designed to encompass all the tasks photographers face (what Lightroom refers to as a photographer's *workflow*), and present them in a seamless, logical, and visual manner. Unifying those tasks under a single interface was significant in and of itself, but the real difference Lightroom brings to the table is in what lies under its hood — a database. Referred to as a "catalog" in Lightroom terms, the database at Lightroom's core is where everything (and I do mean everything) you do to your photos gets stored, and the value it brings is twofold in that it is much faster to read and write to a database than it is to change the actual pixels in your photos, and that it is completely nondestructive since your original source photos are never changed. This approach represents a paradigm shift in digital photo management and editing!

While paradigm shifts offer new ways of doing things and the potential of improved workflows, they can sometimes be disorienting and frustrating to come to terms with at first. My hope is that this book can serve as a resource to keep you out of trouble, on task, and moving forward as you use Lightroom to take your photos from camera to output over and over again.

About This Book

I am more than just a user of Lightroom. Between my roles on the NAPP Help Desk and teaching other photographers, and my participation in various Lightroom groups, forums, and beta testing, I've worked with thousands of photographers. I've tried to understand the problems they faced, and I've helped them find solutions. I wrote this book with the intention of trying to prevent you from encountering the same problems that others have stumbled on, while also sharing the collective wisdom I've gained to make your workflow as efficient as possible.

How This Book Is Organized

Lightroom is a workflow tool by design, and within the macro workflow of capture to output there exist countless smaller workflows that cover all the micro tasks every photographer needs to complete. The very concept of a workflow implies that there is both a natural beginning and a finite end. I mean, you can't start editing a photo if you haven't first pressed the shutter, right?

I organize this book with the larger Lightroom workflow in mind, but each chapter — and even the sections within a chapter — represent all the smaller workflows that make up the larger whole. So, although there's something to be gained from following the structure I lay out in the book, if you're new to Lightroom, my hope is that you can pick up this book when you need it and jump right to the place in your workflow that you want to learn more about.

Part 1: Setting Yourself Up for Success

If you're new to Lightroom — or new to digital photography — you'll definitely want to spend some time in Part I. I've seen too many people get off on the wrong foot with Lightroom and lose time (and sleep) trying to get themselves back on track because they didn't get a few basic concepts under their belt first. I've helped quite a few folks get back on track and I know some of the more common pitfalls, so here's your chance to benefit from my past experience so you can spend more time productively working with your photos.

Part II: Managing Your Photos

Managing data might be the least sexy part of a photographer's workflow; however, it's possibly the most essential. Considering that the volume of photos we photographers are all producing is increasing each year, this is an aspect of the workflow you have no choice but to get right.

Part III: Working in Your Digital Darkroom

This part is where you work to realize the vision you had the moment the shutter clicked. For some, it's as much fun as the capture, but for others, it's a chore to accomplish the greatest quality in the least amount of time. Lightroom can meet the needs of both kinds of people.

Part IV: Sharing Your Work with the World

Unless you're satisfied with the process of only making photographs, you're going to require some form of output and sharing that extends beyond just your eyeballs. Lightroom offers several routes to output, and each has its place.

Part V: The Part of Tens

I want to achieve three things with this part of the book: I want to arm you with the best Lightroom resources available; I want you to become your own help desk; and I want to share some of my favorite Lightroom tips that I can't fit into other parts of the book. This is my favorite section, and I hope it helps to round out your experience with what came before in the previous four parts of this book.

Conventions Used in This Book

Lightroom is wonderfully identical on both Windows and Mac operating systems. I use both operating systems daily, but I create the majority of screen captures in Windows because it's been my experience that there are just more Windows users out there in the world. However, I do include Mac captures where needed to highlight the few places where there are minor differences in the interface or dialog boxes.

In the case of keyboard shortcuts (and there are many), I lead off with the Windows shortcut and always include the Mac shortcut in parentheses right after. All the shortcuts that don't require an additional modifier key are the same on both platforms.

In regards to menu commands, I use the convention of separating each menu command with this cute arrow, ⇨. For example, I tell you to choose File⇨Exit to close the application.

Icons Used in This Book

Scattered throughout this book you find some nifty little icons that point out bits of information that are especially useful, important, or noteworthy.

You see this icon the most. I include many tips to help you get the most from each aspect of the program.

There aren't many of these (thankfully). I only use them when there's a chance you might lose data if you aren't careful.

Whenever a certain piece of information isn't particularly intuitive — but very important to keep in mind — I add this icon to help it stand out.

Where to Go from Here

If you're just starting out, then my advice to you is to visit Part I sooner rather than later. Beyond that, this book is intended to be a reference that you can rely on when you find yourself stuck or that you can use proactively to avoid the most common pitfalls before you go in.

If you're interested in getting some live peer support while you explore what Lightroom has to offer, jump straight to the back of the book and get involved in the Lightroom communities I introduce in Chapter 14.

Part I
Setting Yourself Up for Success

The 5th Wave   By Rich Tennant

"I've got some new image editing software, so I took the liberty of erasing some of the smudges that kept showing up around the clouds. No need to thank me."

In this part . . .

Benjamin Franklin famously said, "An ounce of prevention is worth a pound of cure." Clearly, he didn't have Lightroom in mind, but after helping many people out of the same pitfalls over and over again, I implore you to take those words to heart before you jump into Lightroom. It isn't the things we don't know that often get us into trouble, but rather the things we think we know but get wrong. In Part I, I try to condense the wisdom of those who have gone before you, and although experience can be an excellent teacher, there's no harm in starting out on the right foot.

Chapter 1 introduces you to Lightroom and enables you to find your way around while you move forward. From there, I try to demystify what happens under the Lightroom hood and clear up some wrong assumptions that can lead to confusion when working with the Lightroom catalog (database) model. I wrap up Part I with a review of the essential digital imaging concepts that every Lightroom user should be familiar with before getting in too deep.

Introducing Lightroom

Adobe Photoshop Lightroom — from this point, *Lightroom,* because that's what everybody really calls it — is a workflow tool for digital photographers. Digital photography has come a long way in recent years. The increasing number of people who are moving from shooting in *JPG format* — where the camera processes the data captured by the sensor and produces a JPG file — to shooting *raw* — where you take over processing the "raw" capture data to create the type of file you need — has created a huge need for tools to help manage the processing of large numbers of raw files. Lightroom is not just a raw processing tool though! You can tweak and adjust JPG, TIF, and PSD files, too. And that's just the thing. We have so many files and file types that need to be managed, processed, and delivered! Although many raw-processing applications are on the market, few are as ambitious, multifaceted, and well designed as Lightroom. Add to the mix the idea of an integrated workflow application and you have real state-of-the-art software.

Okay, I've dropped the term *workflow* twice now. It's probably time to get my definition out in the open because you're going to hear me repeat it quite often throughout this book. The goal of a workflow is to increase efficiency when it comes to carrying out the necessary (but often repeatable and at times unexciting) steps required to complete a task. One way to streamline your process is to increase efficiency in the transitions that occur as you move from task to task. Another way is to develop a repeatable methodology for how you do things, so that you always start with task A, then move to task B, and so on. By developing a well-thought out procedure, you don't lose time wondering what to do next or forgetting where you've been. Lightroom comes to our aid on both counts. By providing a unified interface for the full spectrum of digital photography tasks, you aren't juggling three or four different applications at the same time. You can literally plug your camera into one end of Lightroom and produce prints, Web galleries, and more from the other. At the same time, each area — called a *module* — inside of Lightroom is structured to create a logical "start to finish" flow, which makes it really easy to know where you are and where you go next, and that's what a workflow is all about.

Adding Lightroom to Your Photo Toolkit

A photographer at any experience level is going to be carting around a serious amount of gear. Even the accessories have accessories! Although some photographers might derive some pleasure from getting new gear (okay, maybe a lot of pleasure), this stuff isn't cheap! So, each new addition to the family should pass muster and be worthy of being included. Here are some things I try to consider before adding new stuff:

- ✓ **Is it well supported?**
- ✓ **Does it play nicely with others?**
- ✓ **What can it do?**
- ✓ **What can't it do?**

Of course, money is a big factor in any purchasing process, but I assume that if you're at this stage in the decision-making process you've already accounted for your budget. I'm sure you have other considerations as well, but let me address how Lightroom stacks up in my experience.

Is it well supported?

Lightroom first appeared on the scene as a *beta release* back in January 2006, meaning it was incomplete but functional (although not without bugs) software that was free to use and test drive. Over the course of this beta phase (which lasted a year), Adobe was very keen for feedback and the Lightroom development team was actively engaged with the users of the product in a dedicated online discussion forum. Several improved beta versions were released before the final version 1.0 was made available in February 2007. Not only did a better product emerge from this process, but also a community of highly proficient Lightroom users evolved and is still growing strong. An incredible amount of tips, tricks, tutorials, and troubleshooting help has become available online from both Adobe and various users of the product because of this collaborative process.

You can find out more about how to get involved with the Lightroom community and where to find the best-available Lightroom resources in Chapter 14. Trust me; Lightroom is an incredibly well-supported product!

Does it play nicely with others?

Tools don't operate in a vacuum. At the very least, any new tools you adopt need to coexist with and complement your existing toolset. At the end of the day, new tools should help you get more from your old tools by helping you become more efficient, producing better results all around.

Image-editing applications, such as Photoshop or Photoshop Elements, have long been required for working with digital images because you have to push pixels around even when you're just shooting film and scanning. You might have had to correct for red-eye, crop to a new aspect ratio, enhance colors, remove spots, convert to grayscale, or do any number of other routine tasks. Whenever such a task came up, you always turned to your image editor of choice to get the job done — and you'll want to continue being able to do so in the future.

To sift through all those photos on your hard drive, you've undoubtedly used some type of file browser like Windows Explorer, Finder, or Adobe Bridge. You might have also used that file browser for routine maintenance tasks like renaming, moving, and deleting files. Perhaps you also used one of these applications for copying files from your memory card to your hard drive.

You've worked out routines, you know what each tool accomplishes and you know where to find everything. Along comes Lightroom and people rightfully ask, "How will this fit into my routine?" More to the point, folks want to know whether they have to give up something they like in adopting Lightroom and be stuck with doing some tasks in less-productive ways. In hopes of alleviating some of those worries, here's a closer look at how Lightroom stacks up against the image editors and file browsers that you know and use every day.

How Lightroom differs from Photoshop and Adobe Bridge

You can get by without Lightroom — I mean, people managed without Lightroom until recently, right? You can switch between Adobe Bridge (file browser) and Photoshop (image editor), can throw in an FTP (File Transfer Protocol) application when you need to upload Web galleries, or even use a third-party printing application when you want more control over print layouts than what Photoshop provides. You can always cobble together something, but wouldn't it be much more efficient if you could just use a single interface to import your photos from your memory card, add vital metadata, cull the clunkers, rate and group the keepers, throw together a slideshow, upload a Web gallery, and print out a contact sheet? What if you could do all that — and even save steps and settings as reusable shortcuts — from one application?

Wouldn't that change everything about how you work with your digital photos? Yes, of course! This is where Lightroom comes in. As a workflow tool, Lightroom takes over the management of your photos at the point you're copying them from your memory card and then brings them all the way to output and delivery.

Since I began using Lightroom, I've all but abandoned Adobe Bridge for viewing and interacting with my photos. As a file browser, Bridge is a superior tool to Lightroom in many ways except one; Bridge can only show you what you point it at, as Bridge doesn't retain any information about what it has seen in the past. Comparatively, Lightroom is database driven, which means that after you introduce it to your photos (via an "import" process) it remembers everything about them. Being able to leverage the power of a database adds tremendous muscle to the management and processing of your photos.

With regard to editing photos, many people rightly wonder if Lightroom is an adequate replacement for Photoshop. Although I use Photoshop less now that I'm using Lightroom, Photoshop (or another image editor) is still a vital part of my toolkit — as I make clear in a sec. As a raw processor, though, Lightroom is able to leverage its database to work faster and smarter than the combination of Adobe Camera Raw and Photoshop. Because Lightroom and Camera Raw share essentially the same processing engine, you get all the benefits of Camera Raw built into Lightroom.

What kind of benefits, you ask? Okay, time for brass tacks: As an image processor, Lightroom can accomplish many tasks normally done by image editors or other raw photo processors, including the following:

- **Setting white balance**
- **Making tonal adjustments**
- **Reducing noise**
- **Enhancing colors**
- **Cropping**
- **Applying sharpening**

Not bad, right? Yet, although Lightroom covers a lot of ground, it can't do everything you might want to do with your photos. At times, you might need a pixel-editing application in your digital photo toolbox. If you need to perform any of the following tasks, for example, Lightroom would not be your tool of choice:

- **Working with selections**
- **Stitching together panoramas**
- **Creating high dynamic range photos**
- **Working with filters**
- **Combining multiple photos into one**

Adobe Photoshop is the prime tool to complement Lightroom. It gives you the most power and offers the greatest functionality (and tightest integration with Photoshop CS3). However, if you don't need that much power (or don't want to spend that much money), consider Photoshop Elements the next best option. Although not as full featured as its big brother, Elements can push pixels with the best of them. (Truth be told, when you consider all the features in Lightroom against your own needs, you may find that you won't need anything else for most of your work.)

Checking out the Lightroom Modules

Lightroom was built using a *modular* architecture, which means that Lightroom comprises a set of unique applications that share a common interface and that access a common database (or *catalog,* as Lightroom calls it). Each of the applications is referred to as a *module,* and Lightroom has five.

None of these modules can function outside of Lightroom. Although tightly integrated, they each have a set of unique menus, panels, and tools that tailor to the specific function each module is designed to handle.

I drill down into the specific panels, tools, and menus in the chapters ahead, but for now, I'm going to do the overview thing by taking a stab at what makes each module unique and then showing you how to get the most out of the common interface they all share.

What makes each module unique

Lightroom has five modules — but the beauty of modular construction is that the potential exists for more (perhaps many more) to be added. Adobe has opened only limited aspects of Lightroom's guts to third-party developers (just export functionality so far), and the outcome has been very positive.

The potential for extending Lightroom's functionality in the future is something to look forward to, but there's already plenty of power under the hood. Here's a list of the five modules you find in Lightroom:

- ✔ **The Library module:** Your organizational hub, the Library module (see Figure 1-1) is where many of your Lightroom sessions will start and end. Common Library module tasks include

  - *Keywording and metadata entry*

  - *File moving, deletion, and renaming*

  - *Finding, sorting, and grouping*

- ✔ **The Develop module:** The bulk of your image processing takes place in the Develop module. Armed with a powerful array of image-adjustment tools, as shown in Figure 1-2, common Develop module tasks include

  - *Setting white balance and tonal adjustments*

  - *Adjusting contrast and color*

  - *Reducing noise and capture sharpening*

  - *Cropping and adjusting crooked horizons*

  - *Removing red-eye and sensor spots*

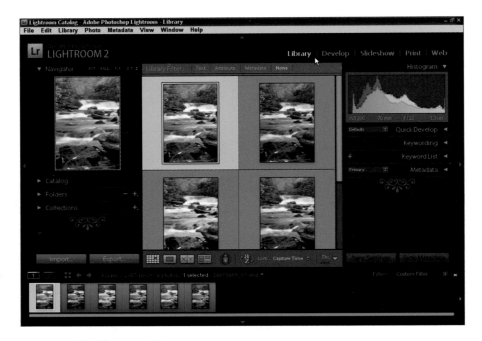

Figure 1-1: The Library module.

Figure 1-2: The Develop module.

✔ **The Slideshow module:** The aptly named Slideshow module, shown in Figure 1-3, is for creating presentations of your photos. The tools in this module allow you to

- *Adjust slideshow layout*
- *Adjust slide transitions*
- *Set the show to music*

✔ **The Print module:** If you print photos, you'll soon find the Print module, as shown in Figure 1-4, to be a valuable addition to your printing workflow. Here you find controls for

- *Creating layouts and print packages*
- *Using output-specific color profiles to ensure the best-looking prints (Chapters 3 and 13 cover profiles in greater depth)*
- *Printing to a local printer or to a JPG file*

✔ **The Web module:** Getting your photos online in some capacity is a requirement these days. The Web module, as shown in Figure 1-5, allows you to manage your Web presence by letting you

- *Choose from various photo gallery styles*
- *Configure the look and feel of your Web gallery*
- *Upload directly to your Web server*

Figure 1-3: The Slideshow module.

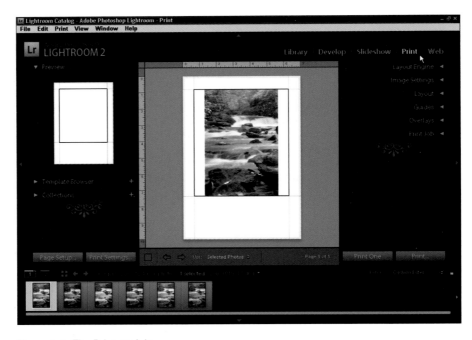

Figure 1-4: The Print module.

Figure 1-5: The Web module.

What the modules have in common

Having all modules share parts of a common interface might make it harder (at first glance) to tell which module is which, but I wouldn't worry too much about that. Clarity will reign supreme when you have Lightroom up and running. Think of it this way: A common interface is in fact one of Lightroom's greatest strengths because keeping the same interface means you don't have to spend time learning five different interfaces! The interface behaves the same and shares the same basic structure no matter where you are.

Check out Figure 1-6 to see what I mean. The Library module shown there sports the following standard interface components — components that each module shares:

- **The Title bar:** Provides an at-a-glance view of the name of the catalog and the module you're in.

- **The Menu bar:** The go-to place for all the commands needed for each module's tasks.

- **The Module Picker:** An easy method to pick the module you want to work with. This area of the interface is also home to the Identity Plate on the left, which you can customize to insert your own graphic, as well as the progress meter that appears when Lightroom performs a task. (For more on the Identity Plate, check out Chapter 5.)

- **The Left Panel group:** Although the content varies with each module, the panels to the left of the interface are generally functions that involve accessing, grouping, and previewing photos and templates.

- **The Right Panel group:** The panels to the right of the interface also vary with each module, but this is where you find controls for adjusting and tweaking.

- **The Toolbar:** Each module has its own set of tools, but the Toolbar is a staple of every module.

- **The Filmstrip:** At the bottom of every module, you always find the Filmstrip, which displays thumbnails of the image grouping you are working with. It also is home to a row of tools — right there along the top — that put a lot of things at your fingertips no matter what module you are in:

    - *Main and Second Window controls.* Click and hold either of these window icons to access a number of shortcuts for controlling each window (more details on the second window function later in the chapter).

    - *Jump to Grid view icon.* No matter where you are in Lightroom, one click takes you to Grid view in the Library module.

- *Go Back and Forward buttons.* Allow you to navigate between previously selected image groupings (folders, collections, searches) you have been viewing.

- *Filmstrip Source Indicator.* Provides an at-a-glance view of the current image grouping and active photo. Click the drop-down arrow at the end for quick access to the special collections found in the Catalog panel as well as a list of recently visited folders and collections.

- *Filters.* When clicked, the Filter label expands to reveal ways to filter the current image grouping by flag, rating, or color label. The Custom Filter drop-down menu provides quick access to all of the Filter Bar options. The last button on the right toggles filtering on and off.

Menu bar   Module Picker

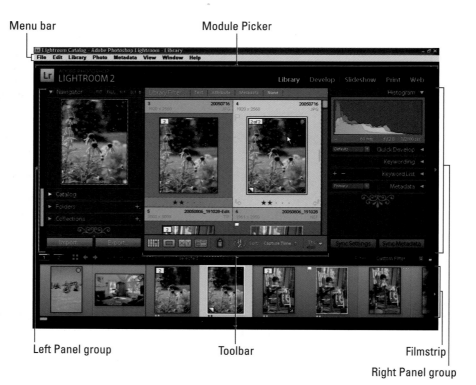

Left Panel group   Toolbar   Filmstrip

Right Panel group

Figure 1-6: The interface components.

Controlling the interface

Lightroom's interface has a number of options for reducing and simplifying the workspace. Here's an example: My publishers forced me to capture the images of Lightroom in this book at a screen resolution of 1024 x 768 (don't ask me why), so things are looking a little cramped. No way would I work at this resolution, though — I'd naturally bump it up to the highest resolution my monitor supports so I could have as much space to work with as possible. However, sometimes there's just not enough room for everything the interface has to offer — usually those times when you really just want to give as much screen real estate to your photos as possible. Imagine trying to work on a project in your shop and being forced to lay all your tools in neat rows on the workbench — I guess it's handy, but you surely won't have as much space as you'd like for the project you're working on. Lightroom has some pretty clever ways of tweaking how your tools are displayed so you can maximize the size of your workspace.

The simplest way to maximize space is to take advantage of working in Full Screen mode. Just like any application you currently use, you're just a keystroke away from maximizing Lightroom to fill the available screen. The neat thing about Lightroom, though, is that it takes this maximizing business a step further by providing two separate Full Screen modes in addition to the Standard Screen mode:

- **Full Screen with Menu:** With this option, Lightroom expands to fill the screen and hide its title bar to gain more space. The Menu bar jumps to the top of the screen. Note that the standard Minimize, Maximize, and Close buttons vanish from the top of the window in this mode.

- **Full Screen:** With this option, Lightroom expands to take over the screen completely. The Menu bar disappears and the taskbar in Windows (the Dock on a Mac) isn't accessible.

- **Standard Screen:** All options are visible and the Lightroom interface can be resized and moved by grabbing the edge of the window just like any other application.

To switch between the three screen modes just press the F key to jump from one view to another. Keep in mind, though, that if it appears as if you "lost" the Minimize, Maximize, and Close buttons at the top of the window (the horror!), what's really happened is that you've simply entered one of the Full Screen modes. (I can't tell you how many panicked e-mails I've received from folks who believe they've somehow lopped off said buttons by mistake, asking whether I could please help them get back their buttons.)

If you still want more space, you can take advantage of the collapsible nature of the Module Picker, Panel groups, and Filmstrip. Refer back to Figure 1-6 for a sec. Do you see the small arrow in the center of the outer edge of each side of the interface? Clicking an arrow once causes that panel to "hide" from view. Now, move your cursor away and then back over any part of that edge and the hidden panel returns, giving you access to the contents of the panel until you move the cursor away again! This is called "Auto Hide & Show." Right-click (Control+click on a Mac) an arrow and you can see the other possible choices:

- **Auto Hide:** When enabled, that panel automatically hides when you move your cursor away from it, but it won't show again until you click the arrow. I personally like this option because the Auto Show kicking in every time I get to close to the edge tends to drive me nuts.

- **Manual:** No Auto Hiding or Showing. Click an arrow to hide and it stays that way until you click again.

- **Sync with opposite panel:** When checked, the settings you apply to one panel will be equally applied to the panel on the opposite side.

I find a more convenient method for showing and hiding these screen elements is the keyboard shortcuts:

- **F5:** Show/hide the Module Picker.

- **F6:** Show/hide the Filmstrip.

- **F7:** Show/hide the Left Panel group.

- **F8:** Show/hide the Right Panel group.

- **Tab:** Show/hide both the Left and Right panel groups.

- **Shift+Tab:** Show/hide the Left, Right, Top and Bottom.

When it comes to clearing the clutter and focusing on your photos, Lightroom has one further cool trick up its sleeve. It's called Lights Out mode and has three states:

- **Lights On:** The normal operating condition, where everything is visible.

- **Lights Dim:** In this mode, your selected photos remain unchanged but the surrounding interface dims. Although dimmed, the interface is accessible and functional (if you know where things are).

- **Lights Out:** Taking the dim view to the extreme, the entire interface is blacked out and only your photos are visible. The ultimate way to reduce clutter!

You can jump through each Lights Out mode by pressing the L key. You set the amount of dimming and the color the screen dims to in the preferences (I cover all the preference settings a little later in the chapter).

Using the secondary display view

The ultimate way to gain more screen real estate is to add another screen! Dual monitor support is a new addition in Lightroom 2.0 and a most welcome one at that. Lightroom's approach to dual monitor support is the addition of a second Lightroom window that you can move to your second monitor. The result is that you have the same primary Lightroom window on one monitor (this is where you access all the modules and do your work) and then your secondary display window provides additional ways to view the photos you are working on. (While it's possible to enable the secondary window on a single monitor system, it is limited in its usefulness as it competes for the same screen real estate as the primary window.)

The secondary display window functions in the same manner with all Lightroom modules. Here are the options available in the secondary window:

- **Grid:** By using the Grid option, you essentially extend the Filmstrip to the second window so that it provides greater access to all the thumbnails of the current group of photos. The secondary window Grid view functions the same as Grid view in the Library module (see Chapter 5 for more information on Grid view).

- **Loupe:** Allows for viewing a single image in its entirety or zoomed in close within the second window. Loupe has three options:

  - *Normal:* Always displays the active photo selected in the primary window.

  - *Live:* Continually displays the photo under the cursor as you move over photos in the main window.

  - *Locked:* Allows you to choose one photo to display continuously in the second window while you view a different photo in the primary window.

- **Compare:** Allows you to compare two or more photos side by side. The secondary window Compare view functions the same way as Compare view in the Library module. (See Chapter 6 for more information on Compare view.)

- **Survey:** Allows you to view multiple photos side by side within the secondary window. The secondary window Survey view functions the same way as Survey view in the Library module. (See Chapter 6 for more information on Survey view.)

- **Slideshow:** Only available when you have the secondary window set to full screen (not possible on a single monitor system). This option allows you to run the slideshow on the secondary display.

There is one other cool option related to the secondary window called Show Second Monitor Preview. (It only works when the secondary window is in full screen mode.) When enabled, it provides a small preview window showing what's being displayed in the secondary window. Huh? It's intended for situations where you might have your secondary monitor facing away from you and toward an audience. This way you can be showing photos to an audience on the secondary display while you work on the primary display, and the preview window lets you have a peek at what your audience is seeing.

You can enable and disable the second window by clicking its icon on the Filmstrip, choosing Window➪Second Window➪Enable from the main menu, or by pressing F11 (⌘+F11 on a Mac).

Getting Up and Running

I'm sure you're chomping at the bit for the opportunity to roll up your sleeves and start putting Lightroom through its paces. I don't blame you! You're gonna love it. However, if you take the time to lay the groundwork so that you get all your ducks in a row, you're sure to start on the right foot (could I cram in any more metaphors?).

Preparing for installation

Don't think of an application installation as being a tiresome chore. Rather, think of it is a perfect excuse to do a little hard disk housekeeping. What better time to do tasks like the following:

- **Freeing up disk space by deleting unused files, clearing caches, moving files to another disk, and emptying the Trash**
- **Running an error-checking application**
- **Running a defragmentation application (Windows only)**

The best reason to clean house before installing is that it might just prevent problems that you'd likely blame on the new application you just installed. So save yourself some aggravation and run those programs now while you're busy reading this book!

I assume you've confirmed that your system meets the posted minimum requirements before you purchased Lightroom (or downloaded the trial), but generally, it's always in your best interest to exceed the minimum whenever possible for best performance. Here's what matters most:

- **RAM:** Maximizing the amount of installed RAM is probably going to give you the most bang for your buck. It's more than likely that you'll be running other applications alongside Lightroom, so the more RAM you have the better for everyone.

- **Processor:** Processing large volumes of huge files takes horsepower. Lightroom is able to take advantage of multi-core processors, so if an upgrade is in your future, put that under consideration.

- **Disk space:** When working with digital images, you just can't have enough disk space. If you're shooting raw on a 10-, 12-, 17+-megapixel camera, you don't want to worry about running out of storage space. Beyond storage, you need ample free space on your startup drive so that all your applications and your operating system have enough elbow room to function. I like using 500 GB external drives because they are relatively inexpensive, and easy to add and remove.

✓ **Monitor:** You might think you're looking at your photos, but you are in fact looking at your monitor. (I actually don't want to think about how many hours in a day I spend basking in its glow.) For the benefit of your eyes and the quality of your editing, consider a monitor upgrade in your future. The truth is, the monitors that typically come bundled with most computers are better suited to word processing, Web browsing, and e-mail. Your choices will be limited to LCD-type monitors (the thin flat kind) as they just don't make the CRT-type monitors (the big TV-like kind) anymore. This is probably a good time to call in a friend to help you shop if you're not sure where to start, but here are a few things to keep in mind:

- *Price:* Quality in a monitor doesn't come cheap. At the high end, you could look at models from Eizo and LaCie, although many people I know are quite happy on the higher end with Dell and Apple. The technology is improving and prices are falling.

- *Size:* Bigger is usually better. Your monitor is your desk space. The bigger your desk, the easier it is to work. 19" - 30" are pretty typical for photo work.

- *Resolution:* A monitor's resolution is expressed by how many pixels across by how many pixels down it can display (such as 1024 x 768). The larger the number, the more pixels will be displayed, which means the more room you have to work, but it also means things will appear smaller. Huh? Here's why. The actual size of the monitor (the inches across) can't change, right? So the only thing that can change is the size of the pixels. The more pixels you add in, the smaller they have to get to fit. A high-resolution monitor might have a resolution of 1920 x 1200. You really have a lot of screen real estate at that resolution. 1920 x 1200 on a 24" monitor is a nice size to work with. 1920 x 1200 on a 17" monitor requires keen eyesight or glasses.

- *Graphics card:* This is the part of your computer that drives the video display. You need to have a powerful-enough graphics card to run your monitor at its native size. You don't want to cart home a monitor your system can't handle. Have all your computer's specifications with you when you shop and ask the salespeople what you will need.

Installing Lightroom is straightforward, whether you download the files from Adobe's Web site or have a disk. You're going to be doing the standard things, like double-clicking the installer file, accepting the end user license agreement, and following the on-screen prompts. You know the drill. I suggest installing in the default location and simply following along with the installation instructions. I also highly recommend taking a few seconds to skim the Lightroom

Read Me file included with the installation files. It contains all the basic need-to-know information about installing the software. It's a good first place to check if you encounter any problems installing or running the application.

Configuring your settings

Lightroom's default preference settings are very good for getting you up and running, but that doesn't mean there aren't a few tweaks that could suit your workflow a little better. You adjust the seat or mirrors in your car every now and then, right? You'll probably want to do the same with Lightroom.

To see what's what with your default settings, first open the Preferences dialog box by choosing Edit➪Preferences (Lightroom➪Preferences on a Mac) from the main menu or by using the keyboard shortcut Ctrl+, (⌘+, on a Mac). The Preferences dialog box appears on-screen in all its glory, as shown in Figure 1-7. What you see here are global preference settings, meaning these preferences are in effect regardless of which *catalog* — which Lightroom database file, in other words — you have open. Although many of these preferences are self-explanatory, a few are worth digging into. I do the digging for you in the next few sections.

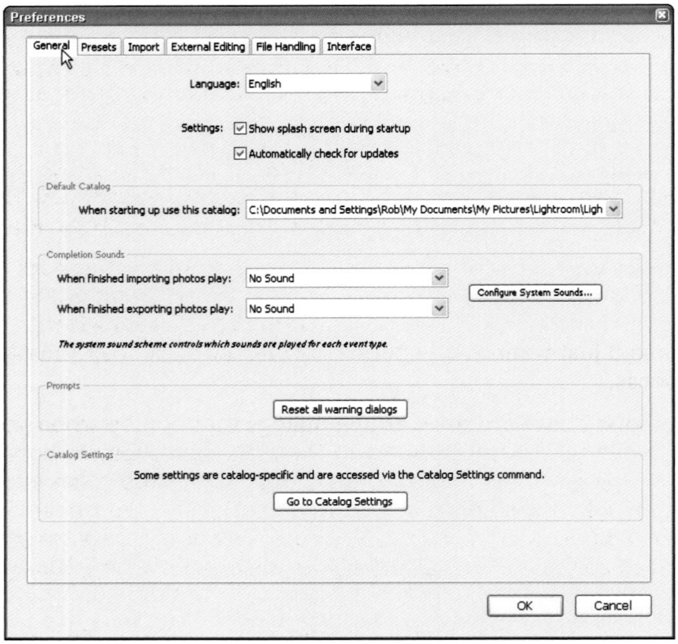

Figure 1-7: The Preferences dialog box.

General preferences

The General preferences tab is kind of like the catchall drawer in the kitchen; it's got all the stuff that didn't fit neatly anywhere else.

- **Language:** Choose the language you want Lightroom to use for its menus and options.

- **Settings:** Here you can choose to tweak two settings: whether the fancy startup screen appears every time you fire up Lightroom and whether Lightroom checks for software updates automatically. The fancy startup screen? That's a personal preference, and I leave that choice up to you. The automatic updates stuff is a bit different. If you cast your mind back to the first time you ran Lightroom, you'll remember that you were asked if you wanted Lightroom to keep track of (and automatically install) any software updates that might come down the pike. If you at first said, "No, thanks" but have since changed your mind, you can enable (or disable) automatic software updates here.

  Software updates aren't minor things, nor are they uncommon. Over the course of the life of Lightroom version 1, there were some significant bug fixes and functionality enhancements released as updates, along with support for newer camera models and their raw file formats. All such fixes and enhancements were made available as software updates.

  Lots of folks like the idea of having Lightroom keep track of any software updates, but if you'd rather be in control of when your applications phone home, then be sure to periodically choose Help⇨Check from the main menu to check for updates.

- **Default catalog:** I cover the use of multiple catalogs in Chapter 2, but in most cases, setting the default catalog to your specific catalog file ensures you always open the same catalog file no matter what.

- **Completion sounds:** The settings for completion sounds are pretty straightforward and entirely personal. Audible prompts are helpful when you start a big import or export and then busy yourself with some other task and just want a little notice of when Lightroom has finished the process.

- **Prompts:** These are the warning dialogs that pop up when you attempt to do things like move photos or folders. Some prompts have a Don't Show Again option to disable them from appearing in the future, which is great when you find the warning prompts slow you down. However, they can help keep you out of trouble, so if you change your mind and want to enable them again, click the Reset All Warning Dialogs button to bring them back.

- **Catalog settings:** The Catalog Settings button is a holdover from version 1, but is worth mentioning. Keep in mind that Lightroom has essentially two types of preference settings: Those that are *global,* meaning they affect the operation of the program (regardless of what catalog is open), and those that are *catalog specific,* which control certain aspects of how each catalog functions. The catalog-specific preferences have moved to the Catalog Settings dialog box, which you can access by clicking the Go to Catalog Settings button or by choosing File⇨Catalog Settings (Lightroom⇨Catalog Settings on a Mac) from the main menu.

The Presets preferences

The Presets tab is shown in Figure 1-8. This is one-stop shopping for all the settings that pertain to Lightroom's default presets and templates, and is broken into three sections, as follows:

- **Default Develop Settings:** These four check boxes control Lightroom's default behavior when it comes to processing photos:

  - *Apply Auto Tone Adjustments:* This setting attempts to automatically adjust the exposure, blacks, brightness, and contrast for best results. The Lightroom team has greatly improved the Auto Tone setting in Lightroom 2, but I wouldn't apply it as a default until you've had some time to test it on your photos to see if you like what it does. If you find it creates a favorable starting point, you can always come back here and enable it.

  - *Apply Auto Grayscale Mix When Converting to Grayscale:* If you use Lightroom to convert to grayscale, you can check this box to let Lightroom take a stab at the best conversion settings, or leave it unchecked and start with the Grayscale Mix sliders zeroed out. Lightroom actually does a pretty good job, so I leave this one checked.

  - *Make Defaults Specific to Camera Serial Number:* If you customize the Camera Calibration tab (see Chapter 8) you can check this box to have the customization apply to each specific camera serial number instead of just by camera model. You'll likely leave this unchecked.

  - *Make Defaults Specific to Camera ISO Setting:* If you customize the Camera Calibration tab (see Chapter 8) you can check this box to have the customization apply to each specific ISO setting instead of the same for all ISO settings. You'll likely leave this unchecked.

- **Location:** By default, Lightroom stores all your presets in a central location that's accessible to any catalog you might have open at the time. This makes the most sense for most Lightroom users. However, if you'd prefer to store your presets folder within the same folder as your catalog file, you can check this box and Lightroom will move them over. Click the Show Lightroom Presets Folder button for quick access to your preset files.

- **Lightroom Defaults:** This collection of buttons serves a single purpose, which is to set each type of preset collection back to its default state. If presets ever seem to go missing, come back here and click the button that corresponds to the type of missing preset.

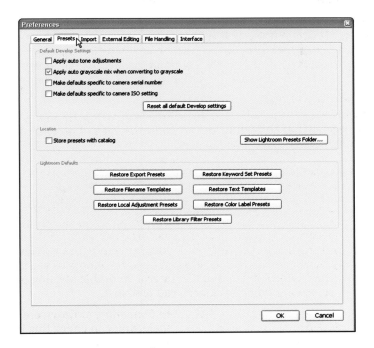

Figure 1-8: The Presets preferences.

The Import preferences

The Import preferences tab, shown in Figure 1-9, controls the settings Lightroom uses when importing photos into your catalog. Here are your choices:

- **Show Import Dialog When a Memory Card is Detected:** I find it very helpful to leave this check box selected because I use Lightroom exclusively for managing my digital photos, so I always want the Import dialog box to open when I pop a card in my card reader. That said, if you find that the dialog box is getting in your way, then by all means uncheck this option and launch the import process manually.

- **Ignore Camera-generated Folder Names When Naming Folders:** I don't know why anyone would want to use the folder names created by their cameras when writing files to the memory cards because such names usually only make sense to the cameras. I recommend keeping this option checked and relying on your own folder-naming scheme.

- **Treat JPEG Files Next to Raw Files as Separate Photos:** By using Lightroom, I no longer find shooting Raw+JPG useful and I prefer having more room on my memory cards for more raw files. (Raw+JPG just doesn't work for me because the way Lightroom renders your raw files won't always match the JPG from the camera.) However, if reasons or habit dictate that you shoot Raw+JPG and you want to import them both as separate files into Lightroom (so that you can work with both versions), then check this box. Otherwise, Lightroom treats the JPEG files as a type of sidecar file and won't display them within Lightroom.

✔ **Import DNG Creation:** These settings pertain to the Copy Photos as Digital Negative (DNG) and Add to Catalog Import option. The lowercase file extension is the norm, so there's no reason to change it. The medium size JPEG preview is a good compromise on file size. The default conversion method settings are great because they preserve the raw data and create a smaller file using lossless compression. The big choice is if you want to embed the original raw file or not. You would want to embed the original raw file if you felt there may come a point in time where you might want to extract the original raw file so that you could process it in software that doesn't work with DNG. The downside to embedding the original raw file is that you double the file's size because you will have the converted raw data (this is what Lightroom will use) and then will add the entire original unaltered file as well (which just sits untouched in case some day it is needed). I prefer to leave this unchecked.

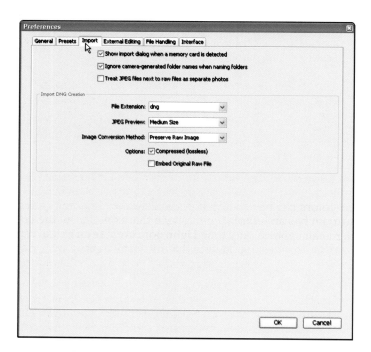

Figure 1-9: The Import preferences.

The External Editing preferences

If you have Photoshop or Photoshop Elements installed, you'll see, as shown in Figure 1-10, that it's configured as your primary external editor. (In my case, it is Photoshop CS3.) You can also configure other applications to have additional editors. However, if you don't have Photoshop or Photoshop Elements installed, you'll only be able to configure the Additional Editor option, as the first slot is reserved exclusively for the two Adobe products.

The purpose of this dialog box is to configure the default settings Lightroom uses when you send a copy of a photo with Lightroom adjustments to an external editor for additional work. Remember, Lightroom never alters your source photos, so if you want to take all the work you have done in Lightroom and apply it to a file so that you can continue working in a different application, then Lightroom has to create a copy of that photo first. These are the settings Lightroom uses to create that copy. You'll also configure what applications (if any) you want to use as an additional editor in this dialog box.

All external editors have the same basic file-setting options (File Format, Color Space, Bit Depth, Resolution, and Compression) to be configured. You do need to configure both editors independently, but this gives you the opportunity to set up each editor differently. The options you choose are going to be determined by your own needs and the type of editor you are using. After giving you a closer look at the file options, I'll go over the steps for adding additional editors. Here are the file options:

- **File Format:** You have two file format options to choose from — TIFF and PSD. Both formats support layers, 16-bit files, and available color spaces. PSD is Photoshop's native file format, but it's a proprietary format and not as widely supported outside the Adobe family of applications. In light of this, my preference is to use TIFF, but there's no wrong choice here.

- **Color Space:** You can find out more about color spaces in Chapter 3, but in a nutshell, a *color space* is a way to define a range of colors so that those colors can be accurately reproduced on different systems. Lightroom has an internal color space that contains all the colors your camera can capture. Any time Lightroom creates an actual rendered copy of your source files, it converts that file from Lightroom's internal color space to the output color space you've chosen. You have three color spaces to choose from:

    - *ProPhoto RGB:* A 16-bit color space capable of holding all the colors captured by your camera, ProPhoto RGB is very similar to Lightroom's working color space, and therefore, the recommended setting.

    - *AdobeRGB (1998):* An 8-bit color space without as many colors as ProPhoto RGB, AdobeRGB (1998) is a common color space for digital photographers who are used to shooting JPG. This is your best choice if you choose 8 bit in the Bit Depth drop-down list.

- *sRGB:* Also an 8-bit color space, but with fewer saturated colors than Adobe RGB, sRGB has its place as an output color space, but it isn't a good choice when sending files to be edited in Photoshop.

✓ **Bit Depth:** This setting determines how much data is contained in a file. The more bits the more information. The more information the better for editing purposes. 16 bit is the recommended option if you're working with raw files. 8 bit is recommended if you're working with JPG.

✓ **Resolution:** Ultimately, the resolution setting only comes into play when you are printing. In this context, it simply sets the resolution tag in the new file's metadata so that it is there if needed. It doesn't affect the number of pixels in the file whatsoever. You'll see 240 as the default setting; however, if your workflow requires that files have a different resolution setting (such as 300) then you can enter that here.

✓ **Compression:** This option is only available when TIFF is selected as the file format. ZIP is a lossless compression format. Your choices here are to use no compression (None) or apply compression (ZIP). Some other applications have trouble handling compressed TIFFs, so if you want a more compatible choice, choose None. If you want to save a bit of disk space, then choose ZIP.

Setting up additional external editors

In Lightroom 1, you could only choose one additional editor, but that functionality has been expanded to allow for multiple additional editors. In a nutshell, you choose an editor, configure its settings, and then save those settings as a preset. You can create as many presets as you need. Here are the steps:

1. **In the Additional External Editor section, click the Choose button.**

2. **Navigate to and select the application you want to use as an editor.**

   You'll see the name of this application listed next to Application back in the Preferences dialog box.

3. **Configure all the file-setting options for the type of files you want to send to that editor.**

4. **Choose Save Current Settings as New Preset from the Preset drop-down menu.**

5. **Give the preset a name and click Create.**

   You'll see this name listed under the Photo⇨Edit in the menu so make it descriptive of both the application and file settings.

You can repeat those steps for any additional editors or configuration of settings for the same editor.

When Lightroom renders a copy to send to Photoshop, it appends a -Edit suffix to the copy by default. You can customize this suffix in the Edit Externally File Naming section at the bottom of the dialog box, but I'd say, unless you have a real need to change the suffix, the default works just fine.

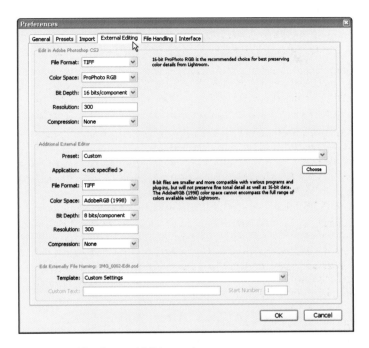

Figure 1-10: The External Editing preferences.

The File Handling preferences

Figure 1-11 shows the File Handling preference settings. This is another one of those catchall collections of settings, so let me go through each section and make some sense of what can be done here:

- ✔ **Reading Metadata:** It is possible to create structure or hierarchies in your keywords (i.e., you might have a keyword "Animal" and then under it you would nest all the types of animals in your photos). There's no single standard for what character must be used to separate hierarchical keywords when they are written into a file's metadata. Lightroom automatically recognizes the | (pipe) character between two words as a means to denote structure, but if you use other programs that use either a . (dot) or a / (slash) as a keyword separator, then check the respective boxes in the preferences; Lightroom respects your choice during import as well, so that your keyword structure is maintained.

- ✔ **File Name Generation:** Different operating systems and even different applications can have problems with certain characters being used within filenames. The settings in the File Name Generation section allow you to configure how Lightroom responds to these characters when it encounters them in a filename. Here's what I recommend for creating a consistent and bombproof approach to dealing with problematic filenames:

- Choose the largest set of characters to treat as illegal.

- Choose either dashes or underscores to be used as a replacement character when an illegal character is encountered.

- Choose the same character you chose in Step 2 to be used as a replacement for any spaces found in a filename.

✔ **Camera Raw Cache Settings:** The intended purpose of any cache is to store (usually temporarily) frequently accessed data to speed up the processes that require that data to function. In this case, Lightroom shares a cache with Adobe Camera Raw, with the primary purpose of helping Lightroom reopen files in the Develop module faster. The default setting is a good compromise between size of the cache and benefit from its use. If you have a drive with a lot of free space, or if you just want to move the cache from its default location, you can click the Choose button and select a different disk. Click the Purge Cache button to clear it and regain space on that disk.

Figure 1-11: The File Handling preferences.

The Interface preferences

Although some of the Interface preferences, as shown in Figure 1-12, are entirely cosmetic, there are some really useful settings here as well:

- **Panels:** I'll leave the Panel End Mark (refer to Figure 1-6 to see the default end mark) decision up to your own sense of flair, but these little decorative icons appear at the bottom of the panel groups in each module and for the most part you won't notice them after awhile (you can even turn them off). In regards to panel font size, if you're finding the panel text a little on the small side, you can try bumping it up a notch. It might not be much, but it's all you can do. Change the Panel Font Size setting to Large and it will take effect the next time you start Lightroom.

- **Lights Out:** I went over the Lights Out function a little earlier in this chapter (press L to cycle through Lights Out modes), but here are its configuration settings. The Dim Level controls how much the Screen Color changes at the first level of dimming (at 80% you can just make out the interface). The defaults work pretty well, but you can increase or decrease the first dim level amount by changing the percentage, or change the color used to hide the interface to different shades of gray.

- **Background:** The area around the photo — but inside the panels — is called the background. The default color is medium gray because that's a neutral color that will have the least influence on how you perceive the colors in your photo. You might try different colors, but I think you'll come back to the default. I'm not sure why there is an option to add an overlay texture to the background, but there is one if you'd like to try it. Perhaps you are the one person who wished there was a way to add pin-stripes to the background?

- **Filmstrip:** When it comes to the Filmstrip settings, I prefer to keep all four of these options checked. I like being able to see ratings (the number of stars assigned), picks (the flag states you can assign), and badges (small icons that appear if keywords, cropping, or develop settings have been applied to a photo) on the thumbnails in the Filmstrip. Additionally, the Image Info tooltips are a great way to see the filename, capture date and time, and dimensions; just hover over an image with your cursor.

- **Tweaks:** The Tweaks section is the one area of the Interface preferences where you'll see a slight difference between Windows and Mac. On the Mac, you find an option to use typographic fractions, but if you wander over to a Windows machine, you find that such fractions aren't available. Therefore, Mac users can have their exposure fractions expressed in a much cuter manner. Don't take this as an unassailable argument for switching platforms, however. Especially because Windows users have a tweak that Mac does not — the Use System Preference for Font Smoothing option. What it means is that Lightroom, on Windows, applies font smoothing (meaning it literally makes the edges of screen fonts appear smoother and rounder) independently of the operating system. So, if you intentionally turned off font smoothing at the operating system level (some people don't like the smooth look) and you want Lightroom to follow suit, then check the Use System Preference for Font Smoothing box.

Both operating systems have a setting in common, though — Zoom Clicked Point to Center. By checking this option, you're telling Lightroom to zoom in and shift the point you clicked to the center of the screen. I prefer to leave this unchecked because when I click to zoom in, I want the point I clicked to remain under my cursor. When Zoom Clicked Point to Center is enabled, the point you click will instead zoom and shift to the center. Give it a test drive if you wish, but I think you'll agree unchecked is better.

Figure 1-12: The Interface preferences.

2

Understanding the Role of the Lightroom Catalog

A key factor separating Lightroom from a pixel editor like Adobe Photoshop and a file browser like Adobe Bridge is Lightroom's use of a catalog file. The *catalog* in Lightroom is essentially a database, and as such it is simply the repository for everything Lightroom "knows" about your photos. Luckily, you don't need to know much about databases to use Lightroom, but if you understand how this particular catalog/database fits into the big picture, you're able to work smarter when managing, organizing, processing, outputting, and safeguarding your photos.

2007-10-19.lrcat

The great thing about a database (unlike my own brain) is that it's able to recall everything that's entered into it. It's equally important to note, however, that a database knows only what's entered into it! To make sure the catalog remains "in the know," you should always use Lightroom for basic file-maintenance tasks (such as moving, deleting, and renaming) of your imported photos. You might use Windows Explorer, Finder, or Bridge for this purpose, but by using Lightroom you ensure the catalog (database) remains up to date because Lightroom (rather than some other application) is doing all the work. If you perform those tasks outside of Lightroom, the database doesn't know what happened, and as a result, will be out of sync with your actual photos. This results in more work for you, which is why understanding how the catalog works is so important.

Catalog Basics

When you install Lightroom, it automatically creates an empty catalog file at the default location as part of the installation process. In fact, Lightroom can't even function without one. You can open Microsoft Word without having a document open, and you can open Photoshop without having an image open, but you can't open Lightroom without opening a catalog. It's integral to Lightroom's operation!

Knowing where the catalog is located

The default installation location for the catalog depends on the operating system you're using:

- **Windows:** My Documents\My Pictures\Lightroom
- **Mac:** Pictures/Lightroom

Inside the Lightroom folder, you find the catalog file, which has a .lrcat file extension, and the file that holds all the previews of your imported images (called the *preview cache*), which has a .lrdata file extension. These two files work together to make Lightroom operational.

If you want to keep your working catalog at a different location than the default (perhaps that default drive is low on free space, or perhaps you prefer to keep all your photo-related files in a different location) then you could simply move the entire Lightroom folder to a new location on your computer and it would work just fine.

A couple of things to keep in mind regarding where a catalog can live happily:

- **Local drive:** The catalog has to be kept on a local drive (external drives are fine). Lightroom can't access a catalog over a network. However, you can access photos over a network.
- **Free space:** Make sure to place the catalog on a drive with a lot of free space (at least 15–20 percent free). The size of your database and its companion preview cache (more on that later) need room to grow as you import new images and process them.

Keep in mind that if you move your catalog, you're going to have to help Lightroom find that catalog the first time you want to open it. Here's how that's done:

1. **Launch Lightroom.**

   If Lightroom can't immediately locate the catalog file, it displays the dialog box shown in Figure 2-1.

2. **Click the Choose a Different Catalog button.**

   Doing so opens the Select Catalog dialog box shown in Figure 2-2.

3. **Click the Choose button.**

4. **In the new dialog box that appears, navigate to the location you chose as the new home for your catalog, select the `.lrcat` file, and then click Choose.**

   You return to the Select Catalog dialog box and the path to the catalog you selected displays prominently in the Catalog Location field.

5. **Click the Select button.**

   Lightroom launches with the catalog at this new location, and will remember it in the future.

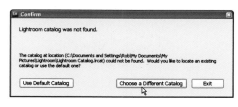

Figure 2-1: The Confirm dialog box; the Lightroom catalog was not found.

Figure 2-2: The Select Catalog dialog box.

An alternative to rewiring Lightroom's institutional memory, as outlined above, is to create a new catalog at the location of your choice and then go back and delete the old catalog. Here are the steps to create a new catalog:

1. **Launch Lightroom.**

   This will open the soon-to-be-deleted catalog, but don't worry; you'll take care of it later.

2. **Choose File⇨New Catalog from the main menu.**

   Doing so launches the Create Folder with New Catalog dialog box.

3. **Navigate to the location on your hard drive where you want to create the catalog.**

4. **Enter a name in the File Name field and then click Save (Create on a Mac).**

   Lightroom closes and relaunches with the new empty catalog.

After you are happily using the new catalog, you can safely go back and delete the Lightroom catalog folder at the default location.

Choosing which catalog to open

Lightroom stores the location of the catalogs you use in its Preferences file. You can configure what catalog to open when Lightroom launches by going to Edit➪Preferences (Lightroom➪Preferences on a Mac) and clicking the General tab shown in Figure 2-3. Clicking the Default Catalog drop-down menu reveals the following choices:

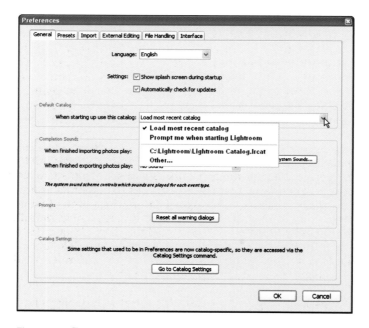

Figure 2-3: The Default Catalog preference setting.

- ✔ **Load Most Recent Catalog:** This is the default. Lightroom simply opens the last catalog that was used.

- ✔ **Prompt Me When Starting Lightroom:** The Select Catalog dialog box (refer to Figure 2-2) appears when Lightroom is launched. From here you can choose to open any catalog or even create a new one.

- ✔ **A specific catalog:** You can configure a specific catalog to always open when Lightroom is launched.

I recommend setting it to use a specific catalog when starting up so that Lightroom always opens the same catalog every time you open it — even if you only have one catalog now. This will make your life simpler down the road because you will know that opening Lightroom always means opening that specific catalog. It's easy enough to switch to another catalog using the FileÍOpen Catalog or FileÍOpen Recent menu if you need to. In fact, you can even force the Select Catalog dialog box to open by holding the Ctrl key (Option key on a Mac) and launching Lightroom.

Caring for the Catalog

You initially enter information about your photos into the catalog with the help of Lightroom's Import function. As each photo is "imported," Lightroom writes its metadata and its location on your hard drive into the catalog. While you continue to work in Lightroom, everything you do with your photos is automatically saved in the catalog in real time (there is no "Save" menu in Lightroom). When I say everything, I mean everything — from keywords and ratings to exposure adjustments to collection membership and virtual copies. Everything.

Because of this design feature, Lightroom is referred to as a *metadata editor,* meaning that you never edit the pixels in your source images. All the adjustments you perform in Lightroom are stored as a set of metadata instructions — in the catalog, of course — that Lightroom uses to render its internal preview files and to create copies of your original files during output. People who shoot raw might be more familiar with this concept, but it's a huge paradigm shift for those who shoot JPG, or who are used to editing JPG, TIF, and PSD files in an image editor like Photoshop. Take a moment to let that sink in because it will make your life much easier moving forward. In light of this, it's vitally important that the catalog is well cared for and protected.

Lightroom has a catalog control panel (of sorts) that displays important information and provides tools for its care. It's called the Catalog Settings dialog box, and you can see it in Figure 2-4. Choosing Edit⇨Catalog Settings (Lightroom⇨Catalog Settings on a Mac) from the main menu gets you there.

The General tab allows you to control the following:

- **Information:** Displays the catalog's location, name, creation date, last backup date, last optimized date, and file size. Click the Show button to open the folder containing the catalog in Windows Explorer (Finder on a Mac).

- **Backup:** Configures the frequency in which the catalog backup function is run.

- **Optimize:** Clicking the Relaunch and Optimize button performs a little database housekeeping on the catalog to reduce its size and improve performance.

Backing up and optimization are important enough topics to warrant their own sections, so I do the smart thing and provide them . . . now.

Figure 2-4: The Catalog Settings dialog box with the General tab active.

Backing up your catalog

It's important to note that Lightroom's backup function does not back up your *photos* (they're never actually inside Lightroom), but it can help protect you against data loss by automating the process of creating backup copies of your *catalog*. A full system backup procedure outside of Lightroom is still required to protect all your data (including your photos). An important note regarding backups for Mac users, Adobe recommends that you do not run Time Machine's backup or restore functions while Lightroom is open.

When the Catalog Backup function runs, it creates a fully operational and identical copy of your working catalog file. Should you ever have a problem with your working catalog (file corruption or data loss) you need to swap the bad .lrcat file with the latest backup .lrcat file. The next time you launch Lightroom, it's in the exact state it was in at the time the backup was created.

I also want to point out that Lightroom does not back up the preview cache in this process, and I suggest that you exclude it from your system backup strategy as well because the cache file will grow quite large as you continue to import new photos (we're talking gigabytes of space here). If you ever "lose" your preview cache, Lightroom automatically creates a new one for you.

Thankfully you can automate the catalog backup process so that you don't have to think about it. In the Catalog Settings dialog box, click the Back Up Catalog drop-down menu to see your scheduling choices, which range from Never to Every Time Lightroom Starts, as shown in Figure 2-5. The first thing you might notice is that the backup can run only when Lightroom starts. If you want to force a backup after a good day's work, set the backup to run Every Time Lightroom Starts; then close and restart Lightroom when you finish working to trigger the backup.

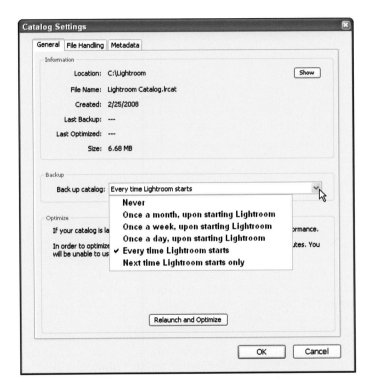

Figure 2-5: The Back Up Catalog drop-down menu.

When considering the frequency with which to schedule a backup, just imagine what would happen if your catalog went kablooey. You'd want your backup catalog to be as fresh as possible, right? Setting it to run once per day is a safe choice. I personally have mine set to Every Time Lightroom Starts. It might seem like overkill, but the backup dialog you get on startup is equipped with a Skip button. The result is that I get a constant reminder to back up every time I open Lightroom and the option to skip if I haven't done much work since the last time I backed up. It also makes it easy to force a backup by simply closing and restarting Lightroom after a big work session.

The next time you start Lightroom in the period for the backup function to run, you're greeted with the Back Up Catalog dialog box shown in Figure 2-6. Here's how you handle this puppy:

1. **Specify where you want the backup catalog saved by clicking the Choose button and then navigating to your desired location.**

   I suggest having your backup saved to a different drive than where your working catalog is located. The reason is that if

   Figure 2-6: The Back Up Catalog dialog box.

   you lose the drive containing your working catalog, you'll be very glad that you had a recent backup safely tucked away on a different drive.

2. **Check the Test Integrity of This Catalog box to have the backup process check for corruption in the database.**

   I know it adds a little time to the backup process, but it's time well spent.

3. **Click the Backup button to begin the process.**

   If you change your mind and just want Lightroom to open, click the Skip Now button to bypass the backup function. Click Exit if you want to cancel the backup and prevent Lightroom from opening.

Each backup function creates a new copy without touching the existing backup files. It's up to you to manage the backup files so that they don't fill the destination hard drive. If you run your backups regularly without clearing the old ones, you might just have several gigs of hard drive space waiting to be recovered! I periodically delete all but the most recent two or three backup copies.

Optimizing your catalog

In the Optimize section of the General tab on the Catalog Settings dialog box (refer to Figure 2-4) you find the Relaunch and Optimize button. If you have a large catalog and notice that it seems a little sluggish, a Relaunch and Optimze operation might give you a performance boost. The whole idea behind Relaunch and Optimize is that it reorganizes the data in the catalog and removes unused space. The end result can be a smaller and faster catalog file.

One click of the Relaunch and Optimize button closes Lightroom, runs the housekeeping functions on the catalog, and then displays a confirmation dialog that it has finished. All you have to do is click the OK button to relaunch Lightroom.

While the whole Relaunch and Optimize process was originally put in place by Lightroom's designers to speed up slow-pokey catalogs, I've seen circumstances where a Relaunch and Optimize has corrected problems ranging from catalog exports to identity plates, so I regularly include this as a troubleshooting step for people with strange catalog behaviors.

Managing the Preview cache

When you're making your way through the Catalog Settings dialog box, you notice the File Handling tab to the immediate right of the General tab. The File Handling tab (shown in Figure 2-7) has three settings to help you manage the size and quality of the preview files that Lightroom creates for all your imported photos.

Before I get into what those controls do, I'd like to talk about what previews are and what they do. I recently was asked a great question by a new Lightroom user who was trying to understand how Lightroom works. She said, "If my source images are never altered and never in Lightroom, then what am I looking at when I'm working in Lightroom?" What a great question! The answer, of course, is preview files. You encounter three types of preview files in Lightroom:

- **Embedded thumbnails:** These are the previews created by your camera and embedded in the raw file. You see these previews before Lightroom renders its version. The quality and size of these previews vary by camera make and model.

- **Standard:** These are what you see in all the modules except Develop. The size and quality of these previews are determined by the settings you choose on the File Handling tab.

- **1:1:** These previews match the pixel dimensions of your source files. These are used when you view images at 1:1 view in the Library.

Therefore, no matter where you work in Lightroom, you're looking at a copy of your source image. While you make adjustments, Lightroom re-renders previews on the fly to show you the effect of the adjustments. All these previews are stored in the Preview cache alongside the Catalog file. Because Lightroom renders the previews as needed, they're not essential files and are not included in the backup process. However, because they're rendered for every photo you import, they require a significant chunk of disk space over time. This brings the discussion back to the File Handling tab of the Catalog Settings dialog box (refer to Figure 2-7).

Figure 2-7: The File Handling tab of the Catalog Settings dialog box.

You can tweak your Preview Cache settings in three ways:

- ✓ **Standard Preview Size:** Use this drop-down menu to choose a pixel size that best matches the resolution of your monitor. Lightroom uses standard-sized previews when you view the image at Fit Screen, meaning you see the entire image on-screen. Because of this, you don't need to generate a standard-sized preview that is greater than the resolution of your monitor. The default 1440 pixels is a good compromise between pixel dimensions and file size.

- ✓ **Preview Quality:** This drop-down menu allows you to determine the amount of JPG compression applied to the standard-sized previews. The default setting of Medium is a good compromise between quality and file size.

- ✓ **Automatically Discard 1:1 Previews:** Use this drop-down menu to configure how long Lightroom keeps the 1:1 previews in the cache. Because they're high-quality, pixel-for-pixel copies of your source files, such preview files can be quite large, so you might not want them lying about on your hard drive for too long. Lightroom, of course, re-renders them if they're needed after having been discarded, but then you have to wait for the render to complete. Leaving the setting to 30 days is a good balance between performance and keeping a damper on the growing size of the cache.

You can force Lightroom to delete 1:1 previews at any time by going to Library⇨Previews⇨Discard 1:1 Previews. Therefore, you're not entirely dependent upon that setting if you find your Preview cache is taking over your hard drive.

"But wait, Rob, what's this Import Sequence Numbers section doing at the bottom of the File Handling tab?" you might ask. Okay, this section's inclusion here might be Lightroom's version of a non sequitur — at least in the context of talking about previews. However, because it *is* here and you're obviously looking at it — and no doubt wondering what it's all about — I tell you:

- **Import Number:** This is where Lightroom tracks the number of imports for use in filename templates when renaming files during import. It only increments when that particular filename token is being used to rename files. You can change the number prior to importing to set it at a different value.

- **Photos Imported:** This is where Lightroom tracks the number of photos for use in filename templates when renaming files during import. It only increments when that particular filename token is being used to rename files. You can change the number prior to importing to set it at a different value. The main use of this value is for when you want to number files incrementally across multiple imports.

I guess they had to put those two guys somewhere. Just keep them in mind when I discuss file naming in Chapter 4.

Metadata options

The Metadata tab, shown in Figure 2-8, doesn't help you care for your catalog file, but it does have the potential to affect how you work. As for what Metadata actually is, think of it as data about the data about your photos. It includes the data that comes from your camera (called "EXIF" data), the data you enter (such as copyright, location, keywords, etc.), and all the settings for the adjustments you make when developing your photos — otherwise known as Develop settings). This metadata is stored in the catalog file, which is why this panel is here. Take a look at the options to see what I mean:

Figure 2-8: The Metadata tab on the Catalog Settings dialog box.

- ✔ **Offer Suggestions from Recently Entered Values:** While you enter various metadata (that is, keywords), Lightroom tries to help you by offering auto-complete suggestions after you type a few characters that resemble a previous entry. Uncheck the box to turn off this feature. Click the Clear All Suggestions Lists button if you want to keep the feature enabled but want to reset it.

- ✔ **Include Develop Settings in Metadata inside JPEG, TIFF, and PSD Files:** Leave this box checked if you want to include the Develop settings (and adjustments you made in the Develop module) with all other metadata when you write to each file's metadata. If unchecked, the Develop settings reside only in the catalog file. The benefit of writing Develop settings to the file itself is that if that file were imported into another Lightroom catalog, the settings would carry over. In addition, Adobe Camera Raw 4 (and up) can read the settings in JPG and TIF files, which would allow you to open those files in Camera Raw and see those adjustments. Develop settings are always written to raw files.

- ✔ **Automatically Write Changes into XMP:** When this box is checked, Lightroom writes to each file's XMP metadata space automatically, and keeps it in sync with the catalog file. (XMP is short for Adobe's *E*xtensible *M*etadata *P*latform, which simply defines how the data is stored in the file.) However, certain things cannot be written to XMP, such as collection memberships, virtual copies, and stacking and develop histories. The benefit of writing to XMP is that you not only keep key metadata and settings embedded in the source files, but the information is accessible to programs outside of Lightroom (Adobe Bridge and Camera Raw, for example). The downside is that the automatic process can include a performance hit (on slower systems) because Lightroom works behind the scenes to write to each file.

✔ **Write Date or Time Changes into Proprietary Raw Files:** This setting only comes into play if you make a change to the capture date/time of a raw file. If the box is checked, then Lightroom will change the capture date/time inside the actual raw file. Some people prefer to keep their raw files completely unaltered, so if the box is unchecked (the default state) then Lightroom will only write the change to the associated XMP file, leaving the source raw file unchanged.

If you're noticing a drag on performance with the Automatically Write Changes into XMP option enabled, you can disable it and then manually tell Lightroom to write to each file's XMP metadata by selecting the file(s) and pressing Ctrl+S (⌘+S on a Mac). The result is the same, but you get to control when it occurs. The downside is that it's up to you to remember.

Working with Multiple Catalogs

I often get asked about the circumstances under which it makes sense to employ a multiple catalog approach to working with Lightroom. There's no absolute right answer, but if you understand the limitations of catalogs, then you can make the best decision for your circumstances.

The single most important factor when considering the use of multiple catalogs is that Lightroom *cannot search* across multiple catalogs. From a management perspective, if you want to access all your photos, it's far simpler to have them in a single catalog, which allows you to leverage all the power of Lightroom's database to find, gather, and work with your photos. It's terribly inefficient to develop a manual (human) system for managing your catalogs just so you know which catalog is responsible for which photos. Yikes!

That said, if you have unique circumstances where groups of photos are so discrete that you might want or need to keep them separate from each other (for example, having a separate catalog for each client or job), then a multi-catalog approach might make more sense. You still need a system for managing all these catalogs so that you can get your hands on the right image when you need it, though.

Some people are concerned about the size of a single catalog as a limiting factor, seeing that as a reason to have many smaller catalogs. There's no limit on the number of photos that can be imported into a catalog. Your system components are a bigger limiting effect on performance when working with large catalogs. Generally, maximizing your RAM, maintaining ample free space on your startup disk, and using fast multi-core processors all improve the performance of working with very large catalogs. I do know of many people working happily with catalogs in excess of 100,000 photos.

I can imagine one scenario, though, where multiple catalogs might make sense: when you're working with a laptop on the road and away from your desktop (and master catalog). Because this set of circumstances is probably common, I think it makes sense to look at what's involved in keeping two catalogs in sync.

Transferring data between catalogs

Okay, in this scenario you have a desktop computer and it contains your master catalog. You do most of your image processing and printing from this workstation. The catalog on this computer is the hub through which all your work passes through. However, as the saying goes, you can't take it with you, so you also have a laptop for working offsite (or while watching TV).

Pretend you're leaving for a week of shooting at some exotic location (hey, you're imagining, so you might as well enjoy it). You need to be able to import and process the photos on your laptop while on location and then get all that work into your master catalog upon your return. Our imaginary Lightroom user (that is, you) is now faced with the following:

- ✔ **Importing and processing new photos into the laptop while on the road.**
- ✔ **Getting all the work from the laptop to the desktop (and master catalog) upon returning.**

Is this possible? Yes, by using Lightroom's catalog Export and Import function. The next two sections give you the blow-by-blow.

You can install Lightroom on your laptop and your desktop. You can legally install Lightroom on two computers as long as you don't run Lightroom on them both simultaneously. So, by installing Lightroom on the laptop you will automatically create a catalog file to go with it. I use the catalog on my laptop as a temporary working catalog while in the field.

Exporting a catalog

Okay, you've returned from the trip with a laptop full of photos and the laptop's catalog full of data. The first part of your (imaginary) process is to get these photos and the catalog data from the laptop to the desktop. Here are the steps:

1. **Open Lightroom on the laptop.**

   This opens your temporary working catalog from the trip.

2. **Expand the Catalog panel in the Library module and click All Photographs.**

   For this example, you'll want to export all the photos in the laptop catalog, and this is the easiest way to gather them up. You'll see the thumbnails of all imported photos display in the content area.

3. **Choose File⇨Export as Catalog from the main menu.**

   Doing so launches the Export as Catalog dialog box, as shown in Figure 2-9.

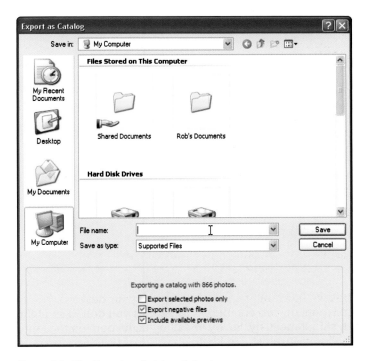

Figure 2-9: The Export as Catalog dialog box.

4. **Choose the location where you want the exported catalog and photos to be saved.**

   The goal is to get the data from the laptop to the desktop. High-speed external drives are great for data transfers of this size. You can export across a network, but a high-speed external drive may be faster if you're moving a lot of data. I like using external drives so I can do the export before I get home and then simply connect the external drive to the desktop for transfer. The choice is yours.

5. **Enter a name in the File Name field.**

6. **Leave Save as Type on the default setting.**

7. **Leave the three check boxes at the bottom on the default setting.**

   Figure 2-9 shows I am exporting a catalog with 866 photos (which is the entire catalog). By clicking All Photographs in Step 2, I told Lightroom I wanted to export everything, so I don't want to check Export Selected Photos Only (or else only the actively selected photos will be included). The Export Negative Files option means that Lightroom will include a copy of every imported photo along with the exported catalog. (This is how we move the photos from the laptop to the desktop.) Including available previews is not required, but it will enable you to see the thumbnails later when you import this catalog into the master catalog.

8. **Click the Save button.**

   Your export begins.

When the progress meter is complete, a copy of your catalog has migrated to the new location you chose. It's a fully functional catalog containing all the data the master catalog has on those exported photos. Look in the exported folder, and you see the folders containing the photos alongside the catalog file.

Phase 1 is done. Time to connect that catalog to the one on your desktop.

Importing from a catalog

Now that you have a folder containing your exported catalog as well as copies of your photos, you need to make it accessible to the desktop computer. In my example, I used an external drive that I moved from the laptop to the desktop. Here are the steps to import from a catalog:

1. **Connect the external drive to the desktop.**

2. **Open Lightroom on the desktop.**

   This opens your master catalog.

3. **Choose File⇨Import from Catalog.**

   The Import from Lightroom Catalog dialog box makes an appearance, as shown in Figure 2-10.

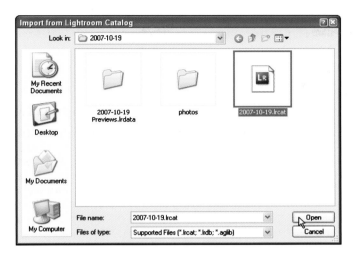

Figure 2-10: The Import from Lightroom Catalog dialog box.

4. **Navigate to the exported `.lrcat` file on the external drive, select it, and then click Open.**

   Doing so launches the Import from Catalog dialog box shown in Figure 2-11; a subtle difference in name from the dialog box in Step 3, but very different functionality. *Note:* The name of the `.lrcat` file you're importing from is shown on the Title bar of the dialog box.

   If your photos aren't visible in the Preview section, select the Show Preview check box.

5. **Choose the Copy New Photos to a New Location and Import option from the File Handling drop-down menu.**

   The goal is to copy files from the external drive to the internal drive and store them with all your other photos.

6. **For the Copy To field, click the Choose button and navigate to a folder on the desktop drive where the photos can be saved and then click OK.**

   The selected location is entered into the Copy To field.

7. **Click the Import button.**

   The import process kicks off. The data from the `.lrcat` file on the external drive is copied into the `.lrcat` file on the desktop. The photos are copied from the external drive to the desktop as well.

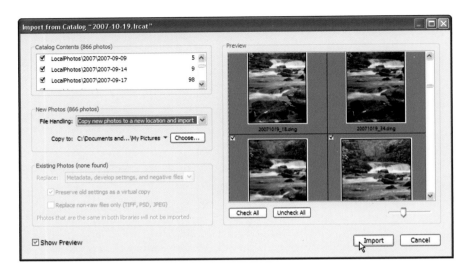

Figure 2-11: The Import from Catalog dialog box.

When your hard drive stops spinning, you've successfully transferred a group of photos (and all the work that has been done to them) from the laptop to the desktop. (Time to congratulate yourself.)

By using Lightroom to perform the data handoff you ensure that Lightroom never loses track of the source photos and that all your work makes it back home. Enjoy!

3

Digital Photo Basics

*L*ightroom is intended as "the professional photographer's essential tool-box," therefore, Adobe assumes its users are already fluent with a certain level of digitalphoto-ese. Although that's certainly true for many users, it's been my experience (through helping many professional photographers with this application) that a person can be quite skilled in the art of photography without knowing a bit from a byte or an NEF from a CR2 or a DNG. I can tell you quite confidently that your experience with Lightroom improves significantly when you increase your working knowledge of a few fundamental digital photography concepts that are integral to Lightroom's operation.

Some of these concepts are complex and involve new words and mind-numbing calculations (done by the computer not you), and some subjects have entire books devoted to just that topic alone. I'm not going to get that in-depth. What I want to do is introduce you to these fundamentals and explain how they affect your Lightroom experience.

Getting Familiar with File Formats

Digital cameras aren't just light-capturing devices, but image-processing computers as well (they even have a tiny built-in LCD screen). The act of clicking the shutter release *does* expose the sensor to light through the lens, but after that the camera's internal computer takes over and creates a digital file. Your camera settings determine what type of file is created and, depending on the file type, the image processing that happens to that file after it's captured. If you're scanning slides, negatives, or prints, you're using a different capture device (the scanner) to create a digital file. In the end, this digital file can move through Lightroom to any number of output destinations.

The file format choice you make has an impact on the amount of information contained in the file, the number and range of colors in the file, and its file size. The next section shows you your Lightroom choices and gives you the information you need to make the right choice for any given circumstance.

Which formats work with Lightroom

Lightroom is a tool designed specifically for digital photography and as such supports only four image formats:

- **JPEG:** The most common file format available on all digital cameras is JPEG (or JPG), which stands for *Joint Photographic Experts Group*. The JPEG format is so popular because you can open it in just about any application, and it can be saved at a range of file sizes. It achieves these various file sizes by compressing the original data contained in the file. The upside of this is that the more you compress an image, the smaller your file size becomes, the more pictures your memory card holds, and your camera can write the data to the card faster. The downside here is that the type of compression employed by the JPEG format is *lossy,* which makes files smaller by removing some of the original data. Too much compression results in too much data loss, which results in a degraded image.

  If you shoot JPEG, use the highest-quality setting and buy larger memory cards. JPEG files are limited to 8 bit per channel (more on that later).

- **Raw:** This (rather unappetizing sounding) file format is available on an increasing number of digital cameras. In fact, any camera falling into the Digital Single Lens Reflex (or DSLR) category has a raw format option, as do some point and shoot models. The upside of shooting raw is that the image file contains all the data that the camera is capable of capturing, and it's saved without being processed by the camera. The downside is that the resulting image has to be processed by software on your computer (hello, Lightroom!) before it's ready for prime time. Raw files come in many different flavors (NEF, CR2, RAF, DNG to name a few) based on the manufacturer and camera model.

- **TIFF:** While TIFF (or TIF), which stands for *Tagged Image File Format*, is occasionally found as an option on some camera models, I don't recommend using it, as the highest-quality JPG setting is almost as good but with a smaller file size. However, TIFF *is* a widely supported and versatile file format that provides either 8 or 16 bit per channel and supports all of Photoshop's features (layers, smart objects, and so on). TIFF can also apply a form of lossless compression (no data is lost) and is a great choice for using when scanning or for saving out processed raw files that will be edited further in Photoshop or other image editors.

- **PSD:** This is Photoshop's native file format (as in PSD, a Photoshop Document). Although it obviously supports all of Photoshop's features, it's a proprietary format, so applications outside the Adobe family might not work with PSD files. Like TIFF, PSD files can be 8 or 16 bit per channel and are not lossy — they don't lose information like JPG files. PSD is a great format when you're exclusively working within the Adobe Creative Suite of products.

JPEG, raw, TIFF, and PSD files are the only files Lightroom can import and export. That means Lightroom ignores any PNGs, BMPs, GIFs, or any other image format. That said, PNG format can be used when creating graphical identity plates, but that's for another chapter.

Making sense of bit depth

Numbers and math are part of any discussion of digital data; numbers are all that computers understand after all. You don't need to understand everything that computers are doing with those numbers, but a basic conceptual framework of what's involved can help inform the decisions you make in your workflow. In the previous section on file formats, I talk about how certain file formats can be 8 or 16 bit per channel. I didn't really explain the bit stuff in detail there, so I'm going to make up for that right now.

At its core, *bit depth* translates into how much data is used to describe a single color (and what could be more important than that?). Further, when it comes to color and Lightroom, you're only dealing with the *RGB color model,* which means that each color in an image is derived from a combination of three colors (called *channels*) — red, green, and blue. An integral concept to remember is that color is created only during *output* — when a color is displayed on your monitor or when ink hits paper. Cameras don't capture in color, but rather they capture various levels of grayscale data in the red, green, and blue channels. Computers combine the grayscale data from each channel to display the color you see on your monitor. The more grayscale data used to describe each red, green, and blue channel, the more colors it can create.

Okay, so if the color of every pixel is determined by the combination of data stored in each color channel, and you can't change the number of channels, the only variable you can control is the amount of data contained in each channel (the bit depth).

A *bit* is just a single unit of data, and in the digital realm, it has one of two possible values, either 0 or 1, which you can think of as either black or white. A single bit doesn't give much data to describe color, so how about using two bits instead. If one bit allows for either 0 or 1, then two bits allows for additional combinations:

```
00
01
10
11
```

Doubling the number of bits (2x2) gives you four possibilities. This translates into white, black, and two shades of gray in between. That still isn't a lot of options to describe all the colors you want to capture, so how about jumping to 8 bits per channel. Now you have 2x2x2x2x2x2x2x2 possible combinations, which translates into 256 possible shades of gray for each channel (with white and black still being two of those possibilities). In an RGB image, that means 256 levels of gray for each red, each green, and each blue channel. When the three channels are combined, it allows for the creation of more than 16 million colors (256x256x256).

Those who are used to creating digital images with a scanner also refer to an 8 bit per channel RGB image as a "24-bit" image. Although this can be a cause for confusion, all it means is that there are three 8-bit channels (3x8 is 24). In regard to file formats, JPEG, TIF, and PSD can be saved as 8 bit per channel files. The important distinction to make is that because of its design, a JPG can *only* be saved as an 8 bit per channel image. It just isn't possible to have a 16 bit per channel JPEG.

Cameras (and some scanners) can capture more than 8 bit per channel. In fact, if you are shooting raw it's more likely that your camera is capturing 12 bit per channel. If 8 bit per channel meant you had 256 shades of gray, then 12 bit per channel (2x2x2x2x2x2x2x2x2x2x2x2) means you have 4,096 shades of gray per channel. Clearly that's a lot more data to work with! So, if the camera is capturing that much data per channel and you want to retain all of that data for processing and editing, your only option is to shoot in raw format because the JPG format is limited to 8 bit per channel. You can also find higher-end DSLRs on the market that can capture in 14 bit per channel.

I hope you are still with me because all this number talk can get confusing. Keep in mind that 8 bits equals one byte. Data is only stored in full bytes, so this is why you only see the option to save files as either 8 or 16 bit per channel. Any file that has more than 8 bits of data is encoded in a 16-bit space. Think of 16 bit as simply a bigger container to hold data. When you have more data than will fit in an 8-bit container (i.e. 10, 12, 14 bit) it has to be put in the next size up, which is 16. Make sense?

Although *more data* probably sounds better than *less data,* keep in mind some practical implications here. More data means larger file sizes. Larger file sizes means fewer photos stored on a given memory card, and it means the camera takes longer to write larger files to the memory card. It also follows that it will take more time to transfer those files from your memory card to your computer, and it will require more hard disk space to store these larger files.

You now see why this information is so critical to the decision you make when you choose what file type to shoot with. Every choice involves a compromise, and it's up to you to decide what best suits your needs.

What is a color space?

In the previous section, I mention that Lightroom deals only with the RGB color model, and I show that the number of gray levels that can be expressed by each channel determines the number of possible colors that can be represented. All great info, but none of it tells what actual color any combination of red, green, and blue will represent. To do that, the computer needs to know what *color space* is being represented. A color space defines the range of colors (called its *gamut*) an image can contain within a given color model (in this case, RGB) and assigns each color within that range a specific numeric value. You encounter the following color spaces in your camera settings or your image-processing software when you deal with digital photos:

- **sRGB:** Contains the narrowest range, or gamut, of colors between these three color spaces. However, this narrow gamut is closest to the range of colors that most display devices are capable of reproducing. sRGB is also the color space best suited for photos being viewed on the Web, which means this is most commonly used for JPG files (which are always 8 bit).

- **Adobe RGB (1998):** Although it possesses the same number of colors as sRGB, Adobe RGB (1998) covers a wider gamut (meaning it has more colors at the more-saturated end of the visual spectrum than sRGB has). This color space was created to match the wider gamut of the offset press better. Adobe RGB (1998) is a more common choice for use with 8 bit per channel file formats going to print because it contains more of these more-saturated colors than sRGB.

- **ProPhoto RGB:** Primarily used with 16 bit per channel file formats, the ProPhoto RGB color space contains more colors (more shades of gray per channel) than 8 bit per channel files, and it has a significantly wider gamut than either Adobe RGB or sRGB. Wide enough to contain all the colors your camera can capture.

These are considered *device-independent* color spaces, which means they're mathematical models whose values remain the same on all display devices. The consistency of values within a device-independent color space is critical because this is what the image-editing software uses to accurately translate and display the colors on your screen. This is different from *device-dependent* color spaces that exactly describe the range of colors a given device can display. (I talk about how device-dependent color spaces are created and used in the upcoming "Importance of a Color-Managed Workflow" section.)

Okay, so what does all this stuff about color spaces mean in relation to Lightroom? Good question. Primarily, decisions about which color space to use are going to affect your decision-making process when configuring your camera settings. The first decision is between JPG and raw. If you choose JPG, then you're choosing an 8 bit per channel output, and it means you're choosing either Adobe RGB or sRGB to define the range of colors in your photos. When your camera produces a JPG file in your chosen color space, that information is embedded in the file so that image-editing applications know what color space the RGB values in the file correspond to.

If you decide to shoot raw, then you're choosing to hold all your captured data and to postpone your color space decision until you process the photo in Lightroom (or any other raw processing application).

The pros and cons of shooting raw

I hope that you're starting to see how your decision to shoot in either JPG or raw affects all aspects of your workflow. Time to see how JPG and raw compare when push comes to shove:

- **JPEG:** Limited to 8 bit per channel output and either sRGB or Adobe RGB color spaces. Results in smaller file sizes, which means faster write times and more bang for your buck on any given memory card because — simply put — you can cram in a lot more photos. Photo output in JPG can still look fantastic both on-screen and in print, and JPEGs are processed in-camera so the output is already in a universally supported format right off the memory card.

- **Raw:** Contains all the data your camera can capture. Results in larger file sizes, which means slower write times and a lower "photo population density" on your memory card because each file takes up so much more room. Raw provides the freedom to decide the color space based on the specific output destination, as well as the freedom to choose the best white balance setting for the lighting in the scene. More data per channel provides greater editing headroom during processing and adjusting, and it's possible to recover more detail in highlights and shadows than with JPEG. Images need to be processed before output is possible.

Raw refers to the fact that the data hasn't yet been processed, but raw isn't a file format like JPG or TIF. (You might have noticed I'm not capitalizing raw here, which is a sure sign that it's not some official term for a file format.) There is no single raw file format. Instead, arrays of raw formats are proprietary to each camera manufacturer. For example, if you shoot Nikon, then you might recognize the NEF format. If you shoot Canon, then you might be familiar with CR2 or CRW. Fuji has RAF and Minolta has MRW. While Adobe keeps Lightroom and Camera Raw (the raw plug-in for Photoshop) updated to support these raw formats (as well as new ones that emerge with new camera models), each camera manufacturer also produces their own raw processing software.

I mention the camera manufacturer software because you should be aware of one advantage they have over Lightroom — Lightroom can't read any of the in-camera style settings (mostly to do with saturation and contrast adjustments) you might set on your camera. The camera manufacturers consider that information to be proprietary, but of course their own raw-processing software can use those in-camera settings. For this reason some people like to be able to use that software, too. Unfortunately, the settings from one application won't work in any other, so you just need to keep that in mind.

In a forward-thinking effort to protect against proprietary formats becoming obsolete, Adobe developed an open raw format called DNG (or Digital Negative). Lightroom has the ability to convert your proprietary raw files into DNG (Adobe also has a free stand-alone DNG converter). The upside is that your raw data can be preserved in a non-proprietary format. The downside is that most proprietary raw processors don't support DNG — you can use DNG to move a proprietary raw file to Lightroom, but then you can't get your DNG file back into your manufacturer's raw processor.

Every decision reflects the set of compromises you're comfortable in making. There really isn't a universally right or wrong answer, only an answer that's best for you. To drive that point home, I'm going to tell you why *I* made the switch to shooting raw and why I feel it's a good fit with Lightroom.

When you shoot JPG, you're handing the processing of the captured data to your in-camera computer. This in-camera computer is bound by the settings you dialed in and applies those same settings to every image that passes through. Don't get me wrong, these cameras can do a heck of job! However, with an application like Lightroom, I finally feel like I have a tool that does just as good of a job and allows me greater creative freedom along the way. I like knowing that I'm working with all the data my camera can capture, and that I can archive that data as a digital negative. I know that computers are getting faster, software is getting better, and storage is getting cheaper. So, when I take into account all that, I don't mind giving the in-camera image processor the day off, and with Lightroom, I really enjoy being in the driver's seat.

Now, you might be saying, "Wait, Lightroom can work with JPG files too!" Yes, this is true, but the important point is that a JPG is a *processed* file. It's already been converted to a specific color space and already has a specific white balance value "cooked" into the pixels when it was rendered. (White balance values determine the color of the light in the scene.) All the adjustments you make to a JPG in Lightroom (or Photoshop for that matter) are relative adjustments to those cooked-in values.

The Importance of a Color-Managed Workflow

When you capture a scene with your camera, you want to reproduce the scene's colors as closely as possible in your output medium. For predictable color reproduction to be possible — as you move from capture device to computer to output device — you need to manage the color each step of the way.

Your monitor and your printer are both output devices. Thinking of a printer as an output device may not be so surprising, because it actually produces something that comes *out* of it, but the image you see on your monitor is just as much an output. Attach a projector to your computer and there's another output. Add a second monitor and there's another output. Okay, that's fine, but what does it matter?

What matters is that every output device has inherent limitations on what colors it can reproduce. Whether it's determined by the components in the LCD display or the inks in your printer, these hard-and-fast limitations can't be overcome — only anticipated. This means that every output device has its own device-dependent color space — its own gamut of reproducible color, in other words. These device-specific color spaces are called *color profiles* and they play an important role in your workflow.

Earlier in the chapter, I talk about color spaces and duly list them as sRGB, Adobe RGB (1998), and ProPhoto RGB. I need to mention one more color space — one you need to factor into the color-management equation — and that's Lightroom's own working space. Essentially, Lightroom's working space is very similar to the ProPhoto RGB space. The important point is that it's a 16 bit per channel space that can encompass all the colors your camera can capture. Lightroom processes all images inside its working space.

By defining the color space in your photo (via the embedded profile chosen on your camera), Lightroom can accurately convert that color information into its working space. By using a custom monitor profile, you can accurately convert that same color data in Lightroom's working space into your display's color space, and at the same time, accurately send the changes you make to Lightroom. Similarly, when you send a photo to your inkjet printer, you employ a specific printer profile that enables Lightroom to convert the colors from its working space to the output space. In the next sections, I show you how to get accurate profiles for your output devices so that everyone — you, Lightroom, and your output device — is on the same page when it comes to color.

Calibrating your monitor

When you unpack a monitor from its cardboard and Styrofoam wrappings, plug it into your computer's output jack, and power it up, you probably don't concern yourself with calibration or profiles. Although you might not realize it, out of the box your monitor has a generic default profile that allows it to display as best it can whatever data your computer throws at it. The generic profile it uses isn't made specifically for the monitor you're looking at, but rather for all monitors of that type. Unfortunately, not all monitors of a given model are going to display exactly the same way because of variations in how they're built.

Lightroom, more so than any other application I've used, relies heavily on the monitor's profile to display your photos accurately. I have seen many users frustrated with display problems after using Lightroom that all relate to a poor and inaccurate generic display profile being used by the monitor.

To make sure you don't end up with display problems, you need to turn to a good hardware calibration and profiling device. This is commonly called calibrating your monitor, although that only tells half the story. Two operations actually take place:

- **Calibration:** This is the process of actually changing how your monitor displays color.

- **Profiling:** After a change is applied, the device creates a new profile so that the display can function in a consistent manner moving forward.

Many calibration devices are available for this purpose — the Datacolor Spyder3, X-Rite i1display2, and Pantone Huey come to mind right off the bat. At the heart of each system is a *colorimeter,* which is a device that measures the actual colors your monitor produces, so that a calibration can be made and a profile can be created. I use the Spyder3 (as shown in Figure 3-1) on both my laptop and LCD panel displays, and it serves me well.

Figure 3-1: Monitor calibration and profiling.

Whichever device you use — and I strongly suggest that you *do* use one — the basic steps are the same:

1. **Warm up your monitor and the device.**

2. **Disable screen savers and power management so that the monitor state remains on and constant.**

3. **Reset the monitor to its factory default settings.**

   Consult the monitor's manual if you're not sure how this is done.

4. **Clean your monitor.**

5. **Launch the software that drives the device.**

6. **Follow the on-screen instructions.**

   At the end of the process, the calibration device will have created the new profile and put it into use.

Don't be afraid to start with the default calibration settings and repeat the process to get the best result. Moreover, one final reminder: It's good practice to recalibrate your monitor on a monthly basis.

Using printer profiles

The inks and the paper being used determine your printer's color space. Unlike monitors, it's possible to get quite functional "canned" profiles for the various paper types your printer can use. The paper manufacturers create these canned profiles, and in many cases, you might get the best results from a printer manufacturer's own paper.

In fact, it's very common for paper profiles to be included with the printer driver installation. That means when you install the printer, you also get all the profiles for that manufacturer's papers. That said, it's always worth your while to download the latest-and-greatest printer driver and paper profiles from the manufacturer's Web site, as new-and-improved versions might have been released since the time the disc included in the printer box was created.

If profiles for the paper you want to use on your printer do not exist, you have two options:

✓ **Create a custom profile:** You can use a profiling device to create a custom profile for installation on your system, along the lines of profiling devices used for monitors. The manufacturers of some monitor calibration devices (Datacolor and X-Rite, for example) also produce hardware for creating these printer profiles. Figure 3-2 shows the Datacolor spectrocolorimeter being used to create a custom profile.

✓ **Have someone else create a custom profile:** If you're not interested in investing in a profiling device, you can have one created for you. This consists of you printing a target provided by the profile creation service, mailing it to them, and they sending you the profile to install. Due to the price and learning curve associated with creating a custom profile, this may be the best option for a beginner.

Figure 3-2: The Datacolor spectrocolorimeter used to create a custom printer profile.

Printer profiles you download from a profile-creation service typically come in an executable file that will install them in the correct location. If not, then you can place them in the correct folder. Each operating system stores the printer profiles in a unique location:

✓ **Windows:** \Windows\system32\spool\drivers\color

✓ **Mac:** /Library/ColorSync/Profiles

The thing to remember when it comes to printer profiles is that you need a specific profile for each printer and paper combination that you plan to use. I go over how to use these profiles when printing from Lightroom in Chapter 13.

Preparing for Hard Drive Failure

I want to wrap up this chapter on a cheery note. It's not a question of *if* your hard drive will fail; it's a question of *when*. To prepare for that moment is not a luxury, but a necessity. By preparing for this eventuality, you also build protection from accidental data loss and other calamities. You do yourself a huge favor when you operate with the mindset that data-storage devices aren't like diamonds or packing peanuts.

If you simply keep your data on a single hard drive, then you must really like to walk on the wild side! If you have your data *mirrored* (meaning copied) on another drive (or on some type of removable media), then you can breathe a little easier. If you also have a third copy of your data stored in a different geographical location, then you not only get a gold star, but you're now protecting yourself against mechanical failure, acts of nature (fire, flood, earthquake, and so on), as well as acts of humankind (theft, vandalism, and toddlers).

The backup basics consist of two key ingredients:

- ✔ **Redundancy:** The more copies of your data you have, the more protection you're afforded against the loss of any one copy. Keep in mind that there *is* a law of diminishing returns here — you don't want to spend all your time creating and managing copies, do you?

- ✔ **Routine:** When you need to restore from a backup copy, you want it to be as fresh as possible. The time between your last backup and actual data loss is directly proportional to the number of tears you'll shed after you realize how much is gone. Whether you have an automated or manual system for creating your backup copies, what matters most is that you incorporate it into your workflow so that it becomes just as important as image capture and processing.

In regards to Lightroom, you need to back up two types of data:

- ✔ **The Lightroom catalog:** This is the database where Lightroom stores every bit of metadata, and every tweak, setting, and adjustment you perform while working in Lightroom. It's critical that you include it in your backup routine. Lightroom does have a backup function that you can configure to run at a set interval. Lightroom's backup function only includes this database file.

- ✔ **Your photos:** Kind of goes without saying, but I want to make the point that Lightroom's backup function doesn't include your actual photos.

I'm sure that your Lightroom catalog and photographs aren't the only precious data on your hard drive. For this reason, you might already have a systemwide backup routine in place. If not, do yourself a huge favor and start today!

Part II
Managing Your Photos

In this part . . .

If you're going to use Lightroom to manage your photos, you first have to establish a connection between the location your photos are stored on your computer and the Lightroom database. This is the essence of the process known as *importing* — and is (rightfully) the entire focus of Chapter 4.

After you're up to speed on how to get your photos into Lightroom, you'll be ready to start tackling all the important management tasks that follow every photo shoot. By the end of Part II, you'll be a master at using Lightroom to keep your portfolio lean, organized, and sorted. All your photos will be just a few clicks away because each file's metadata fields will be bursting with the kind of descriptive information you need to keep a handle on which photo is where.

4

Tackling the Import Process

. . . .

In This Chapter

▶ Understanding the import concept

▶ Getting to know the Import Photos dialog box

▶ Using an import workflow

▶ Setting up an auto import

. . . .

*1*n a Lightroom context, "importing" is commonly thought of as "getting your photos into Lightroom" and on the surface that appears to be what's happening. I use this conversational shortcut as much as anyone does, but it's not a literal description of what's really going on. What's really happening is that data about your photos is being written into your catalog file. The reason I make this important distinction — apart from it being true — is that it's been a source of confusion to many new Lightroom users. Some people make the mistake of thinking their photos are somehow being stored inside of Lightroom, and this just isn't the case. With that in mind, the Import process is where you intro- duce Lightroom to your photos. During this introduc- tion, Lightroom learns everything it can about each photo. (Kind of like what *you'd* do if you were at one of those awkward social gatherings and you met someone new.) The way Lightroom learns is by read- ing each photo's embedded metadata and copying that into its catalog. (Okay, you probably wouldn't do *that* with someone you just met at a party, so the metaphor is starting to fall apart.)

In addition, based on your import settings and the loca- tion of the source files, Lightroom might perform a few other tasks as part of the Import process, including copying or moving photos to a new location and renaming them, applying user-generated metadata (like your copyright), applying keywords, or even beginning the development process by applying a set of adjustments (called "Develop settings"). Importing is a powerful operation that's integral to working with Lightroom. Put another way, you can't work on any photo in Lightroom that hasn't first been through the Import process.

Exploring the Import Photos Dialog Box

Lightroom's Import Photos dialog box, shown in Figure 4-1, contains (going from top to bottom) the following sections and controls:

- **File Handling:** The drop-down menu here gives you four file-handling methods to choose from, with each one having a unique set of options to configure. Note that you see only the file-handling options related to the method you choose:

  - *Add Photos to Catalog without Moving:* This option tells Lightroom to simply note where each photo is stored on your hard disk and add to the catalog.

  - *Copy Photos to a New Location and Add to Catalog:* You're most likely to use this option when you're importing from a memory card, but you can use it any time you want to copy files from one location to another and import at the same time. In fact, when importing from a memory card, Lightroom only offers you the two Copy options — this one and the Digital Negative option.

    Because you're copying files to a new location, you need to choose a location to copy them to as well as a means to organize the folders that are going to be created.

  - *Move Photos to a New Location and Add to Catalog:* The configuration options are the same as with the Copy file-handling method I mention above. The only difference is that Lightroom *moves* the files to the location you choose instead of *copying* them.

  - *Copy Photos as Digital Negative (DNG) and Add to Catalog:* The same Copy/Move configuration options exist with this method as well. The difference is that during this copy process, the files are also converted to DNG format based on your DNG Import Preference settings (set in the preference file).

    For more on DNG Import Preference settings, see Chapter 1.

- **Don't Re-import Suspected Duplicates:** When you check this box, Lightroom won't import any photos that you already have in your catalog.

- **Eject Card after Importing:** Check this box to have Lightroom automatically *unmount* (safely disconnect) your memory card when the import is complete.

- **Backup To:** This option isn't available when importing at the current location. Its primary function is to provide a means to back up your memory card when you "copy and import" from a memory card. Ideally, you would check the box and then choose a backup location on an alternate drive. When the operation is complete, you have your imported files safely copied to two locations at the same time. After you verify the files are unharmed, you can erase and reuse the memory card in good conscience.

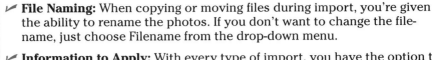

✔ **File Naming:** When copying or moving files during import, you're given the ability to rename the photos. If you don't want to change the filename, just choose Filename from the drop-down menu.

✔ **Information to Apply:** With every type of import, you have the option to get a head start on organizing, personalizing, and processing your photos. Keep in mind that any information you choose to apply at this stage is applied to all imported photos! These settings are also "sticky," which means the choices you make today will become the default for the next import, so always double-check every field! Here are the options:

- *Develop Settings:* These are saved sets of Develop module adjustments that you can create using your favorite settings. You don't need to apply them during import, but it can come in handy if you know what you want to apply to every photo in the import. Set it to None if you want to skip this option. All Develop presets are accessible via the drop-down menu.

- *Metadata:* This is an option you should take advantage of every time. Even if it means only adding your copyright information, you'll be doing yourself a favor by getting that chore taken care of right off the bat. Click the drop-down menu to create a Metadata preset or apply an existing one.

- *Keywords:* Words that describe your photos and then help you find them again later, keywords are relevant to all the photos being imported. You can add keywords that are more specific later, but you're wise to get a jump on the process.

- *Initial Previews:* Although Lightroom renders previews on the fly as it needs to without your intervention, you can configure it to begin rendering Standard-Size or 1:1 previews as soon as the Import process is complete by choosing either option from the drop-down menu. The other two options — Minimal and Embedded & Sidecar — will cause Lightroom to pull in either the low-quality or full-size previews (respectively) from the raw photos first to show you your photos faster, but Lightroom will still eventually render its own previews as you need them after import.

✔ **Preview:** The Preview panel is enabled by clicking the Show Preview box in the lower left of the dialog box. When enabled, you see thumbnail previews of the photos you've selected for import. You can use the Check All and Uncheck All buttons, or check and uncheck individual photos to affect which photos you want to import at that time. The slider below the Preview panel controls the size of the thumbnails.

When you've configured all the options to suit your needs, click the Import button to begin the process. If you change your mind, you can click the Cancel button to bail out. If you're importing from a memory card, you also see an Eject button, which you can use to remove your memory card safely if you change your mind.

Figure 4-1: The Import Photos dialog box set up for copying from a memory card.

Actually Importing Your Photos into Lightroom

Okay, time to introduce Lightroom to some photos! Unless you just happened to pick up this book, the Lightroom software, and your new digital camera sometime earlier this afternoon, I'm guessing you already have some photos on your hard drive that you'd like to import. I'll go further out on a limb and assume that you're going to have new photos in the future to import from your memory card. The workflow is the same in both cases, but the options you encounter are going to have some subtle differences, so it wouldn't hurt to go over the basic process first, and then step through a couple of examples using different import methods.

Employing an import workflow

Things you want to keep in mind before you start importing:

- ✔ **What import method are you going to use?**
- ✔ **Are you going to back up your import?**
- ✔ **Is your metadata template up to date?**

  ↙ **Are there keywords you want to apply?**

  ↙ **Is there a Develop preset that you want to apply?**

  ↙ **Have you created a filename template for the file-naming convention you want to use?**

When you begin the Import process with all your ducks in a row, it saves you a great deal of time down the road. Remember, the Import process provides you with the opportunity to do more than just start looking at your photos in Lightroom. To see what I mean, take a Big Picture look at an import workflow that takes advantage of the Import process's full potential:

 1. **Initiate the import.**

    You can initiate an import a number of ways. The method you choose is partially determined by the location of your photos (memory card versus hard drive), but nothing happens without you taking the first step.

 2. **Select the photos you want to import.**

    No matter where your photos originate, you have to choose which ones to import.

 3. **Configure the settings to meet your input needs**.

    Having answers to the questions at the start of this section allows you to quickly set up this dialog, and click that Import button.

With the Big Picture out of the way, time to sweat a few of the smaller details. The next few sections help you navigate your way through the shoals of the Import process.

Initiating the import

The Import Photos dialog box is the gateway all photos have to pass through and you can open the door a number of ways:

  ↙ **The Import button in the Library module.** This method might be the most common way to launch an import because the big Import button in the Library module is easy to spot (and who doesn't love to click a button). It can be used when importing from any disk or device. (I cover the Library module interface in Chapter 5.)

  ↙ **Connecting your camera or a memory card to your computer.** If you've enabled this feature in Lightroom's Preferences file ahead of time, the Import Photos dialog box automatically launches whenever it detects the presence of a memory card — either solo or as part of a digital camera. This can be a real timesaver if the only time you connect a camera or memory card is when you want to conduct a Lightroom import. A more detailed discussion of Preference settings can be found in Chapter 1.

✓ **Choosing File⇨Import Photos from Disk from the main menu.** Use this option if you're importing files already on your hard disk.

✓ **Choosing File⇨Import Photos from Device from the main menu.** Use this option if you're importing from your camera or a card reader and don't have Lightroom configured to automatically detect a memory card.

✓ **Drag and drop.** You always have the option to drag and drop a folder of images from your file browser right onto the Library module to start the Import process.

Selecting the photos you want to import

If you're importing photos that are already on your hard disk, expect the Import Photos or Lightroom Catalog dialog box to pop up on-screen after initiating the import via the Import button or the File⇨Import Photos from Disk menu option. This is an operating system (OS) dialog box and as such appears differently based on the OS you are using. Figure 4-2 shows the Windows version and Figure 4-3 shows the Mac version.

I've seen a great deal of confusion caused by that dialog box, so I want to take the time to set the record straight. Because it's an OS-level dialog box, it has limitations in functionality that are related to the OS and not Lightroom. The most common problem being that the operating systems aren't so good at displaying raw previews quickly (or at all, in some cases).

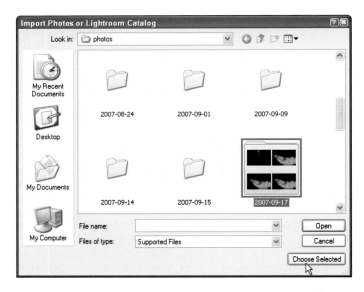

Figure 4-2: Windows version of the Import Photos or Lightroom Catalog dialog box.

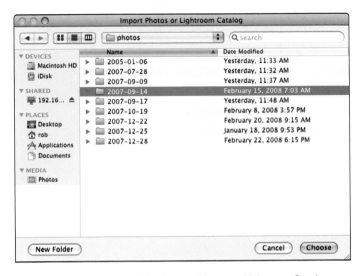

Figure 4-3: Mac version of the Import Photos or Lightroom Catalog dialog box.

The purpose of this dialog box is to provide a means to find and choose the folder(s) or photo(s) that you want Lightroom to import. That's what it does and that's pretty much all it does. In other words, it's just a transitional phase of the Import process, something to help you make your selection and then get out of the way so that Lightroom's Import Photos dialog box can take over and do the heavy lifting — the browsing, previewing, and file naming you love.

On the Mac version the of the Import Photos or Lightroom Catalog dialog box, the button you click after selecting a folder is labeled *Choose,* but the Windows version is labeled *Choose Selected.* Clicking that button — whether it's Choose or Choose Selected — launches the Import Photos dialog box.

That takes care of importing photos already found on your hard drive. When you're importing from a memory card — rather than importing from your hard drive — you already have a smaller pool of photo files you have to deal with. No need, then, to add an extra OS-based dialog box to the mix. Whether Lightroom is configured to detect a memory card automatically or you choose the File⇨Import Photos from Device menu option, you jump right to the Import Photos dialog box, where you see previews for all the photos on the card. Similarly, when you drag and drop a folder from your file browser onto Lightroom's Library module, you're making that photo selection outside of Lightroom; therefore, you jump right to the Import Photos dialog box.

Although it may be true — in most cases — that you'll want to import every photo on the memory card, it's still worth your while to scan through the images using the dialog box's Preview pane to verify that you really want to import them all. Checking the Don't Re-Import Suspected Duplicates box ensures that you don't import the same photos twice, but when scanning the previews you might find you just don't need to waste time importing some of the photos. Uncheck the check box on any folders or photos displayed in the Preview pane that you don't want to import at that time.

Configure the settings to meet your input needs

Now that you know what photos you want to import, it's time to make choices regarding how they're imported and whether you're going to multi-task a little and start processing them on their way in the door.

Back at the beginning of this chapter, when I first start talking about the Import Photos dialog box, I mention that the dialog box gives you four file-handling options. How you initiate the import determines which file-handling options are available. From there, the file-handling method you choose determines what other import options are available. Let me explain.

If you initiate an import from a device (either automatically by inserting a memory card/attaching a camera or manually via the menu or Import button), you see only the following file-handing options:

- ✔ **Copy Photos to a New Location and Add to Catalog**

- ✔ **Copy Photos as Digital Negative (DNG) and Add to Catalog**

If you initiate an import from a disk, then you have all the file-handling options available:

- ✔ **Add Photos to Catalog without Moving**

- ✔ **Copy Photos to a New Location and Add to Catalog**

- ✔ **Move Photos to a New Location and Add to Catalog**

- ✔ **Copy Photos as Digital Negative (DNG) and Add to Catalog**

Here's why. If you're importing from a device (say, a memory card), you don't want the Add Photos to Catalog without Moving option because memory cards are only temporary storage devices. Lightroom knows this and skips this option. The reason moving photos to a new location and then adding to the catalog isn't an option is also based on best practices for dealing with memory cards. First, you don't want to remove files from your memory card until you can visually verify that the files have been copied safely to at least one other disk (two if you want to be safe). The idea here is that you don't want to risk something going wrong in the moving process because you haven't yet created a backup. Second, it's better to use your camera to re-format the card when you're ready to erase the contents than it is to let your computer perform that task. When you reformat the card in-camera, it will be done the best way for the camera, which means less chance of corrupted data when the camera is writing files to the card in normal operation.

The Copy and the Move file-handling options include additional settings not found when adding photos to the catalog without moving. The reason for this is that when you're adding without moving, you aren't changing anything about the photos. You're simply telling Lightroom where they're located and getting on with the business of importing their data. It would follow that if you're choosing to copy or move the photos and then import, you would need to tell Lightroom where you want them to go and if you want to change their names in the process. To that end, when you choose one of the Copy or Move file-handling options, you see the following options appear in the File Handling section of the Import Photos dialog box:

- **Copy/Move To:** Click the Choose button to configure the destination location for the files that are being either copied or moved.

- **Organize:** This option controls the folder structure that is created in the Import process. There are three types of methods:

  - *Into one folder:* This option allows you to put all your photos into a single folder without regard for dates or original folder structure.

  - *By original folders:* This option is useful when you're moving or copying from a disk and you want to replicate the same folder structure on the destination disk.

  - *By date:* Lightroom provides eight date-based folder structures (YYYY\MM-DD, YYYY\Month DD, and so on) to choose from. The capture dates from the photos are used to create the actual dates used, which is reflected in the space below the Organize field. The slash separating some of the date options means a folder and sub-folder structure will be created.

- **File Naming:** Provides the option to change the filenames when placed in the destination folder. Choose Filename from the Template drop-down menu if you want the filenames to keep the original names. An example of how the filenames will look is displayed above the Template field, using the selected template.

Lightroom's file-renaming function is quite powerful and versatile. I feel it's a great option to have during import, but keep in mind that you can rename files later in the Library module. So don't feel pressure to do it at import. Lightroom installs with a number of prebuilt filename templates for you to use, but its true power is unleashed when you use the Filename Template Editor, as shown in Figure 4-4, to create your custom templates. You access the editor by clicking the Template drop-down menu and choosing Edit.

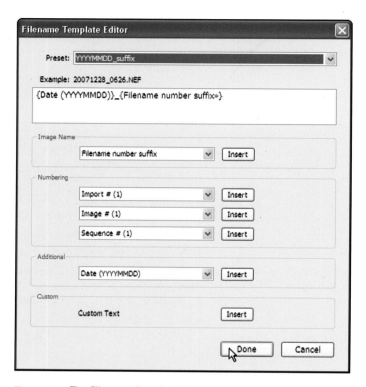

Figure 4-4: The Filename Template Editor.

The editor works by using what it calls "tokens" to represent various text strings that you can assemble into various configurations. There are tokens for image name data, image numbering options, date formats, metadata, and even custom text. The assembled tokens can then be saved as reusable templates anytime you want to rename files. (You'll use the same editor and tokens if you rename after import as well.)

Click through the various sections to get a sense of what data is possible to include in your filenames. I'd like to call your attention to two tokens in particular:

- **Import #:** You can use this token to include the import number in your filename. The Import Number is managed from the File Handling tab of the Catalog Settings dialog box (File⇨Catalog Settings).

- **Image #:** You can include this token when you want to number files incrementally across multiple imports. Controlled by the Photos Imported value, Image # is managed from the File Handling tab of the Catalog Settings dialog box (File⇨Catalog Settings).

I bring these to your attention because it can be hard to draw the connection between what those tokens represent and the Catalog Settings dialog box. (You can learn more about these settings in Chapter 2.)

To see what I'm talking about, follow along as I walk through an example where I create a custom template that combines date information and part of the original, camera-generated filename (refer to Figure 4-4 to see what the template ends up looking like):

1. **Click the Template drop-down menu, and choose Edit.**

   Doing so launches the Template editor. When the editor opens, notice that the active template displays in the Preset field at the top of the editor and that the tokens that make up that template appear in the Editing field. Take a moment to click through the other templates and see how the tokens are constructed.

2. **Delete any tokens that appear in the editing field.**

   Start with a clean slate. Just click into the field behind the tokens and press Backspace (Delete on a Mac). Notice the example above the field changes as you add or remove tokens to preview how the filename will look.

3. **Click the drop-down menu in the Additional section of the editor and choose the Date (YYYYMMDD) token.**

   Just selecting from the menu adds the token to the editing field.

4. **Click the editing field behind the date token and type an underscore.**

   You aren't limited to using just the tokens to build your filenames. You can type right into the editing field. Just remember that with filenames you don't want to make them any longer than you have to and you want to avoid all nonalphanumeric characters except for dashes and under-scores to prevent potential problems down the road. (I prefer the under-score to a dash any day.)

5. **In the Image Name section of the editor, choose the Filename Number Suffix token from the drop-down menu.**

   This is the camera-generated file number. I use it because, when combined with the date, I know it's going to produce a unique filename. That completes the contents of this template.

6. **Click the Preset drop-down menu at the top of the editor and choose Save Current Settings as New Preset.**

   Doing so opens the New Preset dialog box. In case you haven't noticed, the folks at Adobe use the words *template* and *preset* interchangeably. Don't let that confuse you.

 7. **Give the preset (template) a descriptive name and click Create.**

 I usually name my templates so that they mirror somewhat how the file-name will look. In this case, I named it YYYYMMDD_suffix. After you click Create, you see this name appear in the Preset menu.

 8. **Click Done.**

 You're brought to the Import Photos dialog box with your new template selected.

Regardless of the file-handling method you use, you always have the option to apply three different types of information to all the imported files:

- ✔ **Develop Settings:** While some prebuilt Develop settings are available to you out of the box, I don't recommend using any at this point. Applying a Develop setting to all photos at import can be helpful at times (like when you're shooting in a studio and you want to apply a custom white balance setting), but the majority of your imports can do without Develop settings — which means you should leave this set to None.

- ✔ **Metadata:** There's no reason not to apply a basic set of metadata to all imported photos. Create a preset (more on that later) that contains your basic copyright and contact information and apply it every time.

- ✔ **Keywords:** Keywords identify your photos and — when used consistently — provide a powerful means to find specific photos after your catalog grows. It isn't a sexy aspect of the Import process, but do it and you'll reap the rewards. During import, you only want to be careful about getting too specific because the keywords you enter here are going to be applied to every imported photo in the session.

The process for creating a Metadata preset is worth a closer look. You can create an unlimited number of Metadata presets, which can be applied either during import or later in the Library module. I create a baseline preset (meaning information that I want on *all* photos regardless of subject, job, or location) containing all my relevant information (copyright, name, contact info, etc.) as well as additional presets for my wife and my son with their respective information. That way, depending upon whose images are being imported, it's easy to apply the relevant preset right from the start. To create a basic Metadata preset, you do the following:

 1. **In the Information to Apply section of the Import Photos dialog box, choose New from the Metadata drop-down menu.**

 Doing so launches the New Metadata Preset dialog box, as shown in Figure 4-5.

 2. **Enter a name for your new preset in the Preset Name field.**

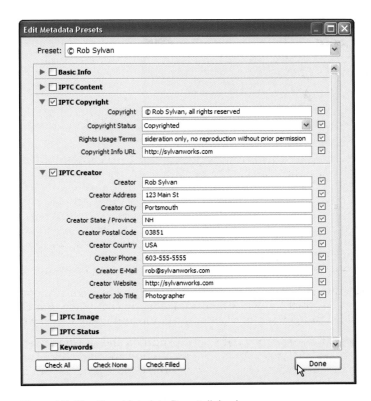

Figure 4-5: The New Metadata Preset dialog box.

3. **Fill out all the fields in the IPTC Copyright and IPTC Creator fields.**

This is the basic information about who holds the copyright to this photo and how to contact them. Adding it here means it's written into the metadata of your exported files and can be written to the XMP metadata of your source files.

I often am asked how to create the (c) symbol so that it can be included in the Copyright field. On Windows, if you have a separate number keypad, hold down the Alt key and press 0169 on the keypad, and then release the Alt key. If you're on a laptop with a keypad overlay on your regular keyboard, hold down the function (Fn) key and the Alt key and press 0169. If you're on a Mac, hold down the Option key and press G.

4. **Click the Create button.**

This saves the preset using the name you entered in Step 1 and closes the metadata editor. You see the new preset in the Metadata field of the Import Photos dialog box.

The last setting to configure before clicking the Import button is Initial Previews. I discuss the role of preview files in Lightroom in Chapter 2, but the main thing to know here is that Lightroom begins rendering the previews after the Import process is complete. This setting determines the size of the previews it starts creating after import. Here are your options:

- **Minimal:** With Minimal selected, the lowest-resolution previews are grabbed from each file as quickly as possible. Lightroom renders its previews only as needed when you are working.

- **Embedded & Sidecar:** Some photos have a larger or full-size preview embedded within it (or its companion metadata file). With this option, that preview is grabbed first, which may provide higher initial quality viewing over Minimal. Lightroom still renders its previews only as needed when you are working.

- **Standard:** In Chapter 2, I discuss how to configure your initial settings for controlling the quality and size of the "standard" preview. This setting tells Lightroom to go ahead and start rendering standard-sized previews based on those settings for all recently imported images.

- **1:1:** This is a full-size, pixel-per-pixel preview of the source file that Lightroom displays when you are viewing photos up close in the Library module. With this option is set, Lightroom doesn't wait until 1:1 previews are needed; instead, Lightroom just starts rendering them after the import is complete.

Note: No matter what setting you use, Lightroom still renders the previews it requires when needed. The main purpose of the setting is to give you a little control over this background process that happens after the import is complete. I routinely set it to Standard.

Putting it all together

The two most common types of imports you perform are the Add Photos to Catalog without Moving and the Copy and Add variants. I'd like to walk through the steps for each type.

When I first started using Lightroom, I had tens of thousands of photos already on my hard drive. I wanted to manage them all with Lightroom, but I wanted to keep them right where they were on my hard drive. This scenario demands that you use the Add Photos to Catalog without Moving file-handling method. Here are the steps:

1. **Click the Import button in the Library module.**

   Note: To get to the Library Module, press G from anywhere in Lightroom.

2. **Navigate to the top-level folder that contains your photos (via the Import Photos or Lightroom Catalog dialog box) and select it.**

I keep all my photos on a separate drive in a Photos folder. Within that folder, I have a subfolder for every year, and within each year, there's a folder for each day I was shooting. I like this date-based approach because it's simple, because Lightroom can automatically generate the structure, and because every photo has a single permanent home. The problem I have with any type of categorical structure is that there's always the possibility that I might have a photo that could fit into more than one category. I don't want to duplicate a file and I don't even want to waste time thinking about where to put it. Therefore, I use dates for storage, and then use keywords and collections to create and access my photos in Lightroom. It works for me.

So, in my case, I'd select the Photos folder. In your case, it might be the My Pictures folder, or whatever folder you use to hold all your photos.

3. **Click the Choose Selected button (Choose on a Mac).**

The Import Photos dialog box appears.

4. **Using the Preview pane of the Import Photos dialog box, scan through the previews and uncheck any photos you don't want to import.**

You might want to import them all, which is fine, but it's always worth a quick scan through the previews.

5. **Choose Add Photos to Catalog without Moving from the File Handling drop-down menu.**

6. **Check the Don't Re-import Suspected Duplicates check box.**

7. **From the Develop Settings drop-down menu, choose None.**

8. **Select an existing preset from the Metadata drop-down menu — or select Edit and create a new one.**

9. **Apply any globally applicable keywords.**

10. **Set Initial Previews as desired.**

This is a personal preference. As I said, I generally set it to Standard.

11. **Click the Import button.**

After that final click, you see the progress meter advancing as thumbnails start appearing in your catalog. Likewise, the Folders panel shows the imported folders. You can start working with photos as they appear, but I usually busy myself with other tasks until Lightroom has completed the job.

After I get all my legacy photos imported, I tend to import all new photos directly from the memory card. I do want to recommend the use of a card reader over directly connecting your camera. A card reader is cheap and portable, doesn't drain your camera batteries, and frees up your camera for taking more photos if you have multiple memory cards. Card readers often provide a faster data transfer rate than most cameras do. Card readers are so common these days that many laptops and monitors have them built right in!

Time to go through the steps for importing from a memory card — no matter how you connect the card to the computer. I'm assuming you've disabled the Show Import Dialog When a Memory Card is Detected preference setting just so I can show you the manual method:

1. **Connect your memory card to the computer.**

2. **Click the Import button in the Library module.**

   This opens the Import dialog box (Figure 4-6). I want to call your attention to it because you only see it when you have a device with a memory card connected and use the Import button in the Library module. Because that Import button works for both import from "disk" and "device," it gives you the option to choose which way to go.

3. **Select your memory card from the Import dialog box.**

   This opens the Import Photos from dialog box, where you see your incoming photos.

4. **Scan through the previews and uncheck any photos you don't want to import.**

5. **Choose the Copy Photos to a New Location and Add to Catalog option from the File Handling drop-down menu.**

6. **For the Copy To line, click the Choose button and navigate to where you want the photos copied to.**

7. **Click the Organize drop-down menu and choose how you want the photos organized.**

   I made my case for a date-based structure, but choose what suits your needs best.

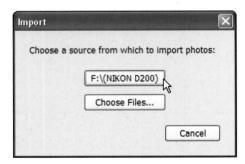

Figure 4-6: The Import dialog box.

8. **Check the Don't Re-import Suspected Duplicates check box.**

9. **Check the Eject Card after Importing check box.**

10. **Check the Backup To check box and configure a backup location.**

    This isn't a required step, but I highly recommend you consider a work-flow that involves backing up your memory card during import. You only need it once for it to prove its value.

11. **Choose a file-naming template from the Template drop-down menu.**

12. **From the Develop Settings drop-down menu, choose None.**

    You are free to choose one if it suits your needs.

13. **Click the Metadata drop-down menu and select an existing preset — or create a new one.**

14. **Apply any globally applicable keywords.**

15. **Set Initial Previews as desired.**

    This is a personal preference. As I said, I generally set it to Standard.

16. **Click the Import button.**

The Import process is now underway. After the progress meter is complete, it's safe to remove your memory card. Always visually verify all the photos are where they're supposed to be before formatting that memory card!

Automatic Import

Under Lightroom's File menu, you find an Auto Import option. Any time you can automate a repetitive process, it's a good thing! Lightroom's Auto Import is handy when you're shooting *tethered* (meaning your camera is connected to your computer while you are shooting) or when you just want to set up a folder that will trigger Lightroom to import files as soon as they appear in the folder (such as images you create while working in another application).

To open the Auto Import Settings dialog box (shown in Figure 4-7), choose File⇨Auto Import⇨Auto Import Settings from the main menu. The Auto Import Settings dialog box performs the same function and is identical to the Import dialog box, with the following exceptions:

- ✔ **Watched Folder:** The idea here is to save in this folder the photos you take. As soon as Lightroom sees a photo hit this folder, it initiates the Auto Import process. If you're shooting tethered, this is the folder where you should save the photos from your camera.

- ✔ **Destination:** This location is where Lightroom moves your photos to during the Import process. This keeps the watched folder empty. The Destination folder appears in your Folders panel after the import.

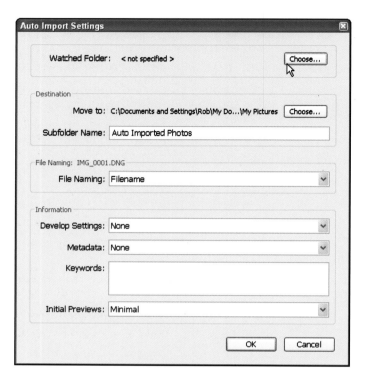

Figure 4-7: The Auto Import Settings dialog box.

There's no preview because this needs to be configured before you have photos ready to import. In fact, the watched folder needs to start empty for the process to function correctly.

Just like a normal import, you want to configure your filename template and metadata template, add keywords, configure previews, and even apply a Develop preset if needed. If you're shooting tethered, this might be a great time to apply a Develop preset. If you're going to be working under the same lighting for the duration of the shoot, you could take a test shot and import it. Correct the white balance in the Develop module and save it as a Develop preset. You could then apply that preset to the rest of the images when they're imported!

Because shooting tethered is the most common use of Auto Import, it makes sense for me to go through what's involved and what steps are required.

The most critical component of the Auto Import operation isn't even in Lightroom. In fact, Lightroom doesn't interact with your camera at all. What you need is software that allows you to control your camera from your computer. Some camera manufacturers bundle this type of software (or a limited version of it) with your camera, but others make you pay for it. (Check with your camera manufacturer.) Third-party applications also provide camera-control support for many cameras (check out bibblelabs.com, for one prominent example). The purpose of this software is to allow your camera to save photos directly to a specified location on your hard drive (that is, the watched folder) instead of on the camera's memory card. After you have that software installed and operational, you're ready to move forward.

Here are the steps to setting up Auto Import for tethered shooting:

1. **Choose File⇨Auto Import⇨Auto Import Settings from the main menu.**

2. **Click the Choose button next to Watched Folder and select the empty folder you want Lightroom to watch.**

3. **Click the Choose button in the Destination section and select the folder you want Lightroom to move the imported photos into.**

4. **Choose a filename template from the File Naming drop-down menu.**

5. **From the Develop Settings drop-down menu, choose a Develop preset, if applicable.**

   I mention earlier that this scenario is a great candidate for applying a Develop preset during import. It's beyond the scope of this chapter to cover the creation of Develop presets, but check out Chapter 7 for in-depth coverage.

6. **Choose a Metadata preset from the Metadata drop-down menu.**

7. **Apply globally applicable keywords to this import session.**

8. **Configure the Initial Preview setting.**

9. **Click OK.**

10. **Choose File⇨Auto Import⇨Enable Auto Import from the main menu.**

    At this point, Lightroom is ready and waiting for that first photo to land in the watched folder.

11. **Connect your camera to your computer.**

12. **Launch your camera control software and configure it to save photos into the watched folder you configured in Step 2.**

    This process is going to vary with each camera-control software, but the end goal is the same. Double-check that photos are being saved into the watched folder before moving to the next step.

13. Take a test shot with your camera.

You should first see an indication from the camera software that the file is being transferred to the computer. After that transfer is complete, Lightroom should automatically begin the import.

If your test shot was successful, then you're ready to begin shooting your job. If the test was unsuccessful, double-check that you enabled Auto Import in Step 10, that the camera is actually saving photos to the watched folder, and that the watched folder starts out empty.

Viewing and Finding Photos in the Library

*J*ust like your friendly local public library, the Library module is the place you go to find and check out your photos. Except in this case, you're also the head librarian and that means you have the power to organize and manage the contents as well. The Library module is Lightroom's hub — all your photos pass through here on their way to the other modules and beyond. Feel free to make as much noise as you want.

You can do a heck of a lot to your photos in the Library module — hopefully good things, but you never know. This chapter focuses primarily on the operations performed with the organizational panels. For help on sorting, developing, and applying various types of metadata to your photos, you need to turn to Chapter 6.

Exploring the Library Module

When you first enter any building, you need to become oriented to the lay of the land. Although each of Lightroom's modules contains tools and options that are task specific, the layout of the interface is essentially the same. This common interface is designed to help you become acclimated to the modules as you move through them. More importantly, the common interface clues you in that you can modify many elements of the interface the same way across modules. Refer back to Chapter 1 for a complete rundown of the interface controls.

Getting to know the panels and tools

The Library module, shown in Figure 5-1, is sure to become a frequent stop in your workflow. Every imported photo makes at least a brief appearance here, even if it's their last. The top of the interface provides the means to access menus and move between modules. The left set of panels provides the main access route to your photos; whereas, the right set of panels helps you mess around with your photos. Smack-dab in the middle is the content area, which is *the* place to get a closer look at your photos. As for the other elements, the following list details the ones you should probably spend some time getting to know. (For those following along using Figure 5-1, I'm starting in the top-left corner and moving down.)

Figure 5-1: The Library module.

- **Identity plate:** Also the *vanity plate,* this is a customizable component of the interface that you can use to make Lightroom your own.

- **Navigator panel:** Displays a preview when you move over photos in the Filmstrip. Sets the zoom level in Loupe view.

- **Catalog panel:** Contains a small set of collections for quick access to imported photos. In Lightroom terms, a collection is just a special grouping of photos. The ones that appear in this panel are automatically created by Lightroom. You can create your own using the Collections panel (discussed below).

- **Folders panel:** Provides direct access to the folders that contain your photos on your disk.

- **Collections panel:** Contains all your collections and provides tools for organizing and creating additional collections.

- **Filmstrip:** Displays thumbnails of all the photos in the current grouping.

- **Filter Bar:** Harnesses the power of the Lightroom catalog to find and filter your photos based on a wide range of criteria.

- **Content area:** Where your photos display in each of the Library module view modes.

- **Toolbar:** Contains a set of tools for completing organizational tasks — stuff like applying ratings, changing the sort order, and switching between Library module views (to name a few).

- **Module Picker:** Allows for quick movement between various Lightroom modules.

- **Histogram:** Displays a graph of the tonal values contained in the active photo.

- **Quick Develop panel:** Allows for the application of Develop settings and presets while working with photos in the Library module. I cover this panel in greater detail in Chapter 6, but the real Developing tools are covered in Chapters 7 and 8.

- **Keywording panel:** Provides a display of keywords applied to selected photos as well as a means to apply additional keywords.

- **Keyword List panel:** Displays a list of all the keywords contained in your catalog as well as tools to create, edit, and remove them.

- **Metadata panel:** Metadata is data about the data about a photo, if that makes any sense. Basically, we're talking about camera-generated information that gets recorded when you press the shutter (f-stop, shutter speed, etc) as well as photographer-generated information to go along with it (title, description, location, etc). This panel provides a means for viewing, adding, and editing each photo's metadata.

Becoming familiar with the menu options

There's often more than one way to perform any single task, but the menu options are usually the single location that contains all the options. What's more, the menu options provide the added benefit of displaying the associated keyboard shortcut (if there is one). Therefore, it's worth becoming familiar with the menus to get a good sense of what is possible in each module. The Library and Metadata menus are unique to the Library module, the Photo menu pops up in Library and Develop, but their siblings — File, Edit, View, Window, Help — appear in all:

- **Lightroom (Mac only):** Contains the commands for opening Lightroom's preferences, catalog settings, and identity plate setup.

- **File:** Provides access to all the import and export commands, controls for quick collections (one of the special collections in the Catalog panel) as well as the plug-in manager and plug-in extras.

- **Edit:** You find the Undo and Redo commands here as well as all the selection commands. If you have a Windows machine, this is where you go to edit Lightroom's preferences, catalog settings, and Identity Plate Setup.

- **Library:** Home to the commands for creating new collections and folders as well as advanced filtering options and preview controls.

- **Photo:** Go here if you want to do stuff to your photos, like opening them in your file browser or an external editor, stacking them with other photos, creating virtual copies of them, rotating them, applying flags, ratings or labels to them, or removing them from Lightroom and your disk.

- **Metadata:** Here you find controls for adding and managing metadata, which also includes keywords.

- **View:** Commit this one to memory, as it contains the most used keyboard shortcuts for switching between various views across modules. Equally important are the view options for Grid and Loupe views (more on those later).

- **Window:** Use the Window menu to access commands for switching between modules, changing screen modes, and selecting options for the secondary display.

- **Help:** Here you find commands for accessing the Help file (both locally and online), checking for updates, and module-specific shortcuts.

You can access many of these same options by right-clicking (Control+click on a Mac) a thumbnail, which calls up a contextual menu similar to the one shown in Figure 5-2.

Open in Loupe
Open in Survey

Lock to Second Window

Show in Explorer
Show in Folder in Library
Show in Collection ▸

Edit In ▸

Set Flag ▸
Set Rating ▸
Set Color Label ▸
Add Shortcut Keyword

Add to Quick Collection

Stacking ▸
Create Virtual Copy

Develop Settings ▸
Metadata Presets ▸

Rotate Left (CCW)
Rotate Right (CW)

Metadata ▸
Export ▸

Delete Photo...

View Options...

Figure 5-2: Contextual menu options.

Creating a custom identity plate

In going over the menu options under the Edit menu (Lightroom menu on a Mac), I mention an item called Identity Plate Setup that deserves more attention. This menu option controls the appearance of the Module Picker. Beyond the Module Picker, the identity plate (also, a *vanity plate*) can appear in a few other places within Lightroom:

- **In a slideshow**
- **In print layouts**
- **In Web galleries**

In all cases, the identity plate provides you with an opportunity to personalize or "brand" both Lightroom and the work you output from Lightroom. In this section, I show you how to customize your Module Picker, but do keep in mind that the design you come up with here is going to show up in other places too.

Basically, you have two types of identity plates:

- ✒ **Styled text:** Allows you to type in the text you want to use and then configure the font face, size, and color.

- ✒ **Graphical:** Allows you to include your own logo — image or text — that you design as a graphic in Photoshop. Keep in mind that you only have 57 pixels in height to work with, although it can extend behind the Module Picker buttons if that's what you want. Graphics can also contain transparency, which allows the black background to show through. As for which file format to use, I'd say the PNG file format is best suited for creating a graphical identity plate on either Windows or Mac.

The first three steps for customizing the identity plate are the same for either styled text or graphical identity plates:

1. **Choose Edit⇨Identity Plate Setup (Lightroom⇨ Identity Plate Setup on a Mac) from the main menu.**

   Doing so launches Identity Plate Editor as shown in Figure 5-3.

2. **Check the Enable Identity Plate check box.**

   This box has to be checked to enable any changes you make in the editor.

3. **Click either the Use a Styled Text Identity Plate radio button or the Use a Graphical Identity Plate radio button, depending on your preference.**

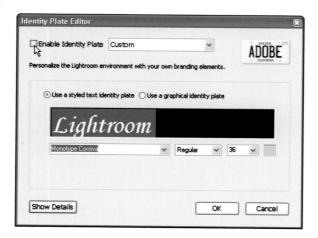

Figure 5-3: The Identity Plate Editor.

What happens after that depends on the type of identity plate you create. If you're creating a text identity plate, you do the following:

1. **Still in Identity Plate Editor, select the text in the Editor window.**

   The changes you make are going to affect only the selected text.

2. **Type the text you want to display.**

3. **Reselect the text and then choose your desired font from the Font drop-down menu.**

4. **Choose the look for your font from the Font Style drop-down menu.**

   Some fonts have additional styles beyond Regular, such as Bold or Italic.

5. **Choose the font size you want from the Font Size drop-down menu.**

   You can also highlight the number and enter a new value.

6. **Click the color swatch to launch the Color Picker and choose the color of the text.**

Because changes are applied only to the selected text, you can choose to style individual words (and even characters) with different colors and font faces. Mix, match, and experiment!

If you're creating a graphical identity plate, you do the following after clicking the Use a Graphical Identity Plate radio button:

1. **Still in Identity Plate Editor, click the Locate File button.**

2. **In the dialog that appears, navigate to the location of the graphic you want to use.**

   Graphics in PNG format are your best choice here because they offer transparency, reasonable file size, and work equally well on Windows and Macs. Remember the 57 pixels height limit!

3. **Select the file and click Choose.**

After you have the identity plate looking how you want (either text or graphic), you can also modify the Module Picker buttons to better suit the look of your plate. Click the Show Details button at the bottom of the Identity Plate Editor to reveal the Module Picker button options as shown in Figure 5-4. Here are the steps to modify the buttons:

1. **Choose your desired button font from the Font drop-down menu.**

   When you select a font, the preview in the Editor updates to reflect the choice. Select a new font if you're not happy with how it looks.

2. **Choose the look for your font from the Font Style drop-down menu.**

   Some fonts have additional styles beyond Regular, such as Bold or Italic.

3. **Choose a size for your font from the Font Size drop-down menu.**

4. **Click the left color swatch to open the Color Picker and choose the color of the active button state.**

   This color indicates the active module.

5. **Click the right color swatch to open the Color Picker and choose the color of the inactive button state.**

   This color indicates the inactive modules.

After you have the Identity Plate and Module Picker buttons looking how you want, click the drop-down menu at the top of the Editor and choose Save As. Give this configuration a name and click Save. Click OK to close the Editor and apply the new look.

Figure 5-4: Customizing the Module Picker buttons.

Choosing the Right View for the Right Task

You have a couple choices when it comes to seeing your photos while working in Lightroom, but more likely than not the view mode you choose will be determined by the task you're performing. Expect to spend most of your time working with thumbnails in Grid view, with frequent dips into Loupe view to check focus at 1:1. That's how I use Lightroom, at least.

Grid view and Loupe view work hand in hand, and a few important keyboard shortcuts make toggling between the two views rather seamless:

- **Press G to jump to Grid view no matter what module you are in at the time.**

- **Press E to jump to Loupe view from anywhere in Lightroom.**

- **From Grid view, select a photo and press Enter to jump to Fit Screen in Loupe. Press Enter again to jump to 1:1. Press Enter one more time to return to Grid view.**

- **From Grid view, select a photo, and then press and hold the Z key to jump directly to 1:1 view. Release the Z to return to Grid view.**

Working with thumbnails in Grid view

Grid view could also be called "Thumbnail" view because thumbnails are
what make up the grid. Grid view is the workhorse of view modes, the place
where you spend the majority of your time when you're performing these
common organizational tasks:

- ✔ **Organizing**
- ✔ **Sorting**
- ✔ **Moving**
- ✔ **Renaming**

You do perform those tasks now and then, don't you? Whether you're watching a new import roll in, clicking into a folder or collection, or performing a
keyword search of your portfolio, you're going to end up seeing thumbnails.
The size of the thumbnails — and, by extension, how many thumbnails fit
within the content area — can be changed with the Thumbnails slider on the
Toolbar or by using the + and – keys on your keyboard.

If you can't see your Toolbar, press T to toggle it on (and off if you don't want
to see it). Click the drop-down arrow on the right end to enable/disable the
tools that appear on it.

Changing the look of the thumbnails

You have three different grid styles to choose from, all of which offer varying
amounts of additional data to appear with each thumbnail:

- ✔ **Compact Cells**
- ✔ **Compact Cell Extras**
- ✔ **Expanded Cells**

You can cycle through each cell style by pressing the J key and can configure
what information you want to appear in each cell style from the Grid View
Options dialog box. Here's how:

1. **Choose View⇨Grid View Style⇨Compact Cells from the main menu.**

2. **Choose View⇨Grid View Style and uncheck Show Extras in the menu.**

   You're now looking at unadorned thumbnails. This view is great when
   all you want to see are photos and nothing but the photos. If this strikes
   you as a bit too stark, keep on reading.

3. **Choose View⇨View Options.**

   Doing so opens the Library View Options dialog box, as shown in
   Figure 5-5, with the Grid View tab active.

Figure 5-5: The Library View Options dialog box.

The reason I want you to go through Steps 1 and 2 here are that this is a live dialog box, meaning that while you enable options in the dialog box, you see them appear on the thumbnails. By entering the dialog from the most compact state, you see that all but two options are disabled. Those are the only options for Compact Cells with no extras. I recommend leaving them checked. Now you only have Compact Cell Extras and Expanded Cell Extras to configure.

4. **In the Library View Options dialog box, check the Show Grid Extras check box.**

   Compact Cells should be displayed in the Show Grid Extras drop-down menu and all the options are now configurable. Notice that the thumbnails are now showing large index numbers behind them. You are now in Compact Cell Extras view. Ignore the Expanded Cell Extras section for now.

5. **Using the Compact Cell Extras section of the dialog box, configure Compact Cell Extras as desired.**

   How you configure this style is up to you, but the only change I make is to uncheck Index Number. The index number is a count of each photo in the grouping you're looking at. I find it to be useless and confusing because the number changes based on the filtering and sort order you're using. If you find it helpful, by all means, keep it. Otherwise, I recommend just going with the defaults.

6. **Choose Expanded Cells from the Show Grid Extras drop-down menu.**

   Note that the thumbnails change to Expanded Cells view style in the background.

7. **Using the Expanded Cell Extras section of the dialog box, configure Expanded Cell Extras as desired.**

   Again, Index Number appears as a default header label. Notice that the header label drop-down menus are arranged in the same way they appear within each thumbnails header. Click each drop-down menu to choose the data you want to display. You have a wide range of metadata to choose from — you can even choose None, which is what I do in place of the Index Number.

8. **Click the dialog box's Close button.**

   Because the settings are applied while you work, there's no need to save them. After the dialog is closed, press the J key to cycle through each style and see if it works for you. Change as needed.

Refer to the Cheat Sheet in the front of the book for a complete diagram of a grid cell and all the icons, badges, and labels.

Changing the sort order

How your thumbnails are arranged within the content area is the *sort order*. You can change the sort order with the controls in the Toolbar or by choosing View➪Sort from the main menu. Capture Time is the most common sort order, but the others can be useful, too. The one that causes the most confusion is User Order, which is when you manually click and drag photos into a custom order — confusing because it only works under specific conditions. You can only apply a User Order when

- ✔ **You're working within a collection.** Not collection sets or smart collections, though. Only when working within a single (regular) type of collection.

- ✔ **You're working within a single folder.** That folder cannot have any subfolders (even empty ones).

With that in mind, here's what you do to change the sort order manually:

1. **Click into a single folder or collection containing the photos you want to sort.**

If you want to sort photos that reside across a range of folders, you first need to put them into a single collection.

2. **Click the center of the photo you want to move and hold the mouse button.**

   Although it's a photographer's natural tendency, don't grab the photo's frame (no need to worry about fingerprints here) because it won't work.

3. **Move the photo to the new location in the order you want and release when the separator line at that location darkens.**

   While moving the thumbnail, you'll see the cursor change to a hand holding a small thumb. Watch the lines between each photo darken as you pass over them.

Making efficient use of space with stacks

Stacking is a folder-specific function that allows you to group photos into a virtual "stack" so that only the top photo is visible. This is helpful in situations where you have multiple shots of the same subject and want to group them under a single thumbnail, like when shooting for a panorama or HDR. (But really, any reason that works for you is fine — you don't have to justify anything!)

To stack photos together:

1. **Select all the thumbnails you want to group together.**

   You can select multiple photos either by holding the Shift key and clicking the first and last photo in a series to select them all, or by holding the Ctrl key (⌘ on a Mac) and individually clicking each photo you want to select.

2. **Choose Photo➪Stacking➪ Group into Stack from the main menu.**

   Lightroom brings the selected photos together into a collapsed stack.

Stacked photos are identified by a bar on either end of the group of stacked photos, as shown in Figure 5-6. You can expand and collapse the stack by clicking either of those bars, or by selecting one of the stacked thumbnails and pressing S.

Figure 5-6: Stacked photos indicator.

Taking a closer look in Loupe view

When viewing a thumbnail isn't adequate for the job, it's time to switch to Loupe view. The easiest way to switch is to press E, which switches you to Loupe view at the Fit setting. The Navigator panel, as shown in Figure 5-7, is Loupe view's best friend, in that it displays a thumbnail of the active photo. At the top of the panel are the various zoom levels you can use in Loupe view. The default zoomed-out state is Fit, which means the entire image fits in the content area, and the default zoomed-in state is 1:1, which means actual pixel view (or 100 percent). Click each zoom level to activate, or click the drop-down menu at the end to zoom in some more. (All the way to 11 for you Spinal Tap fans.) When Fill is selected, the photo is zoomed in just enough to fill the entire content area.

Figure 5-7: The Navigator panel.

The choice you make at the top of the Navigator panel will become the default zoomed-out and zoomed-in state. I find Fit and 1:1 to be the most useful.

When you zoom in beyond Fit, you can click and drag the photo to inspect different areas of the photo, or click and drag the white square in the Navigator panel to pan across the photo. Here's an alternative (and more efficient) method to inspect all areas of the photo when you zoom in beyond Fill:

1. **Click the photo to zoom in.**

   1:1 works very well for this.

2. **Press the Home key on your keyboard to jump to the upper-left corner of the photo.**

3. **Repeatedly press the Page Down key on your keyboard to move over the photo.**

   Each press of the Page Down key moves you an equal amount until you reach the bottom, where one more press brings you back to the top but over to the right. You can continue to press the Page Down key until you've viewed the entire photo down to the lower-right corner.

4. **Click on the photo to zoom out.**

In practice, this process goes by rather quickly, and you're guaranteed not to miss one pixel of the photo this way.

Just like in Grid view, it's possible to display some important information about the active photo. Here it's called the Loupe Info Overlay, and two versions allow for different sets of information to be displayed (but not at the same time). You can cycle through each overlay and back to the Off position by pressing the I key.

To set up your Loupe Info Overlay, choose View⇨View Options from the main menu to launch the Library View Options dialog box. It should open to the Loupe View tab, as shown in Figure 5-8.

Each Info Overlay can be configured by clicking its respective drop-down menus and choosing the data you want to see. (Remember you get to set up two sets of information.) The check box in the General section toggles on and off the display of the loading and rendering messages that appear when photos are opened in Loupe view. I find the messages to be a helpful reminder that there's something going on behind the scenes when first viewing a low-quality preview, so I leave that box checked — and recommend you do the same.

Figure 5-8: The Loupe View tab of the Library View Options dialog box.

Using the Panels to Access Your Photos

The Catalog, Folders, and Collections panels provide multiple ways to view, organize, and access your portfolio. Each offers a unique set of tools to help you stay in control of your portfolio. The next few sections examine each panel in turn.

Getting the 20,000-foot view from the Catalog panel

The Catalog panel, shown in Figure 5-9, provides quick access to a few special collections of your photos:

- **All Photographs:** Provides quick access to all imported photos.

- **Quick Collection:** A temporary holding place for photos. See the upcoming section on collections for more information.

- **Previous Import:** Shows the most recently imported photos. Each new import clears the last batch and adds the newest.

Figure 5-9: The Catalog panel.

- **Previous Export as Catalog:** A temporary collection created with the last photos you exported as a catalog. (This collection only appears after a catalog export has been made.) Right-click (Control-click on a Mac) the collection title to access the Remove option.

Using the Folders panel like a file browser

The Folders panel, shown in Figure 5-10, displays a listing of all the folders of photos that you've imported as well as the disk (or volume) where the folders reside. Volumes and folders can be expanded or collapsed as needed to access the contained photos. Volumes are arranged in the order in which they're imported; whereas, folders within each volume are arranged in descending alphanumeric order — an ordering that cannot be changed.

The *Volume Browser* — the bar that appears above your top-most level

Figure 5-10: The Folders panel.

folder — indicates the name of the volume (disk) that your folders reside on as well as a number of other functions:

- ✔ **Shows at a glance where your photos reside.** Previously, if you had two folders of the same name on two or more disks, it could be confusing trying to remember which folder was on which disk.

- ✔ **Can be configured to display disk space, photo count, or online status.** Mine is set to disk space in Figure 5-10. Right-click (Control+click on a Mac) and choose the information to be displayed.

- ✔ **Provides a color indicator (think dashboard warning light) of how much free space is on that disk.** Green means plenty of space, but it will turn to orange when it starts to get full, and then red when it is very low, and black if that disk is offline.

- ✔ **Allows for all the folders on a given volume to be collapsed under one heading.**

If your imported folders reside on more than one disk you'll see a Volume Browser for each disk (I have two disks showing in Figure 5-10).

Although the Folders panel looks a lot like your file browser (Windows Explorer or Finder), it's fundamentally different. The difference is that the Folders panel shows only the folders and photos that have been through the Import process. Your file browser, comparatively, simply browses the folder and shows its contents. That difference aside, the Folders panel reflects the reality of your actual folders in the following ways:

- ✔ **The actual folder names are shown in the Folders panel.**
- ✔ **Changes made in the Folders panel are reflected on the actual folders.**

Unfortunately, changes that you make to the folder structure outside of Lightroom aren't updated automatically in Lightroom. This is an area where you can create problems for yourself. To avoid creating problems, only make changes to the imported folders (and photos) from within Lightroom.

Adding new folders and subfolders to the Folders panel

Lightroom only shows the folders that have been imported; therefore, you might decide at some point that you want the parent folder of one of your imported folders to appear in the Folders panel. The quickest way to bring the parent folder into Lightroom is to right-click (Control-click on a Mac) the child folder in the Folders panel and then choose Add Parent Folder. The parent folder immediately appears in the Folders panel; however, any photos that it might contain will not be visible until they're imported.

Another option is simply to create a new folder entirely. The benefit of doing this in Lightroom is that not only is the folder created, but it's also imported at the same time. You can either create a new folder inside of one of your existing folders (also referred to as a *subfolder*) or create a new folder in an entirely different location. Here's how the new subfolder thing works:

1. **Select the folder you want to use as the parent folder for the new subfolder.**

2. **Click the + symbol at the top of the Folders panel and choose Add Subfolder.**

   The Create Folder dialog box appears, as shown in Figure 5-11. Note that in the Folder Options section, the name of the folder you select appears checked.

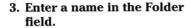

Figure 5-11: The Create Folder dialog box.

3. **Enter a name in the Folder field.**

4. **Click Create.**

   The new folder appears in the Folders panel under the previously selected folder.

The process for creating a new folder in a new location is slightly different:

1. **Click the + symbol at the top of the Folders panel and choose Add New Root Folder.**

   Doing so launches the Browse for Folder dialog box.

2. **Navigate to the disk location where you want this folder to be created.**

3. **Click the New Folder button to create a new folder, give it a name and click OK (Choose on a Mac).**

   The new folder appears in the Folders panel.

The most common reason for adding a new folder to Lightroom is so that you can move photos or folders into this new location. Folders can be moved by clicking and dragging them to the destination folder of your choice within the Folders panel. You can also move individual photos by clicking and dragging them from Grid view to the destination folder in the Folders panel. After you drag a file or folder to a new location, Lightroom prompts you to make sure you want to complete that action, as shown in Figure 5-12. Click the Move button to proceed.

Figure 5-12: The Moving a File warning.

Along with adding new folders, you might also feel the need to remove folders as well. If the folder you want to ditch is empty of photos and subfolders, then right-click (Control+click on a Mac) the folder and choose Remove. The folder disappears from Lightroom as well as from your Mac hard drive. (On a Windows machine, that folder remains on your disk until you remove it via your file browser.) If you remove a folder that contains photos or subfolders, it is removed only from Lightroom. (Both Mac and Windows machines keep such folders on their hard drives.)

Keeping the catalog in sync with the folders

If you're outside of Lightroom and you decide to use your file browser to add new photos to a folder that has already been imported into Lightroom, the photos will not appear in Lightroom automatically. All photos have to go through the Import process first. Lightroom's Synchronize command is great for making Lightroom take a closer look at a given folder and, if necessary, opening the Import dialog to bring any additions into the catalog. Here's how it works:

1. **Right-click (Control+click on a Mac) the folder you want to check.**

2. **Choose Synchronize Folder from the contextual menu that appears.**

   Figure 5-13: The Synchronize Folder dialog box.

   Doing so opens the Synchronize Folder dialog box, as shown in Figure 5-13. Depending on the number of files contained in the folder, Lightroom might take a couple minutes to compare what it knows about the folder to what is actually in the folder and to determine what action(s) need to occur to get the two in sync.

3. **Check the boxes for each operation you want Lightroom to perform.**

   You can have Lightroom

   - Import new photos (with or without showing the Import dialog box).

   - Remove any missing photos from the catalog file — photos that were in the folder but might have been moved to another folder.

   - Check for any metadata updates that might have occurred from editing in a different application (such as adding keywords via Adobe Bridge).

4. **Click the Synchronize button.**

   Lightroom closes the Synchronize dialog box and performs the tasks you assigned.

Grouping photos into collections

The Collections panel, shown in Figure 5-14, is found just below the Folders panel. ***Note:*** I created a few custom collections for demonstration, but by default you would only see a set of smart collections (more on those later). Although, on the surface, collections appear to function just like folders, they have a critically important difference; they don't exist outside of Lightroom. You can open a file browser, navigate to a folder, and see what it contains, but you could search your entire hard drive and never find a collection.

Folders are real, recognized by file browsers the world over. Collections are *virtual* folders, created out of thin air by Lightroom for its purposes. In the real world, if you want to place a photo into more than one folder, you have to make copies of the source file and place one copy into each folder. With collections, all you do is create *pointers* to the source file. That way, a single photo can be placed into as many collections as you care to create without ever needing to duplicate the source photo.

Figure 5-14: The Collections panel showing several custom collections.

Collections can contain photos from all corners of your portfolio, which makes them a powerful organizational tool. You might have a collection containing all your best work, or all photos of a given subject, or perhaps one for each client. The purpose collections serve and how you might name them are entirely up to you. I find that they provide a very natural way to quickly access groups of photos around a specific theme.

You can create a collection a number of ways:

- ✐ **Click the + symbol at the top of the Collections panel and choose Create Collection.**

- ✐ **Choose Library⇨New Collection from the main menu.**

- ✐ **Press Ctrl+N (⌘+N on a Mac).**

You can organize collections within the Collections panel by putting them into a *collection set*. (A collection set is simply a grouping of collections.) For example, if you shoot weddings, you might have a collection set for each client. Within that collection set, you might have a collection for the bride, another for the groom, another for the family, and so on.

To add a collection set, click the + sign at the top of the Collections panel and choose Create Collection Set from the menu that appears. After you give the set a name, it appears in the Collections panel. You can then drag and drop existing collections into it. Collection sets cannot contain photos, only collections.

Quick Collection

The Quick Collection, a useful variation on the Collections idea, can come in handy when you just want to set some photos aside without putting them in a permanent collection. Quick Collection resides in the Catalog panel, and you place photos into the Quick Collection by doing one of the following:

- **Selecting the photos and pressing the B key.**

- **Clicking the tiny Quick Collection indicator that appears in the upper-right corner of each thumbnail.**

   This indicator, shown in Figure 5-15, is only visible when you place your cursor over a thumbnail. (I take that back: You can also see the indicator on photos you've already included in the Quick Collection.)

- **Choosing Photo⇨Add to Quick Collection from the main menu.**

Those same options also work in reverse to remove photos from the Quick Collection. You can clear all photos from a Quick Collection by choosing File⇨Clear Quick Collection. If you decide that you want to make a Quick Collection permanent, you can save it by choosing File⇨Save Quick Collection. After giving the collection a name, it appears where all well-behaved collections end up — in the Collections panel.

Quick Collection indicator

Figure 5-15: The Quick Collection indicator button.

Smart collections

The addition of smart collections to Lightroom 2 is a great example of how to leverage the power of a database to do work for you. True, you already have all kinds of ways to group your photos by virtue of data they have in common — just think of the Filter bar. However, smart collections take that power to the Collections panel.

Now, instead of having to manually select photos and put them in a collection, you can create a smart collection that automatically pulls photos into it based on the criteria you choose to include. To get you started, Lightroom comes installed with five default smart collections:

- ✓ **Colored Red:** All photos with a red color label are included.
- ✓ **Five Stars:** All photos rated five stars are included.
- ✓ **Past Month:** All photos containing a Capture Date within the last month.
- ✓ **Recently Modified:** All photos with an Edit Date within the last two days.
- ✓ **Without Keywords:** All photos with an empty keyword field.

If none of these starter smart collections appeals to you, you can easily delete them. Just select one (or more) and then click the minus sign in the Collections header bar. Poof, they're gone. If you want to see the rules governing a smart collection, you can right-click any smart collection and choose Edit. Doing so launches the Edit Smart Collection dialog box, which spells out in gory detail the parameters the smart collection is using. Feel free to tweak the settings to better fit your needs and then click Save!

You can create as many smart collections as you need — and you don't need to start with one of the default sets. You can create one from scratch. One smart collection that I use as a sort of safety net is designed to collect any photo that is not marked as copyrighted in its metadata. Even though I include the copyright setting when I import photos (see Chapter 4) there are times when some photos lose that setting after being edited in an external editor (see Chapter 9), so this simple collection automatically collects any photos that would otherwise remain unnoticed. Here's how to set up that type of smart collection:

1. **Click the plus sign on the Collections header bar and choose Create Smart Collection from the contextual menu that appears.**

   Alternatively, you can choose Library⇨New Smart Collection from the main menu. This launches the Create Smart Collection dialog box shown in Figure 5-16.

2. **Enter a descriptive name in the Name field.**

3. **Choose a Collection set to put the collection in.**

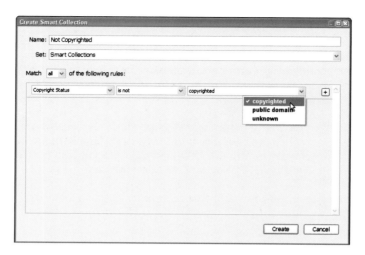

Figure 5-16: Create Smart Collection dialog box showing a finished example.

4. **Select All from the Match drop-down menu.**

   The idea here is that a photo has to match all the provided rules to be included in the collection.

5. **Choose Copyright Status from the First Rule drop-down menu — the menu directly underneath the Match drop-down menu.**

   So, your first rule is now about *Copyright Status.* When you make that first choice about what criteria you want to use for your rule, the contents of the subsequent drop-down menus update automatically with relevant criteria until the rule is complete. Next, you need to define what is it about copyright status that you want to take notice of. In this example, you want all photos not marked as copyrighted, so you'll change that in the next step.

6. **Choose *Is Not* from the bordering drop-down menu — the next part of our first rule.**

   Great, so now you need to answer the question, is not what? Which you'll do in the next step.

7. **Choose Copyrighted from the far-right drop-down menu — the last part of our first rule.**

   So your smart collection is set to grab all photos whose copyright status is not copyrighted. Perfect, that's exactly what you want to happen.

8. **Click the Create button.**

   The new collection appears in the Collections panel.

Creating Multiple Versions with Virtual Copies

Virtual copies are based on all Lightroom adjustments being recorded as a set of instructions waiting to be applied at output. A *virtual copy* is essentially an alternative set of instructions that references the same source file as the original. Here's a simple example: You have a color photo and wonder how it might look in grayscale, so you create a virtual copy and convert the copy to grayscale. In Lightroom, you see two versions of that source file, one color and one grayscale. If you look in the folder where the source file is saved, you see only the original. The grayscale copy is simply an alternative set of instructions that is stored in Lightroom's catalog waiting to be applied during output.

A preview version of the virtual copy was created and stored in the preview cache, but even at 1:1 size, the preview file requires far less disk space than your original file (especially if it was raw).

You can recognize a virtual copy in Grid view by the page curl effect in the lower-left corner, as shown in Figure 5-17.

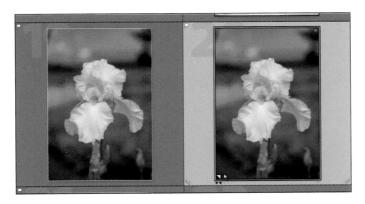

Figure 5-17: The page curl effect represents a virtual copy.

You can create a virtual copy three separate ways:

- ✔ **Choose Photo⇨Create Virtual Copy.**
- ✔ **Right-click (Control+click on a Mac) and choose Create Virtual Copy from the contextual menu that appears.**
- ✔ **Press Ctrl+' (⌘+' on a Mac).**

If you decide that you prefer the virtual copy to the original, you can make it the new master version of the file and make the old master into a virtual copy. With the virtual copy selected, choose Photo⇨Set Copy as Master. You see the page curl effect "jump" from one thumbnail to the other.

6

Organizing and Developing from the Library

In This Chapter

▶ Using different viewing modes to evaluate your photos

▶ Leveraging the adjustment tools in the Library module

▶ Applying flags, ratings, and labels to manage, organize, and sort

▶ Adding metadata

▶ Batch renaming with templates

▶ Using keywords to describe your photos

▶ Applying information with the Painter tool

▶ Finding photos with the Filter bar

*O*ne of the first tasks I perform when working with a batch of newly imported photos is to weed out the worst of the bunch. I keep anything that has at least some redeeming quality, but any poor exposures or photos with improper focus are sent straight to the trash. I do want to note that, even though photos I flag as rejected are deleted from disk, I *do* retain an archived copy of my original import as a fallback. This provides me with enough peace of mind to be a tougher critic of my own work, which I feel is integral to my own growth. That's one of the things I really like about Lightroom; it gives me the tools I need to evaluate my work in an efficient manner.

An additional result of this tough love editing process is that I won't have to spend any time organizing, sorting, or applying additional metadata and keywords to photos I'm not going to keep. But that is just *my* approach to this process. I've structured this material in the context of a common workflow scenario to illustrate how certain functions work, and I encourage you to develop and refine a workflow that best suits your style and needs.

Evaluating Photos

The Library module has four view modes — Grid, Loupe, Compare, and Survey. I covered Grid (press G) and Loupe (press E) — the workhorse view modes — in Chapter 5. You'll still be using them as you move between Compare and Survey (which I'll tackle in just a bit). Each view can serve a variety of purposes, but I find that when it comes to evaluating photos, the Survey and Compare views are the ones I reach for most. They still work hand in hand with both Grid view and Loupe view, but they offer different ways to interact with — and see — your photos in relation to other photos.

Although not a "view mode" per se, you do have one other way to see your photos from the Library module — the Impromptu Slideshow. With this feature, you can launch a full-screen slideshow and also apply flags, ratings, and color labels as the images transition past. I talk more about Impromptu Slideshow — as well as the more traditional view modes — in the next few sections.

Survey view

Survey view, as shown in Figure 6-1, is great when you want move from Grid view to look only at a small group of photos by themselves. To enter Survey view, just select the thumbnails that you want to look at together while in Grid view, and press N. Don't ask me why N is the shortcut, and don't ask me why it's called Survey view, for that matter. I'm just here to tell you what's what. As an alternative (there's always an alternative) you can enter Survey view by selecting photos and clicking the Survey view button on the Toolbar, choosing View⇨Survey View from the main menu, or right-clicking (Control+click on a Mac) a selected photo and choosing Open in Survey from the contextual menu that appears.

Lightroom automatically arranges the selected photos to fit within the available content area. The more photos you select, the smaller each photo will appear; whereas the more screen real estate you provide to the content area, the larger the photos will appear. For this reason, you might find it helpful to maximize the content area by

- ✓ **Pressing F to jump to full screen.**
- ✓ **Pressing Tab to collapse both side panels.**
- ✓ **Pressing F5 to collapse the Module Picker.**

The photo with the white border is the *active* photo (the one that any flags, ratings, metadata, or adjustments will be applied to). You can use the arrow keys on your keyboard to change the active photo or just click a different photo to make it the active one.

Figure 6-1: Three photos shown in Survey view.

If you want to zoom in to take a closer look at any photo, just click it to make it the active photo and press and hold the Z key to zoom to 1:1. As long as you hold the Z key, you can pan around the photo (by clicking and dragging) for closer inspection. When you're done, just release the Z key to return to Survey view. If you don't want to keep holding the Z key down, you can just press it once to jump to 1:1 Loupe view, examine the photo at your leisure, and then press the Z key to return to Survey view. Either way, Lightroom provides you with a free round trip ticket to Loupe view and back.

You can also remove photos from this view (not the catalog) by clicking the X icon that appears in the lower-right corner when you move your cursor over the photo or by Ctrl-clicking (⌘+click on a Mac) the photo itself. As photos are removed from view, Lightroom adjusts the remaining photos to fill the newly available space.

Compare view

The most useful view mode for side-by-side comparison of one photo to another is the aptly named Compare view. This view is best for situations where you have multiple shots of the same subject and you want to determine — after careful consideration — which one you like best. To get Compare view up and running, start out from Grid view, select the thumbnails you want to compare and then press C. (You can also enable Compare view from the button on the Library Toolbar, the main menu, or via the contextual menu.)

You can see an example of Compare view in action in Figure 6-2. Similar to Survey view, Compare view fills the available content area. The trick here is that Compare view limits itself to showing two photos at a time. Collapsing panels to maximize your content area allows the photos to be as large as possible.

Figure 6-2: Two photos in Compare view.

The first photo you select before entering Compare view will be labeled the Select. The Select is the photo you are comparing against all the others. When the other photos appear in the content area, they're referred to as the Candidate. The Select is always on the left and the Candidate is on the right. You can see the Select and Candidate label appear as an overlay on the photos themselves. (Refer to Figure 6-2.) Additionally, the Select has a black diamond icon display on its thumbnail in the Filmstrip; whereas, the Candidate displays a white diamond icon in the Filmstrip. The diamond icons are helpful visual cues when you have a large selection of photos to compare. You can use your arrow keys on your keyboard to swap other photos into the Candidate position.

The active photo has a white border around it in the content area. (The Select is active in Figure 6-2.) Click either the Select or the Candidate in the content area to set it as the active photo. When the Select is active, clicking another photo in the Filmstrip sets it as the new Select. Likewise, when the Candidate is active, clicking another photo in the Filmstrip sets it as the new Candidate. The active photo is also the one that can have flags, ratings, labels, quick develop settings, and metadata applied to it.

To aid the evaluation process, you can also zoom into each photo by either clicking into the active photo or by using the Zoom slider on the Toolbar. If the Lock icon on the Toolbar is closed (that is, locked), then both the Select and Candidate zoom by the same amount. While zoomed and locked, you can click the active photo and pan around, which results in both photos panning in sync. If the Lock icon is open (that is, unlocked), you can zoom and pan each photo independently of the other. Clicking the Sync button next to the Zoom slider results in both photos being zoomed to the same section of each photo. The Z key shortcut I describe in the Survey view section works here, too.

You can have the Candidate become the Select and the Select become the Candidate by clicking the Swap button on the Toolbar, as shown in Figure 6-3. You can also promote the Candidate to become the Select by clicking the Make Select button on the Toolbar. (It's the button just to the right of the Swap button.) You can exit Compare view by either switching to a different view mode or by clicking the Done button on the Toolbar.

Make Select button

The Swap button

Figure 6-3: The Compare view Toolbar buttons.

Impromptu slideshow

Sometimes it's nice to just sit back and watch a show; a slideshow, that is. An impromptu slideshow can be launched from any module, but I find it to be especially useful in the evaluation process. You can launch a slideshow either by clicking the Slideshow button on the Toolbar, by pressing Ctrl+Enter (⌘+Return on a Mac), or via the Window menu.

When you launch a slideshow, Lightroom displays the photos you selected using the existing settings from the Slideshow module. If you want to make any changes in how the impromptu slideshow performs, you need to change the default settings in the Slideshow module.

While the slideshow is running, you can use keyboard shortcuts to apply flags, ratings, and color labels to the on-screen photo. (Not sure about which keyboard shortcuts to use? Don't worry; I go over the keyboard shortcuts for each in this chapter.) When you apply items, an icon for the applied item flashes briefly in the lower-left corner of the screen as a visual cue that it's been set. Press the spacebar to pause the show (press it again to resume) and the Esc key to exit. Nothing to it.

Adjusting Your Photos in the Library Module

Although not intended to take the place of the Develop module, the combination of the Histogram and the Quick Develop panels in the Library module can provide valuable information about your photos and allow for tweaks that can further inform your selection process. Quick Develop panel adjustments can be applied while in the Grid, Loupe, Survey, or Compare views.

Using the Histogram to analyze your photos

A *histogram,* in the digital photo world, is a graph representing all the tones in a selected photo. The left side of the graph represents the darker tones and the right side represents the lighter. In the Lightroom interface, the Histogram panel has a place of honor — first position — on the right.

At a basic level, a histogram can give you an indication of the overall exposure of a photo. An overexposed photo shows points all stacked to the right edge (see Figure 6-4); whereas, an underexposed photo shows points bunched on the left (see Figure 6-5.). That said, Figure 6-6 shows a photo that, although properly exposed for the moon, has a histogram with bunches of points to the right because most of the image is dark. The moral of the story here is to keep the subject in mind when viewing the histogram.

Figure 6-4: An example of an overexposed photo and its histogram.

Figure 6-5: An example of an underexposed photo and its histogram.

Figure 6-6: An example of a properly exposed photo of a primarily dark scene.

The bottom of the Histogram panel displays the ISO, focal length, aperture, and shutter speed of the active photo to aid in that photo's evaluation. With all this information, you can use the tools in the Quick Develop panel to make adjustments without leaving the Library module. To see what kind of adjustments I mean, check out the next few sections.

Making adjustments with the Quick Develop panel

The default Lightroom rendering of your raw photos may not always be enough to judge the potential of a given photo. Perhaps a photo was slightly underexposed, or perhaps the wrong white balance was selected in-camera. Those issues (among others) can be corrected relatively quickly and should not be the cause for you tossing out an otherwise good photo. The Quick Develop panel, shown in Figure 6-7, gives you the tools to do some quick rehab work on deserving photos.

The Quick Develop panel contains three subsections that can be collapsed or expanded by clicking the arrow at the top of each subsection:

- **Saved Preset:** Provides quick access to all Develop presets, while also letting you crop to any aspect ratio and switch between color and grayscale.

- **White Balance:** White balance is the setting that compensates for the color of the light used to capture the scene so that subjects appear in the photo the way our eyes see them (our brains do this for us automatically). *Note:* The White Balance preset options are different for raw photos and rendered photos (JPG, TIFF, and PSD files). When working with raw data, an absolute white balance hasn't been "cooked" into the pixels, so it's possible to switch the absolute white balance value as needed. However, all rendered photos have a white balance value cooked into the pixels when the file is created, so all future white balance adjustments are relative. When working with a rendered file, your White Balance preset choices are limited to As Shot, Auto, and Custom.

✓ **Tone Control:** This final subsection contains all the adjustments affecting the tonal range of the photo.

The Reset All button at the bottom of the panel removes *all* adjustment settings, including any adjustments made in the Develop module. However, you can reset any single Quick Develop adjustment by double-clicking the label of that particular adjustment.

You can apply adjustments to the active photo while in the Loupe, Survey, and Compare views. When in Grid view, any adjustments you make are applied to all selected photos (not just the active photo). This "one fell swoop" approach is handy during not only the evaluation process, but also a real timesaver when you want to apply the same adjustment to a large group of photos.

Figure 6-7: The Quick Develop panel with all subsections expanded.

A good example of a bulk application of the Quick Develop panel is applying a new aspect ratio to a group of selected photos in Grid view. Here's how:

1. **Press G to jump to Grid view.**
2. **Select all the photos you want to crop to the new aspect ratio.**
3. **Expand the Saved Preset section of the Quick Develop panel.**
4. **Select the desired aspect ratio from the Crop Ratio drop-down menu.**

You see the thumbnails of the selected photos change to reflect the new crop ratio. When you apply the crop in this manner, you center the crop in each photo. Press R to jump to the Crop tool to tweak each crop for best composition. (I cover the Develop module's Crop tool in detail in Chapter 7.) The benefit of starting from the Quick Develop panel is that the aspect ratio is already set when you enter the Crop tool, which greatly speeds the process.

Along the same lines, if you adjust a single photo (whether using Quick Develop or the Develop module) and want to apply the same settings to multiple photos, you can use the Sync Settings button located at the bottom of the right panel group. Here's how:

1. **Press G to jump to Grid view.**
2. **Select the adjusted photo first.**
3. **Select the other photos you want to sync with the same settings.**
4. **Click the Sync Settings button.**

    Doing so launches the Synchronize Settings dialog box, as shown in Figure 6-8.

5. **Check only the boxes that correspond to the settings you want to apply to the other photos.**
6. **Click the Synchronize button.**

You see all the thumbnails of the selected photos update to reflect the newly applied settings from the first photo.

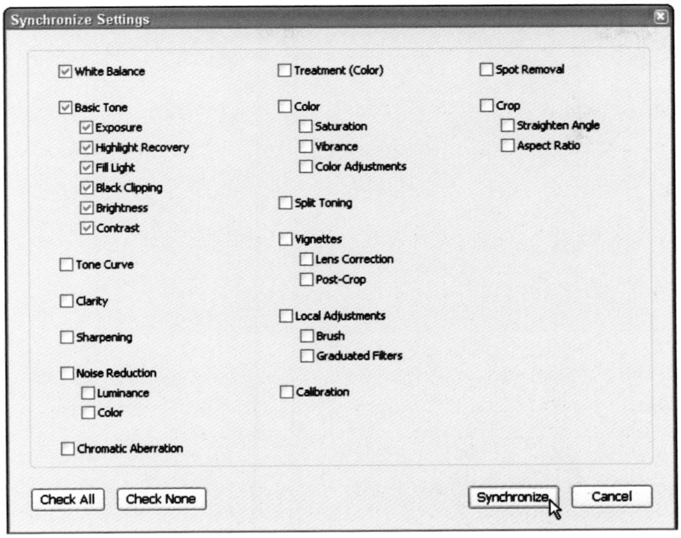

Figure 6-8: The Synchronize Settings dialog box.

Making Choices: Flags, Ratings, and Color Labels

Having all the various view modes and their associated tools at your disposal won't do you a lick of good if you can't integrate them into your workflow in a way that makes the process of evaluating your photos more efficient. I've come up with my workflow model, but don't think of it as carved in stone. Perhaps you already have a system of, say, color labels or ratings that works for you. By all means, do what works. In these next few sections, I cover what organizational tools are available to you and how they work in a typical Lightroom workflow. Feel free to pick and choose the pieces that fit your needs.

Using flags to pick the winners from the losers

Flags are a fantastic tool for quickly making a first-pass edit of your photos so that you can separate the shots you want to keep from the ones that no one else needs to see. You have three flag states to choose from, represented by the flag icons shown in Figure 6-9:

- **Pick:** These are your keepers, and are marked with a White Flag icon.
- **Rejected:** These are on the chopping block, and are marked with a Black Flag icon.
- **Unflagged:** These haven't been evaluated, and do not show an icon.

Figure 6-9: Three photos showing picked, rejected, and unflagged photos from left to right.

Flags (of each type) can be applied to one or more selected photos at a time. Unflagged photos do not show a flag, but if you position your cursor over an unflagged photo, you can see the outline of the flag icon. This clickable target can be used to set a flag. Click the icon once to set it as picked and click again to unflag. You can also apply flags by

- **Clicking either the Pick or Rejected Flag icon on the Toolbar.**
- **Right-clicking (Control+click on a Mac) a photo and choosing Set Flag and then choosing one of the three flag states from the contextual menu that appears.**
- **Keyboard shortcuts — P for Pick, X for Rejected, and U for Unflagged.**
- **Choosing Photo⇨Set Flag from the main menu.**

Flags don't tag along with photos when you put them into a collection. In other words, if you apply a Pick flag to a given photo and move it to a collection, you see that its flag did not come with it. The intention is to allow greater flexibility with how you might use flags, but I've found that most people just consider it confusing — and I agree.

The easiest and most efficient method to apply flags is by using the keyboard shortcuts. This process is expedited by choosing Photo⇨Auto Advance from the main menu. With this feature enabled, Lightroom automatically advances to the next photo after applying the flag.

Here's a real quick workflow using the Filter bar (which I'll cover in more detail later) for making your first-round selections:

1. **Press G to jump to Grid view.**
2. **Press Shift+Tab to hide all panels and maximize content area.**

3. **Adjust the Thumbnail Size slider on the Toolbar as needed to get a good size for evaluating each photo.**

   When you need to quickly see a 1:1 view of your photo while working in Grid view, press and hold the Z key to zoom. While holding the Z key, you can even click and drag the photo to inspect other areas. When you release the Z key, you return directly to Grid view.

4. **On the Filter bar, click the Attribute label to display the Attribute filters, and then right-click (Control+click on a Mac) anywhere on the flag icons in the Attribute filter and choose Flagged and Unflagged Photos from the contextual menu that appears (refer to Figure 6-10).**

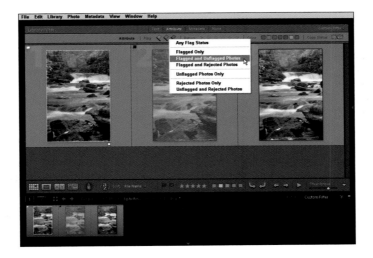

Figure 6-10: The Filter bar showing the Attribute filters.

This sets a view filter (more on the Filter bar at the end of the chapter) that tells Lightroom to only display photos that are either flagged as a Pick or Unflagged, which results in Lightroom hiding (not deleting) any photos that are flagged as Rejected. This way, when you flag a photo as Rejected, it immediately vanishes from view and advances you to the next photo (don't worry though; you can bring it back later).

5. **Choose Photo⇨Auto Advance from the main menu.**

   You can also enable Auto Advance by pressing Caps Lock before flagging, but the advantage of using the Auto Advance menu is that you don't have to worry about turning Caps Lock off before you start typing somewhere else.

6. **With the first image selected, evaluate and flag as either a Pick or Rejected.**

   Press P for Pick and X for Rejected. Lightroom automatically advances to the next thumbnail. If you just can't decide, press U (Unflagged) to advance to the next photo. I show you how to deal with unflagged photos later.

7. **Continue applying flags until you reach the last image.**

   At this point, you should only see photos that are flagged as Pick or Unflagged. Skip to Step 10 if you didn't leave any photos Unflagged.

8. **On the Filter bar, right-click (Control+click on a Mac) anywhere on the flag icons and choose Unflagged Photos Only.**

   Now, all picks and rejected photos are hidden from view, and you are left with only unflagged photos.

9. **Flag the remaining photos as either a Pick or Rejected.**

   When photos are flagged, they're hidden from view because of the Unflagged Photos Only filter. You know you're finished when you don't have any photos left.

10. **On the Filter bar, right-click (Control+click on a Mac) anywhere on the flag icons and choose Rejected Photos Only.**

    Photos flagged as rejected are going to appear faded; this is normal and helps them to stand out when you see a mix of flag states.

11. **Verify that you're satisfied with your Rejected photos and change any to Pick if needed.**

12. **Press Ctrl+Backspace (⌘+Delete on a Mac) and choose Delete from Disk.**

    This is the keyboard shortcut to delete rejected photos — you find the same command under the Photo menu.

13. **Press Ctrl+L (⌘+L on a Mac) to turn off all filters.**

    You should now be left with all the photos you flagged as Pick!

Deleting photos from Lightroom

Lightroom is very careful (as it should be) in its approach to deleting photos from disk. You're always prompted with a confirmation dialog box, as shown in Figure 6-11, before a deletion is allowed to take place. When prompted, click the Delete from Disk button to complete the

Figure 6-11: The Confirm dialog box appears when attempting to delete photos.

deletion process and have Lightroom move the selected photo(s) to the Recycle Bin (Trash on a Mac). Clicking Remove removes the photo from the Lightroom catalog only.

You can only delete a photo from disk with the Delete key when you're working in a Folder view. If you're working in a Collection view and press Delete, the selected photo(s) are removed from that collection only. (For more on Folder views and Collection views, check out Chapter 5.)

Using ratings to rank images

Ratings provide another means to sort your photos by subjective criteria. There's no hard-and-fast rule on what criteria correlates to any number of star ratings. It's entirely up to you to develop your system! Because I use a flag system to cull all the bloopers first, I don't use ratings to mark which photos stay or go. I find ratings helpful for quickly identifying the best of the best, while ignoring the photos that aren't so bad to warrant deletion but at the same time, just aren't good enough to do much with.

In the interest of keeping things simple, the more I like a shot, the more stars I apply. To prevent a lot of hemming and hawing over the difference between a 4-star photo and a 5-star photo, I typically use a 0–2 star scale. If I think it's a useable shot, I assign one star; if I think it's really good, I assign 2 stars; and if I can't decide, I leave it at 0. I find this helps me refine and focus my energy on processing instead of ranking. Develop a system that works for you.

As with most Lightroom tasks, there's more than one approach to accomplishing the same result. After selecting the photo, you can apply ratings in the following ways:

- ✔ **Press the number keys, 0–5, depending on the number of stars you want to apply.** Each number key corresponds to the number of stars applied.

- ✔ **Click the appropriate star under each photo cell in Grid view.** Press J to cycle through Grid cell styles if you don't see rating stars under the thumbnails.

- ✔ **Right-click (Control+click on a Mac), select Set Rating from the contextual menu that appears, and then choose your desired rating from the menu.**

- ✔ **Choose Photo⇨Set Rating from the main menu and then choose your desired rating from the menu.**

After you apply a rating and still have the photo(s) selected, you can use the [key to decrease or the] key to increase the rating. When it comes to applying ratings, I find it goes quicker when you enable automatic advancing (Photo⇨Auto Advance) and then use the number keys to move through an entire shoot.

Applying color labels to differentiate images

Color labels provide a visual that you can use to further sort and organize your photos. How these are used is entirely subjective, and perhaps you might not use them at all. They do offer some unique benefits:

- ✔ **Labels are very flexible.**
- ✔ **Labels can be shared between Lightroom and Adobe Bridge (the file browser bundled with Photoshop).**
- ✔ **Labels can be used as criteria in the creation of smart collections.**
- ✔ **Labels can be used as a filter on the Filter bar.**

I've seen people use labels to assign a different color to each photographer for easier sorting after an event with multiple shooters. I've seen others assign different colors to different states in the editing process (such as a color for Needs Keywords, another for Ready to Deliver, and so on).

I find labels useful for labeling groups of photos that I intend to send to other applications for additional processing. For example, I have a color for photos I plan to stitch into a panorama, another color for photos I want to combine into a high dynamic range photo, and so on. I then set up a smart collection for each color label to provide quick access to these special groupings.

Instead of trying to remember what each color means in your system, you can create a Custom Label Set with names that make sense to you. Here's how to create your custom label set:

1. **Chooose Metadata⇨Color Label Set⇨Edit from the main menu.**

   Doing so launches the Edit Color Label Set dialog box, shown in Figure 6-12.

2. **Enter a name for each color in the set that you want to use.**

   In my example, I used Panoramic for red, HDR for yellow, and so on.

3. **Choose Save Current Settings as New Preset from the Preset drop-down menu.**

   The New Preset dialog box appears.

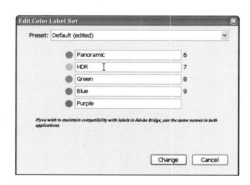

Figure 6-12: The Edit Color Label Set dialog box.

4. **Enter a name and click Create.**

   The preset name appears in the Preset drop-down menu of the Edit Color Label Set dialog box.

5. **Click Change to close the editor and begin using that set.**

You can use only one color label set at a time, so when you change to this new set, you won't see any color labels applied with a previous color set. A color label is simply a tag in the file's metadata. By applying a color label, you're entering the color label into the file's metadata. When that label matches the color label set in use, Lightroom displays the corresponding color. Changing the set doesn't change the label that's applied; you just won't see Lightroom display a color. You can change color label sets by selecting them from the Metadata⇨Color Label Set menu.

If you use Adobe Bridge in conjunction with Lightroom, you might want to create the same color label set in Bridge so that both applications use labels the same way.

Moving Beyond Camera-Generated Filenames and Metadata

With every shutter click your digital camera creates a file, assigns it a name, and embeds all the settings used to make the capture into the file's metadata space. When you begin to work with your photos, you want to add additional custom metadata (such as your contact information) to your files. When doing so, you might discover that the camera-generated filenames don't particularly fit your needs. Lightroom has an excellent set of tools to aid you in managing this aspect of your portfolio.

It's possible to both rename and apply custom metadata during the Import process. However, that doesn't fit everyone's workflow. For some, the Import process is just getting photos off the memory card as quickly as possible, and everything else can come later. For others, it only makes sense to apply a minimal amount of custom metadata at import and then complete the job after the first round of edits, so that time isn't wasted working on files destined for the trash heap. Similarly, you might want to wait to rename all photos until after you remove the duds so you don't end up with any gaps in the filenames. Whatever your reason or workflow, Lightroom allows for a flexible approach.

Batch renaming with filename templates

After you import your photos to Lightroom, it's in your best interest to perform all your renaming tasks from within Lightroom because Lightroom
stores each file's name in its catalog. If you were to rename files outside of
Lightroom, the data in Lightroom's catalog wouldn't match the new names,
and Lightroom then would consider those files missing or offline. While it *is*
possible to reconnect Lightroom to the newly named files, it's an onerous
task that I wouldn't wish on anyone. I can't tell you how many times I've seen
people do this. Please don't fall into that trap!

Thankfully, the renaming function within Lightroom is powerful, extremely
configurable, and easy to use. Lightroom comes installed with a number of
file-naming templates that you can use as-is, or you can create custom templates to fit your needs. Each file-naming template is comprised of *tokens* —
little widgets that represent a chunk of data used to build your filename.
These tokens include

- ✔ **Custom text**
- ✔ **Date/time values**
- ✔ **Sequence numbers**
- ✔ **Metadata elements**
- ✔ **Existing filename**

These tokens are assembled and arranged with Lightroom's Filename
Template Editor, which is best explained by walking through an example.
Here's how to create a custom naming template comprised of the capture
date and a sequence number:

1. **Select the photos you want to
   rename from Grid view.**

2. **Choose Library⇨Rename
   Photo from the main menu (or
   press F2).**

   The Rename Photos dialog box
   appears, as shown in Figure 6-13.

Figure 6-13: The Rename Photos dialog box.

3. **Choose Edit from the File Naming drop-down menu.**

   Doing so launches the Filename Template Editor shown in Figure 6-14.

4. **Select and delete any existing tokens from the Editor window.**

   The active template always appears in the editor. You can use the existing tokens as a starting place for a new template, but I usually find it
   simpler to start from scratch. That said, if you want to see how other
   templates are constructed, you could click the Preset drop-down menu
   and select other templates to load into the Editor window.

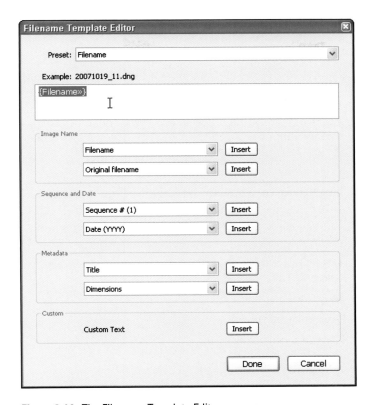

Figure 6-14: The Filename Template Editor.

5. **Choose the desired date format token from the Date drop-down menu.**

   Personally, I'd go for Date (YYYYMMDD), but you can mix and match any configuration of date elements that best suits your needs. *Note:* When selecting an item from the drop-down menu, you don't need to click the Insert button; the token is added to the template automatically. You only need to click the Insert button if the element you want to use is the default menu item showing.

6. **Click the Editor window after the date token and type an underscore.**

   Yes, you can hard-code text right into your template! It's a filename after all, so don't go crazy, but if there's some naming convention you want in a template you can either hard-code it by typing it or add a custom text token for greater flexibility. I use an underscore because I don't believe in having spaces in filenames.

7. **Choose the desired sequence format from the Sequence drop-down menu.**

   I often work with a three-digit sequence number, so I chose the Sequence # (001) token.

8. **Choose Save Current Settings as New Preset from the Preset drop-down menu.**

   Doing so opens the New Preset dialog box. Custom file-naming templates are going to be available to you during import, export, and as part of the Rename Photos dialog box regardless of where the templates are created, so it makes good sense to save them for reuse.

9. **Enter a descriptive name in the Preset Name field and then click Create.**

   In the Filename Template Editor, the name you chose appears in the Preset drop-down menu.

10. **Click Done to return to the Rename Photos dialog box.**

    The name of the template you created appears in the dialog box's File Naming drop-down menu and the example at the bottom left of the dialog box reflects your new template.

11. **Click OK to apply that template to the selected photos.**

Keep in mind that renaming photos in Lightroom renames the actual photos, too.

Creating metadata templates to embed information into each image

The Metadata panel (see Figure 6-15) is great for displaying any metadata embedded in an image, but you can also use it to add new metadata, edit some existing metadata, or access other photos that share common data points. Because so much data about each photo can be displayed, the Metadata panel has a number of different view options that are accessible via the drop-down menu in the panel's header. This enables you to pick a view that shows only the type of metadata you're interested in, which makes work much easier.

The Preset drop-down menu at the top of the panel gives you access to your custom metadata templates — as well as the controls to create *new*

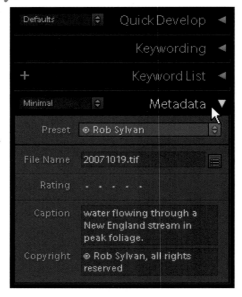

Figure 6-15: The Metadata panel.

templates. Any templates you've created via the Import dialog box are also accessible here. To create a new metadata template

1. **Choose Edit Presets from the Preset drop-down menu.**

   The Edit Metadata Presets dialog box appears, as shown in Figure 6-16. You can also access this dialog box by choosing Metadata⇨Edit Metadata Presets from the main menu.

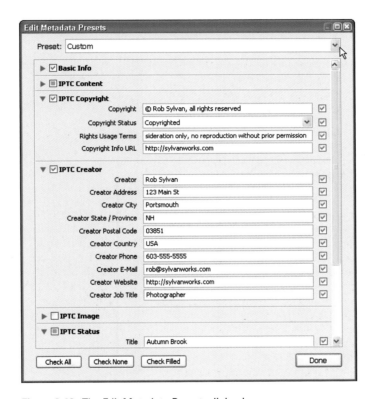

Figure 6-16: The Edit Metadata Presets dialog box.

2. **Complete all applicable fields.**

   Depending on your needs, you can complete as much or as little of the dialog box before saving it as a template.

3. **Choose Save Current Settings as New Preset from the Preset drop-down menu.**

   Doing so launches the New Preset dialog box.

4. **Enter a name in the Preset Name field and click Create.**

   The name of the preset appears in the editor's Preset drop-down menu.

5. **Click Done to close the editor.**

You can apply a preset by selecting your photos in Grid view, and then selecting the desired preset from the Metadata panel's Preset drop-down menu. Lightroom prompts you with the Apply Metadata Preset dialog box, shown in Figure 6-17, where you can choose to apply the preset to just the active photo or to all selected photos. Select the Don't Show Again check box if you don't want to be prompted in the future. (The choice you make becomes the default behavior when the prompt is turned off.)

Figure 6-17: The Apply Metadata Preset dialog box.

Keywording

I don't know anyone who loves the task of adding keywords to their photos, but I also don't know anyone who isn't glad to have well-keyworded photos when it comes time to find them. *Keywording* is your chance to describe the contents of your photos with words that aid you in finding them. By doing so, the words you use form a structure of their own inside your catalog. If you're thorough and consistent in the application of keywords, you'll reach a point where you can find all photos of a given subject with just a click (or two).

Although it's possible (and often helpful) to start keywording at import, you'll find the Library module is where you do most of your keywording activities. Both the Keywording panel and the Keyword List panel have supporting roles in this process.

If you weren't a user of Lightroom 1, then you can skip this paragraph because I just want to bring former Lightroom users up to speed on an interface change. The Keyword Tags panel of Lightroom 1 has moved from the left side of the interface to the right side, and is renamed Keyword List. The Keywording panel remains on the right side with the same name.

The Keywording panel, shown in Figure 6-18, is made of three sections:

- **Keyword Tags:** The top section of the panel, Keyword Tags, provides a means to enter new keywords and to display the applied keywords of a selected photo. Use the Keyword Tags drop-down menu to access other options for displaying keywords.

✏ **Keyword Suggestions:** While you add keywords to your photos, Lightroom begins generating a list of suggested keywords based on other photos that have similar keywords applied to them. This is a new addition to Lightroom 2, and not only speeds up the keywording process, but also helps you remain consistent. Click any suggested keyword to add it to the selected photo.

✏ **Keyword Set:** Another keyword entry aid. You can create an unlimited number of keyword sets of up to nine keywords in each. Lightroom comes installed with three common sets that you can use or modify to fit your needs. Holding the Alt key (Option key on a Mac) reveals the keyboard shortcuts for each word in the set. This makes for speedy keywording by selecting photos and pressing Alt+number. Use the Keyword Set drop-down menu to access an existing set, or choose Edit Set to create a new one.

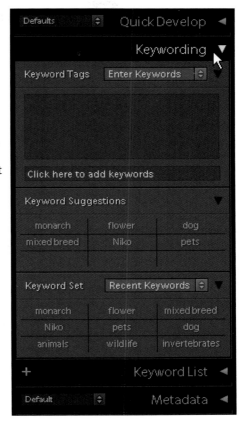

Figure 6-18: The Keywording panel.

The Keyword List panel, shown in Figure 6-19, consists of the following items:

✏ **Add/Remove keywords buttons:** Click the + or – buttons in the Keyword List header to add or remove keywords.

✏ **Filter Keywords:** Your keyword list can grow quite large. Enter a word (or part of a word) in the Filter Keywords field to display the keywords containing only that word (or part of that word).

✏ **The master list of keywords.**

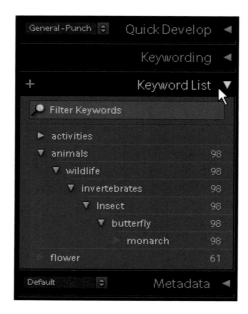

Figure 6-19: The Keyword List panel.

Adding and organizing keywords

You can add keywords to selected photos in the Library module a number of ways:

- ✓ **Drag selected photos onto a keyword in the Keyword List panel.**
- ✓ **Drag selected keywords onto selected photos.**
- ✓ **Select photo(s) and enter keywords via the Keywording panel.**
- ✓ **Use keyword shortcuts.**

You can't say Lightroom doesn't give you choices! Just to narrow down the realm of possibilities, though, I walk you through *one* way — creating and applying a keyword in the same step:

1. **Select a photo to keyword from Grid view.**

   In this example, I use a photo of my dog, Niko (see Figure 6-20).

2. **Expand the Keywording panel and then click the Click Here to Add Keywords field.**

   Always use this field to add new keywords.

Figure 6-20: Applying keywords to a photo using the Keywording panel.

3. **Enter a keyword and press Enter.**

   In this example, I simply enter **dog** and press Enter.

At its most basic level, that's all there is to it. The keyword *dog* has been applied to the photo, and the keyword now appears in the Keyword List panel. If I have another dog photo, I can drag the photo onto the keyword (or vice versa) to apply the keyword to the photo. Alternatively, if I prefer to type the keyword, I can repeat the steps above; however, as soon as I type **d,** Lightroom kicks into auto-complete mode and displays possibilities from my keyword list that I can then choose from, as shown in Figure 6-21.

You can assign multiple keywords to selected photos by entering them into the Click Here to Add Keywords field, separating each word with a comma. For example, I could also type **pets, baseball, Niko** and then press Enter. As more keywords are added to each photo, they appear in the Keyword List panel.

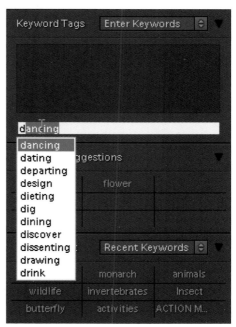

Figure 6-21: Keyword auto complete example.

TIP

As you can imagine, the Keyword List panel keeps growing as each new word is added, so much so that, pretty soon, it becomes rather unwieldy. To maximize the effectiveness of your keywords, you might want to consider arranging them into a hierarchical structure that adds both additional meaning and organization to your keyword list.

To put your existing keywords into some kind of order, you can drag and drop keywords onto each other, which puts them into a parent/child relationship. For example, I originally added *baseball, dog, pets,* and *Niko* to the photo back in Figure 6-20. If I want to start building a structure with those words, I'd probably select *dog* in the Keyword List panel and drag it to *pets.* (I'm such a logical guy.) After releasing *dog,* it's nested under *pets,* as shown in Figure 6-22.

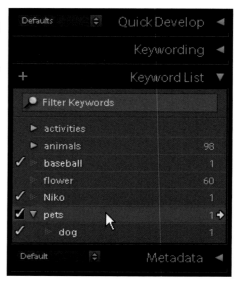

Figure 6-22: Nested keyword structure.

Instead of creating your structure after you add words to your photos, you can reverse the process and create the structure first. This gives you the benefit of thinking about how you want to arrange your keywords beforehand and generally leads to a much more thorough keywording process. The Keyword List panel provides the tools to aid you in the creation of new keywords. For example, to continue building on the "pets" structure I want to add the keyword *cat* and nest it underneath *pets* in anticipation of future cat photos. Here's how:

1. **Select the parent keyword.**

   In this case, I select *pets* because I want to add *cat* as a child keyword.

2. **Click the + symbol at the top of the Keyword panel to open the Create Keyword Tag dialog box shown in Figure 6-23.**

3. **Enter the keyword in the Keyword Tag field.**

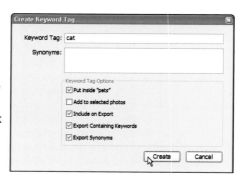

Figure 6-23: The Create Keyword Tag dialog box.

4. **Enter any synonyms.**

   Separate each synonym with a comma. Synonyms aren't searchable inside Lightroom, but they can be included as a keyword in exported copies.

5. **Check the Put Inside box.**

6. **Uncheck the Add to Selected Photos box.**

   In this case, I'm adding a keyword in anticipation of a future photo, not adding a keyword to any photos I have selected, so I uncheck this option. Of course, you can leave it checked if you want to apply it as part of the process.

7. **Check the Include on Export box.**

   If you want this keyword included in the exported copies, you need to check this box. If you just want the keyword to exist as an organizational aid in your catalog (such as a high-level category heading), then leave this box unchecked.

8. **Check the Export Containing Keywords box.**

   The parent keyword will also export. In this case, I want to ensure *pets* exports as a keyword along with *cat*.

9. **Check the Export Synonyms box.**

10. **Click Create.**

My new keyword, *cat,* is now added to the Keyword List panel under *pets*. The process is the same for adding other new keywords while you flesh out a keyword structure.

Using the Keyword List to find photos

Now that you've added a few keywords and have begun creating an organizational structure, you can use the Keyword List panel to jump right to a group of photos that share the same keyword. Figure 6-24 shows my first dog photo selected and both the Keywording and Keyword List panels. Notice that the four keywords in the Keyword Tags field have check marks next to them in the Keyword List. Those check marks identify all the keywords applied to the selected photo. Also, notice that the cursor is hovering over the Dog keyword in the list. I want you to know about two important options:

- **The Check Mark inside a Box business.** When you move your cursor over any keyword, you see a check box appear. Unchecking a keyword removes it from the selected photo. Adding a check mark applies that keyword to the selected photo.

✔ **The Right-facing Arrow next to the Counter business.** Clicking that arrow applies a Library filter that displays only the photos in the catalog that have that same keyword. Click None on the Filter bar to turn the filter off.

Figure 6-24: The Keywording and Keyword List panels.

Before I wrap up this chapter with a look at the Filter bar there is one more cool tool I want to introduce you to that will make adding all these various types of flags, metadata, and keywords a lot more fun.

Using the Painter Tool

The Painter tool is the little spray can icon in the Grid view Toolbar, as shown in Figure 6-25. You can use it to apply keywords, labels, flags, ratings, metadata, develop settings (the same Develop presets you saw in the Quick Develop panel), or photo rotations. You can even use it to assign a photo to a specific collection. It's quite simple to use if you prefer a more hands-on approach to adding the same piece of information to a large group of photos.

Here's the basic process — it's going to work the same for each data type:

Painter tool

Figure 6-25: The Painter tool in the Toolbar.

1. **Click the Painter tool to activate it.**

   Your cursor changes to the Painter icon and the Toolbar now shows only the Painter-specific settings.

2. **Choose the type of data you want to apply from the Paint drop-down menu.**

   In Figure 6-26, you can see I selected Rating. Whichever option you choose from the Paint menu results in its available options being displayed as the next setting to configure (in my case, stars appeared).

Figure 6-26: The Painter tool options.

3. **Choose the actual data you want to apply to your photos.**

   What you choose here will depend on the type of data you selected in the Paint drop-down menu. In my example I chose a rating of 2 stars. If keywords were chosen from the menu then I would type in keywords and so on. Think of this as loading the paint can with actual paint you are going to spray.

4. **Click and drag the Painter tool across the photos you want to apply that data to.**

   You apply the chosen information as you move the cursor across each photo. Just one click and drag (as if you are spraying) across the photos is all it takes.

If you "overspray" and get paint on the wrong photo, you can remove that data by clicking that photo with the Painter tool. Actually as soon as you move the Painter over an already-painted photo, the cursor changes to an eraser!

5. **Click the Done button in the Toolbar or press Esc to put the Painter tool away.**

Finding Photos with the Filter Bar

Okay, you've invested a lot of time in managing your portfolio, so you might as well take a look at one of the ways you can start to get a return on that investment. Let me introduce you to the Filter bar, shown in Figure 6-27 — a new addition to Lightroom. It combines what was the Metadata Browser and the Find panels in Lightroom 1, but takes those panels to a new level (and a new location). With the Filter bar embedded in the top of the content area, it feels much more integrated with the process of finding and filtering your photos. The downside is that it eats into the content area's real estate, but this can be alleviated with the use of a secondary display window set to Grid view. The Filter bar display can be toggled on and off by pressing the \ key. This doesn't turn off any active filter; it just hides the bar to maximize the content area. Filtering is turned on and off by pressing Ctrl+L (⌘+L on a Mac) or by clicking None on the Filter bar.

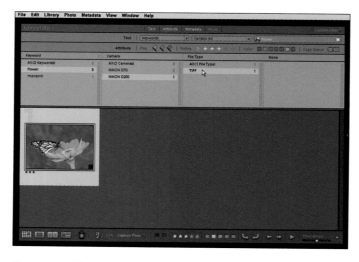

Figure 6-27: The Filter bar.

The Filter bar allows you to drill down into your portfolio in the following ways:

- **Searching text fields:** Not limited to searching by keyword, you can search on filenames and metadata fields as well.

- **By status indicators:** Clicking Refine reveals the options for "refining" your view using flags, ratings, labels, and master versus virtual copy status.

- **Leveraging metadata:** Enabling the metadata filter opens worlds of possibilities for gathering photos based on information about or embedded in each file, such as capture date, file type, aspect ratio, shutter speed, location, camera used, and more!

Filters can be used singly or in multiple mix-and-match combinations. I could have a hankering, say, for all TIF files with the keyword *flower* that were taken with my D200 and that have a rating of three stars or greater. Here's how I'd use a filter to satisfy that hankering:

1. **Select All Photographs from the Catalog panel.**

2. **Press \ if the Filter bar isn't visible.**

3. **On the Filter bar, click the Text label.**

   Doing so causes the Filter bar to expand and show the Text filter.

4. **Choose Keywords from the Search Target drop-down menu.**

   You could leave it set to Any Searchable Field because it's unlikely that *flower* would appear anywhere and not be a keyword, but I want to point out how specific you can focus your searches.

5. **Enter** flower **into the Search field.**

   When you begin typing, the content area updates to show only those results that match the filter.

6. **Hold the Ctrl key (⌘ on a Mac) and click the Attribute label.**

   Doing so causes the Filter bar to expand and show the Attribute filters.

7. **Click the third rating star.**

   Only photos with the *flower* keyword that are rated three stars or higher are left in the results.

8. **Hold the Ctrl key (⌘ on a Mac) and click the Metadata label.**

   The Filter bar expands further to include the Metadata options. The Default Columns view is displayed, which does include the camera model, but I also want to limit the results to only TIF files. You can customize the metadata columns to show different data — would anyone like to change the Lens column to File Type?

9. **Choose File Type from the drop-down menu located next to Lens.**

   I can change any column to File Type, but because Lens isn't criteria I'm concerned with in this example, I chose to ditch Lens. Now, I can see the file types as well as the camera models that represent the photos showing in the content area.

10. **Click the TIFF label.**

    Now, only TIF files are showing.

11. **Click the Nikon D200 label.**

    Now, only TIF files, shot with the D200, rated three stars or higher, that contain the *Flower* keyword are showing.

If this was a filter type that I thought I would use often, I could choose Save Current Settings as New Preset from the Custom Filter drop-down menu and give my new preset a name. It would then appear in the Custom Filter drop-down menu and be just a click away. Press Ctrl+L (⌘+L on a Mac) or click None on the Filter bar to turn off that filter and return to an unfiltered All Photographs.

Part III
Working in Your Digital Darkroom

The 5th Wave   By Rich Tennant

"If I'm not gaining weight, then why does this digital image take up 3 MB more memory than a comparable one taken six months ago?"

In this part . . .

Whether you're shooting raw or JPG (or both), you won't be able to escape having to perform some level of digital tweaking of your photos. Chapter 7 introduces you to the Develop module and the most common tasks you undertake when processing your photos.

After you master the basics, you'll be ready to dig into the more advanced Develop module tools covered in Chapter 8. The tips and tricks I highlight here can help you achieve the vision you hold for your photos in your mind's eye.

Depending on your artistic vision and the demands of your project, you might also find that you need an external image editor to complete the job. Chapter 9 covers all the improved integration features with Photoshop CS2 and shows you how to take your photos out of Lightroom and bring them back in again.

7

Develop Module Basics

In This Chapter

▶ Getting familiar with the Develop module

▶ Switching between view modes

▶ Applying settings to multiple photos

▶ Preserving editing states with snapshots

▶ Using develop history to undo adjustments

▶ Performing basic tonal adjustments

▶ Cropping to an aspect ratio

▶ Removing spots and red-eye

▶ Understanding the Graduated Filter

▶ Making local corrections with Adjustment Brush

*W*elcome to the Develop module! This is where Lightroom's real magic happens. You find some amazing additions to the Develop toolset in this version of Lightroom, and some of the existing tools have been upgraded. The need to send photos to an external editor has been decreased significantly. (In fact, you might no longer need an external editor for most photos!) Because this module has so much to offer, I split the coverage of the Develop module between this chapter and Chapter 8.

In case you are puzzling over the use of the word *develop* here, you need to keep in mind that Lightroom was primarily designed to work with raw photos, which by definition have not yet been processed for final output. So, Lightroom approaches photos with the mindset that photos first need to be *developed* before they are ready to leave Lightroom and face whatever comes next.

Aside from getting oriented to where everything is in the Develop interface, you get a chance to focus on the most common Develop tasks (from adjusting exposure levels to removing red-eye), as well as how to go back in time, batch process hundreds of images, and save your settings for reuse.

Exploring the Develop Module

At first glance, it's easy to be a little overwhelmed by all the panels, sliders, and buttons in this module. Don't be! The layout is essentially the same as all the other modules. You find the Module Picker across the top; the left side holds the panels that pertain to saved settings and different states of your photos; the right side contains all the adjustment controls. In the center, you find the content area and the Toolbar, and the ever-present Filmstrip runs along the bottom. Refer back to Chapter 1 for ways to modify the interface to suit your needs.

Getting to know the panels and tools

To know the Develop module is to love it, so go ahead and get acquainted with the interface, shown in Figure 7-1. Here's an overview of what you can find lying about:

Figure 7-1: The Develop module interface.

✔ **Identity plate:** Also known as the *vanity plate,* this is a customizable component of the interface that you can use to make Lightroom your own.

✔ **Navigator panel:** Displays a preview of your presets as you move the cursor over the contents of the Presets panel.

✔ **Presets panel:** On the left side, the Presets panel contains all the preinstalled and (soon to be created) custom Develop presets.

✔ **Snapshots panel:** A "snapshot" is a means to preserve a specific state in your editing process. Snapshots are great for creating multiple versions of a single file and storing them for easy access later.

✔ **History panel:** Still on the left, the History panel records a running history of every tweak and adjustment you make to each photo. This allows for an unlimited "undo" because you can always step back through the Develop history to any point in time.

✔ **Copy and Paste buttons:** Allow you to copy and paste Develop settings from one photo to another.

✔ **Filmstrip:** Strung across the bottom, the Filmstrip primarily displays thumbnails of all the photos in the current grouping, but also contains shortcuts for controlling both the primary and secondary windows, quick access to other photo groupings, and tools for filtering the active photo grouping.

✔ **Content area:** This is your workspace, which provides a live preview of the photo you're working on.

✔ **Toolbar:** Just below the content area, the Toolbar contains the buttons for switching between view modes, along with additional tools available via the Toolbar drop-down menu for navigating between photos, playing an "impromptu" slideshow, controlling zoom level, and applying flags, ratings, and labels.

✔ **Module Picker:** At the top right of the interface lies the Module Picker, which allows for quick movement between various Lightroom modules.

✔ **Histogram panel:** Provides a way to visualize your image data through an interactive graph of the all the tones contained in the active photo.

✔ **Tool Strip:** This is the collection of adjustment-tool icons nested under the histogram. The Crop, Spot Removal, and Red Eye Correction tools were pulled from their original location on the Toolbar of Lightroom 1 to join the new Graduated Filter and Adjustment Brush here in the Tool Strip.

✔ **Basic panel:** Why basic? Well, you touch these adjustments almost every time you bring a photo into the Develop module. You need to get these settings straight (such as White Balance and Exposure) before you can move on to other tasks.

- **Tone Curve panel:** This is the best tool for adjusting brightness and contrast.

- **HSL / Color / Grayscale panel:** Allows for the tweaking of individual colors as well as conversion to grayscale.

- **Split Toning panel:** Provides control over the color in the shadows and highlights of your photos. This can be used for creative color modifications or neutralizing existing color casts.

- **Detail panel:** Contains the tools for increasing sharpening, reducing noise, and correcting that annoying purple fringe (that is, *chromatic aberration*).

- **Vignettes panel:** This is both a practical correction tool for fixing dark edges that can appear because of lens configurations and for applying creative darkening (and brightening) to a photo's edges.

- **Camera Calibration panel:** Provides the ability to chose a default profile for rendering raw photos as well as the means to create your default rendering settings.

Becoming familiar with the menu options

The File, Edit, View, Window, and Help menus remain consistent across all modules, but the Develop module has a dedicated set of menu options. Menus are certainly useful for accessing specific functions, but they also serve to remind you about all the options and their respective keyboard shortcuts. Over the course of the two Develop module chapters (this chapter and Chapter 8), I cover all the functions in their context, but here's an overview of what you find in the Develop module menus:

- **Develop:** Contains the commands for creating new snapshots, presets, and preset folders, erasing the contents of the History panel, applying new Develop default settings for raw files, and navigating between photos.

- **Photo:** This group of commands pertains to stuff you can do to the active photo, such as adding it to the Quick Collection (or other target), showing its location, sending it to an external editor, creating virtual copies, rotating and flipping, applying flags, ratings, or labels, writing and reading the metadata stored in the photo, and deleting.

- **Settings:** Provides access to all the commands for copying, pasting, syncing, and applying Develop settings.

You might find it more efficient in many cases to use the contextual menus that appear when you right-click (Control+click on a Mac) various panels, settings, and photos. Don't be shy — click around and see what you find!

Understanding the view options

Working in the Develop module is obviously a visual process. You can scrutinize every nudge of every slider to get your photos looking how you want. Lightroom offers two view modes (with multiple options) to help you see what you're doing and how far you've come:

- **Loupe view:** This is the default working view when you enter the Develop module, and is where you will do almost all of your work. Just like the Loupe view in the Library module, you'll only see one photo at a time in the content area. You can zoom in or out by clicking the photo, using the controls in the Navigator panel, or the Zoom slider in the Toolbar. You can jump to Loupe view in the Develop module by pressing D no matter where you are in Lightroom.

  The word *loupe* refers to the film-based practice of looking at negatives through a magnifying lens called a loupe.

- **Before and After view:** Allows you to switch out of Loupe view for a comparison between the work you've done and the photo you started with. There are a number of variations on how you can arrange photos for comparison (which I'll cover in a bit) to give some choice over which might work best for a given photo. Press D to switch back to Loupe view.

No matter which view you're working in, to cycle through the Info Overlay displays — that little summary of information about the active photo that displays in the content area — press the I key, or choose View➪Loupe Info menu. To customize the information shown in the overlay, press Ctrl+J (⌘+J on a Mac).

Okay, you have the overview out of the way — time to take a closer look at each view mode.

The Loupe view

Just like in the Library module, the Navigator panel, shown in Figure 7-2, controls the zoom level. The default is Fit (the entire photo fits in the content area), with a zoomed-out level of 1:1 (as in 100 percent, or actual pixel view). You can change the zoom level by clicking the labels in the Navigator panel. When zoomed beyond Fit view, you can pan around the photo by clicking and dragging in the content area or by clicking and dragging inside the Navigator preview.

The Before and After views

Although much of your work happens in Loupe view, sometimes it's hard to appreciate how far

Figure 7-2: The Navigator panel's zoom controls.

you've come until you look at where you started. You can compare Before and After views several ways:

- ✔ **Left and Right:** Choose either a side-by-side view of the whole photo showing each state, or a split view (shown in Figure 7-3) that shows the Before image on the left and the After image on the right.

- ✔ **Top and Bottom:** Choose either to have the entire Before image on top and the After image on the bottom, or a single photo split between the two views.

- ✔ **Before Only:** This option is great for toggling between Before and After views for a quick peek by pressing the \ key.

These views aren't just for looking, though! All the adjustment sliders are still active and can be applied while looking at the Before and After views.

You can access all these view options from the button on the Toolbar (or the View menu). *Note:* When you're in Before and After view, three additional icons appear in the Toolbar. (Refer to Figure 7-3.) Here's what they do (from left to right):

- ✔ **Copy Before's settings to After:** If you decide you want to start over, you can quickly revert your After state's settings to how they were before.

- ✔ **Copy After's settings to Before:** If you're satisfied with the After state, you can save it as the new Before state so that you can press on with additional edits and have this state to compare against (and revert to).

- ✔ **Swap Before and After Settings:** This is handy if you want to create a new version that goes in a different direction from the original Before state, and preserves the current After state for later comparison.

Figure 7-3: Before and After split view.

These commands are also accessible from the View menu and can be applied from the Loupe view, too, if needed.

Applying settings to other photos

Okay, I'm sure your itching to dive in to the Editing tools (and you will!), but I really want you to have the big picture in mind before you start pushing sliders around. I promise you'll be knee-deep in adjustments soon enough.

I want to call your attention to the two buttons at the bottom of the left panel group and the two buttons at the bottom of the right panel group. (Again, refer to Figure 7-3.) Here's what they do:

- ✔ **Copy:** Allows you to copy settings from the active photo so that they can be pasted on to other photos (one at a time).

- ✔ **Paste:** Applies the copied settings to only to the active photo when clicked. For multiple photos, use Sync/Auto Sync, which I cover in a bit.

- ✔ **Previous:** Applies all the settings from the last photo you worked on to the currently active photo. This button is only visible when you have a single photo selected in the Filmstrip.

- ✔ **Reset:** Removes all Develop settings.

The Copy/Paste function is great when you want to keep a collection of settings ready to be pasted to any single photo when needed. However, when you want to apply a collection of settings across a selection of photos, you need to use either the Sync button, or its alter ego, the Auto Sync button.

If you have more than one photo selected, either in the Filmstrip or if you are using the secondary window in Grid view, you notice that the Previous button has changed to Sync. When you click the Sync button, it opens the Synchronize Settings dialog box, shown in Figure 7-4. This functions just like the Copy button in that it allows you to choose which settings in the active photo you want to apply, but in this case, the settings are applied to the other photos you select. After checking the boxes next to the settings you want to "sync," click the Synchronize button.

You can synchronize settings across any number of selected photos, which is most effective when you want to selectively synchronize a subset of settings across multiple photos. If you're in a situation where you have a grouping of photos that you want to process exactly the same way and in real time (almost), then you want to change the Sync button to Auto Sync by holding the Ctrl key (⌘ on a Mac) and clicking Sync. As soon as you press that key, you see Sync change to Auto Sync — clicking the button makes the transformation complete. After you turn on Auto Sync, every adjustment you make to the active photo is automatically applied to the rest of the selected photos. You see the thumbnail previews update as you work. This is a huge timesaver!

Here's the catch — once Auto Sync is on, it's on until you turn it off (just click it again without holding any key). I have to tell you that I've accidentally auto-sync'd a bunch of files more than once. Thankfully, there's that faithful Undo shortcut, Ctrl+Z (⌘+Z on a Mac)!

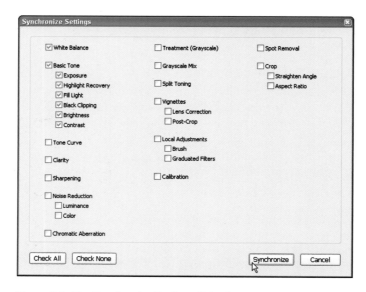

Figure 7-4: The Synchronize Settings dialog box.

The Presets, Snapshots, and History Triple Play

Understanding how the Presets, Snapshots, and History panels function greatly improves your understanding of how all the Develop module settings are applied.

Lightroom is a *metadata editor,* which means that every adjustment you make is recorded as a set of instructions to be applied during some form of output. You see a live preview of the changes you make, but it's just that, a preview. None of the changes actually "happen" until you do something such as export a copy or print.

The Presets, Snapshots, and History panels allow you to interact with the set of instructions Lightroom comes up with in some pretty cool ways. The next few sections fill you in on the details.

Saving time with presets

The Presets panel, shown in Figure 7-5, is where you can save a collection of settings to be reused on other photos. A small collection of presets is preinstalled and listed under the Lightroom Presets section of the panel. Any new presets you create (see the next section) are going to be stored under the User Presets section by default, or you can create new folders to store them.

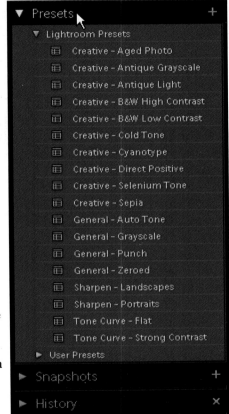

Creating your own presets

Because a preset is simply a collection of settings pulled from the active photo, the first thing you need to do is apply some adjustments to said photo. After you take care of that business, here's how you save those adjustments as a new preset:

1. **Click the + icon at the top of the Presets panel.**

   Doing so launches the New Develop Preset dialog box shown in Figure 7-6.

2. **Enter a name for your new preset in the Preset Name field.**

3. **(Optional) Click the Folder drop-down menu to choose where to place the preset.**

Figure 7-5: The Presets panel.

This step is optional because all presets are placed in the User Presets folder by default. You only need to change the location if you want them somewhere else.

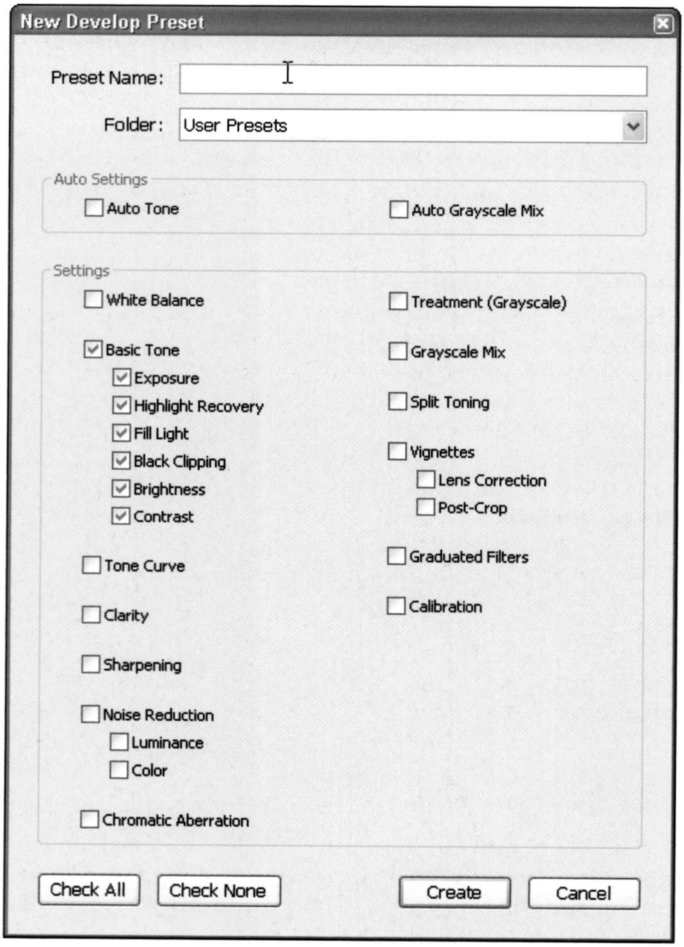

Figure 7-6: The New Develop Preset dialog box.

4. Check the box next to each setting you want to include in the preset.

The Check All and Check None buttons at the bottom of the dialog box can speed the selection process.

5. Click Create.

The new preset appears in the Presets panel within the folder you select. Move your cursor over any preset to see a preview of its effect in the Navigator panel.

If you realize you forgot to add a particular setting or made a new adjustment and want to add it to the preset, just right-click (Control+click on a Mac) the preset and choose Update with Current Settings from the contextual menu that appears. This launches the Update Develop Preset dialog box (which is the spitting image of the New Develop Preset dialog box). Check and uncheck any settings and click Update. To delete a user preset, right-click (Control+click on a Mac) the preset in the Presets panel and choose Delete.

Freezing time with snapshots

The Snapshots panel, shown in Figure 7-7, is a way to collect different states of a photo and store them so you can revisit a state later. Whatever state a photo is in can be saved as a snapshot. Just click the + icon at the top of the Snapshots panel, and give the new Snapshots listing a name. Create as many snapshots as you need.

If you make some additional tweaks after saving a snapshot and like that version better, right-click (Control+click on a Mac) the snapshot and choose Update with Current Settings from the contextual menu that appears. To remove a snapshot, just select it and click the – icon at the top of the panel.

Figure 7-7: The Snapshots panel.

Going back in time with the History panel

It's never too late for a do-over in Lightroom. The History panel, shown in Figure 7-8, records every adjustment and tweak you make in the Develop module. You can open a photo anytime and step to any earlier point in its Develop history by clicking an earlier History step. You can even save a History state as a snapshot by right-clicking (Control+click on a Mac) and choosing Create Snapshot from the contextual menu that appears.

Enough of the overview, already. Time to look at how you go about "developing" your photos.

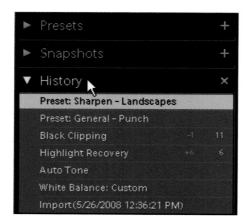

Figure 7-8: The History panel.

Development Essentials

Lightroom's Develop module is both an image processor and an image editor. I'll tell you where I draw the line, but I'll be the first to admit that the distinction has blurred, thanks to Lightroom. When your camera is set to capture in JPG mode, it takes the raw capture data and processes it by using the in-camera settings (such as contrast, saturation, and sharpening) to produce a rendered JPG version of the captured image data. The benefit of shooting JPG is that you're using the camera for both capture and processing, which can certainly be a timesaver. The downside is that the original *raw* capture data is lost after the JPG version is created. If you bring that JPG into Lightroom's Develop module, you're not processing the capture data, but rather editing the rendered image data. Of course, with Lightroom the actual pixels in the source file are never changed, so technically, only the pixels in exported copies are edited, but I hope you can see the distinction.

Here's why it matters. In contrast to JPG, when you shoot raw, you take the camera out of the processing business. The result is that the camera is primarily a capture device that saves the raw capture data to your memory card. That raw capture data needs to be processed by some type of raw-processing software. I'll assume you're using Lightroom for that task. When you bring a raw photo into Lightroom, you take over the image-processing tasks formerly performed by the camera in the JPG example. You decide how much contrast, saturation, and sharpening (to name just a few settings) are going to be applied to create a rendered version of the photo (during output).

The benefit is that you can customize those settings to maximum effect on a photo-by-photo basis, and you never lose the original capture data! You can reprocess the raw data any number of ways. The downside is that you need to add that processing step into your workflow, which takes time.

The reason the line between processing and editing has blurred is that Lightroom can perform a much wider range of adjustments on your photos than any camera could dream of performing. Red-eye removal, cropping, and spot removal used to be tasks that could be done only in a pixel editor (like Photoshop). With the introduction of the Graduated Filter and Adjustment Brush in Lightroom 2, the line between processing and editing is almost erased.

That said, the place where the rubber meets the road (as far as each Lightroom user is concerned) is that when you bring a rendered file (JPG, TIF, or PSD) into Lightroom, you're working with processed data. Therefore, all the adjustments you make in Lightroom are made relative to whatever processing decisions have previously been made. When you bring a raw file into Lightroom, the adjustments are absolute settings — no prior processing has been done — giving you much more leeway in how you process each photo.

Using the Histogram panel

The Histogram panel, shown in Figure 7-9, is another way to look at your photo by displaying it as a graph of all the tones it contains. When this information is used in conjunction with the live view of the photo in the content area, it greatly informs the adjustment decisions you make.

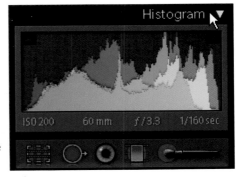

Figure 7-9: The Histogram panel.

Although the actual graph is the same as what is shown in the Library module, the Develop module's Histogram panel has a few additional features:

✔ **It's interactive:** When you move your cursor over the histogram, you see how each area of the histogram relates to the tonal adjustment sliders in the Basic panel:

- *Blacks:* The far-left end of the graph showing the darkest shadows.

- *Fill Light:* The tonal range between the darkest shadows and the midtones.

- *Exposure:* Covers the midtones to the beginning of the highlights.

- *Recovery:* The far-right end of the graph showing the brightest highlights.

Similarly, if you place your cursor over each of the four tonal adjustment sliders in the Basic panel, you see the respective sections of the Histogram panel brighten. You can click and drag within the histogram to make tonal adjustments, and when you do so, the respective sliders adjust in tandem.

✔ **It has clipping indicators:** The arrows at either end of the histogram are white when data in all three channels has been clipped, or are a color when only one or two channels are clipped. (*Clipping* means that pixels in the image have exceeded the tonal range on an end of the histogram — shadows or highlights — and no longer contain any image data.) In some instances, this is okay, such as shadow aeas you want to be all black, or bright highlights — reflections of the sun or chrome, for example, or the catch lights in someone's eyes. However, other times, clipping isn't nice at all — such as when all the detail in a white wedding dress is lost due to overexposure.

In addition to the histogram indicators, you can enable a visual clipping indicator that displays in your photo. Press the J key to enable the clipping indicator. When enabled, areas that are clipped on the shadow end are shown in blue, and areas clipped on the highlights end are shown in red. Figure 7-10 shows an image with both shadow and highlight clipping.

✔ **It's great for RGB readouts:** The photo you see in the content area is made from the image data contained in the Red, Green, and Blue channels of the photo. Lightroom uses a scale that ranges from 0 percent (black) to 100 percent (white).

Figure 7-10: An example of shadow and highlight clipping indicators.

The relationships between the histogram, the basic tonal adjustments, the clipping indicators, and the RGB readouts make the histogram an important tool for evaluating what's happening in your photos, which is why the Histogram panel remains visible at the top of the right panel group no matter how far down you scroll to the other adjustment panels.

Making basic adjustments

It's almost a given that you're going to be making certain kinds of adjustments to almost all your photos. These adjustments are grouped into four sections in the Basic panel, as shown in Figure 7-11:

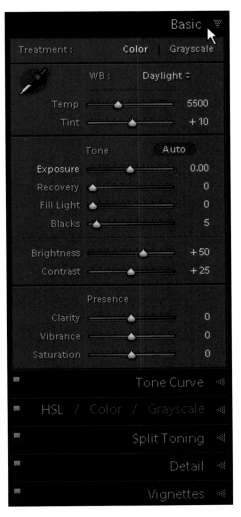

- **Treatment:** Choose between working on a color or grayscale photo. All the controls in the Basic panel apply to grayscale images as well. I cover grayscale conversions in the next chapter.

- **White Balance:** Provides tools you can use to neutralize color casts or to creatively interpret the lighting conditions that existed at the moment of capture. White balance is subjective. Have fun with it.

- **Tone:** Contains the controls for adjusting the range of tones in the photo. You can set highlight and shadow-clipping levels and adjust midtone brightness levels as well.

- **Presence:** These three controls have a big effect on how people respond to your photo. The Clarity slider is essentially a local contrast adjustment (which can improve apparent depth and sharpness), whereas Vibrance and Saturation adjust the colors. I go over each in more detail a little further on.

Figure 7-11: The Basic panel.

With that overview in mind, make your way through the next few sections where I delve deeper into the Basic panel.

Controlling color casts

White balance adjustments — where you attempt to make objects that appeared white when you saw them in person appear white in the finished photo — are subjective. How you process your photos is how you express your vision of the scene that you captured. The color of the light has a big impact on how others will react to the image. I had a conversation recently with an extremely successful wedding photographer. He was lamenting the fact that too many assistants are trained to neutralize the color casts in the photos they're editing. He wanted to capture the feeling of the light that was present at the time of capture, so the photos matched memories of those moments. Of course, others are sure to prefer that color casts be neutralized. The choice you make is going to depend on your vision.

Lightroom offers three methods for adjusting the white balance:

✔ **White Balance Selector tool:** This neutralizing tool is located in the White Balance section of the Basic panel. You can activate it by pressing W or by clicking the eyedropper icon. Your goal is to find and select a highlight that is close to being *neutral;* that is, all three RGB values should be pretty close to each other. The Selector tool has a special Loupe — the gridlike object behind the cursor shown in Figure 7-12 — that shows you the pixels and their RGB values under the tool while you move the eyedropper to find the right spot to click. RGB values in the 80s usually work best. Lightroom attempts to neutralize the color cast by adjusting the R, G, and B channels at that location to equal values.

When active, the Toolbar contains the following options, as shown in Figure 7-12:

- *Auto Dismiss:* By default, the White Balance Selector tool goes away after clicking on a spot. However, at times, you might want to try sampling multiple locations before manually dismissing the tool. Uncheck this box to stop Auto Dismiss.

- *Show Loupe:* The Loupe is a helpful tool, but you can also see the RGB values display under the histogram. Uncheck this box to turn off the Loupe.

- *Scale:* Adjusts the size of the grid in the Loupe.

- *Done:* Exits the White Balance Tool when not using Auto Dismiss. Pressing Esc also works.

✔ **White balance preset:** When working with raw images, you can set the absolute white balance based on the lighting at the time of capture using the appropriate preset, or choose Auto to let Lightroom work its magic. The absolute white balance value has already been set in rendered files (JPG, TIF, or PSD), so your preset options in Lightroom are limited to either leaving it as is (As Shot) or letting Lightroom try to adjust auto-matically (Auto). Custom is displayed if the White Balance Selector tool or the Temp and Tint sliders are used to make a manual adjustment with both raw and rendered files.

⌐ **Temperature and Tint sliders:** Make manual adjustments to the color temperature and its tint.

Figure 7-12: The White Balance Selector tool.

I often find that a combination of each of these tools provides me with the most pleasing results. Your starting point is always going to be the As Shot setting, and if that looks good to you, then don't feel compelled to continue adjusting. When it doesn't feel right, you need to make some decisions. My preference is to reach for the White Balance Selector tool and attempt to achieve a neutral result, and then, based on the scene, adjust the Temp and Tint sliders until it looks how I think it should. When I'm working on one photo that's part of a series shot under the same lighting conditions, I'll use the Sync button to apply the same setting to those photos as well.

After you settle on a white balance setting that you like, you can move on to making tonal adjustments.

Adjusting tonal range to bring out the best

The tone adjustments in the Basic panel provide you creative freedom to make the most of the settings you used in the camera to capture the image data. I talk about the relationship between the tonal adjustments and the histogram earlier in this chapter, and now you're going to utilize all the tools at your disposal.

The Tone section of the Basic panel (refer to Figure 7-11) contains the following adjustments:

- **Auto:** The Auto setting got a complete overhaul for Lightroom 2 and actually works quite well for many photos. This is Lightroom's attempt to optimize the tonal settings based on the data in the histogram. It can make for a great starting point.

- **Exposure:** The slider's scale is based on f-stops. Adjustments will affect the entire tonal range, but the biggest impact is on the highlights. Adjust as needed to improve overall image brightness. If some highlight clipping occurs, it might be possible to correct with the Recovery slider.

- **Recovery:** Use this adjustment to recover detail in extreme highlights by reducing highlight values until they no longer extend past the end of the histogram.

- **Fill Light:** Helps to open detail in the light shadow areas with minimal impact on the darkest values (to help keep blacks black).

- **Blacks:** The darkest shadows. Use this slider to determine what areas of the image (if any) to clip to all black (no detail).

- **Brightness:** This adjustment acts very much like the Exposure adjustment I mention above, but is primarily intended to brighten midtone values. It can be helpful in small doses, but you might get better results from adjusting the tone curve (which I cover in Chapter 8).

- **Contrast:** Increases or decreases contrast in the image. This is a bit of a legacy adjustment whose functionality has largely been replaced by the tone curve.

How you approach these adjustments largely depends on how well the image was exposed in-camera. Are you compensating for over- or underexposure or just optimizing a proper exposure? Does the scene contain really bright highlights as well as dark shadows? This is where you need to make an evaluation based on what you see in the content area (in conjunction with the histogram) to decide how to get from where you are to where you want to be. Here's a basic workflow you can apply to each photo:

1. **Evaluate the image.**

   Note problem areas, such as clipped highlights, clipped shadows, and muddy midtones. Compare them to how you intended the photo to look. Can you get there from here?

2. **Click Auto in the Tone section.**

   This function has improved so much that I now include it as a Develop preset on import because it can serve as a good starting point.

3. **(Optional) Press J to turn on the clipping indicators.**

   They're easy to toggle on and off and they show you exactly what area of the photo is being clipped.

4. **Adjust the Exposure slider.**

   Your goal is to set the white point and thereby overall image brightness. Additionally, you can hold the Alt key (Option on a Mac) while you drag the Exposure slider to get an alternative view of any image areas that might be clipping in the highlights.

5. **Adjust the Blacks slider.**

   You always have much less detail in the shadow areas than in the highlights. In many cases, you can create a more-pleasing image by clipping the darkest shadow areas to black. As you can with the Exposure slider, you can hold the Alt key (Option on a Mac) while dragging the Blacks slider to see just the areas of the image that are clipping to black.

6. **(Optional) Adjust the Recovery slider.**

   Not every image will need to have the highlights pulled back, but for those that do, the Recovery slider is a fantastic tool. Adjust as needed until there is no longer any clipping in the highlights.

7. **Adjust the Fill Light slider to brighten the darker areas of the photo.**

   Almost all images can benefit from a little bump in the Fill Light to open up shadows a little more.

A quick way to return any slider to its original state is to double-click its label. This works for all sliders in Lightroom.

I left out the Brightness and Contrast sliders from that process because I tend to leave them as a "finishing touch" at the end of my developing process, and I prefer the control offered by the Tone Curve panel. There's no one right way to approach this, so if you prefer using the Brightness and Contrasts sliders, by all means, do so.

Making images pop

Every image won't need the adjustments found in the Presence section, but they make a big impact on the ones that do. However, precisely *because* they can have such a big impact, you need to be careful not to overdo it. It's easy to get hooked on their power!

With that warning out of the way, take another look at Figure 7-11, casting your eyes to the three sliders in the Presence section of the Basic panel:

  ✓ **Clarity:** This contrast adjustment is designed to give the image a little oomph. When it was in development, Adobe considered naming it "punch" because that seemed an apt description of its effect. This adjustment is best applied while zoomed to 1:1 to better gauge its affect on the detail in the image. Like most things in life it is best used in moderation.

✔ **Vibrance:** A more sophisticated saturation adjustment that mostly affects the less-saturated colors while protecting skin tones and preventing clipping in the most-saturated colors. This is a great all-around color booster.

✔ **Saturation:** Use this slider to adjust the saturation of all colors equally in both directions. Decrease saturation by dragging to the left and increase saturation by dragging to the right. Not great for skin tones.

A great starting point for Presence settings is contained in the preinstalled Develop preset called General - Punch. Expand the Presets panel and look under the Lightroom Presets collection (refer to Figure 7-5). Just click it one time to apply it to the selected photo. All it does is set Clarity to +50 and Vibrance to +25. It really does live up to its name!

Fixing Common Problems

Just below the Histogram panel is a collection of editing tools referred to as the Tool Strip, as shown in Figure 7-13. If you're familiar with Lightroom 1, you'll recognize a few of the tools (although they were previously located in the Toolbar), but a couple of new additions are here as well. The Tool Strip contains:

✔ **Crop Overlay:** Allows for cropping to a specific aspect ratio; it also functions as a straightening tool.

✔ **Spot Removal:** Functions similarly to the Clone and Heal tools in Photoshop, which primarily allow for the basic removal of sensor spots and skin blemishes by borrowing pixels from another part of the image.

✔ **Red-Eye Correction:** Handy for those times when you just had to use on-camera flash.

Figure 7-13: The Tool Strip.

✔ **Graduated Filter:** Enables the application of multiple adjustment settings in a user-controlled gradual fade across any area of the photo. For example, you can correct an overcast sky by applying a gradual exposure compensation and saturation boost to just the sky and having it fade naturally at the horizon.

✔ **Adjustment Brush:** Provides the ability to "paint" with multiple adjustment settings. Think of it as a Dodge and Burn tool on steroids! A good example is the application of additional sharpening to the eyes in a portrait without sharpening the surrounding skin, but that just scratches the surface of what this tool can do.

Need some practical tips on how to use all these tools? Read on and become enlightened.

Creating strong compositions through cropping

Cropping in-camera might be the goal, but it isn't always the reality. However, even if you do get it "right" in-camera, there might still be occasions where you need to produce an image with an aspect ratio that is different from the aspect ratio of the original photo. The only way to change the aspect ratio is to crop. The Crop Overlay tool provides both a means for practical corrections as well as creative composition adjustments.

It's worth mentioning that the histogram always reflects the area of the photo inside the crop rectangle. In some cases, you might want to make cropping your first adjustment if you aren't planning to keep some areas of the photo in the final composition. This way, the histogram can reflect just the data you are keeping and, therefore, be more accurate when you're performing basic tonal adjustments.

You can jump into the Crop Overlay by clicking its icon in the Tool Strip, but I prefer the keyboard shortcut R because it works in any module. This is especially handy after applying a crop ratio to a batch of photos via Quick Develop in the Library module — press R to jump into Crop Overlay to finesse each photo.

As soon as you press R, the Crop Overlay appears over the photo and the following cropping options appear in the Tool Strip, as shown in Figure 7-14.

- ✔ **Crop Frame Tool:** Click this tool (the icon next to Aspect) to draw freeform cropping rectangles as an alternative to readjusting the default resizing handles.

- ✔ **Aspect Ratio drop-down menu:** Access a list of preinstalled aspect ratios or create a custom aspect ratio when you need the crop to fit a determined output aspect ratio.

- ✔ **Aspect Ratio Lock:** When closed, the crop rectangle can be resized, but the aspect ratio will not change. When open, you can resize and change aspect ratio as needed. Press A to toggle between open and closed.

- ✔ **Straighten Tool:** Allows for quick straightening. Select the tool (the icon next to Angle) and then click and drag along any straight line in the photo that should be either vertical or horizontal (say, the horizon or edge of a building). When you release the mouse, the photo rotates accordingly.

- ✔ **Angle slider:** Click and drag to rotate a photo. Click the slider handle once and use the left/right arrow keys to nudge the rotation, or click into the number field and use the Up/Down arrow keys for a finer amount of rotation.

- ✔ **Reset:** Returns the image to its uncropped state.

- ✔ **Close:** Click to exit the Crop Overlay. (I prefer to simply press D.)

Straightener tool

Crop Frame tool

Figure 7-14: The Crop Overlay.

You'll notice the crop rectangle, its resize handles, and a guide overlay inside the content area. You can resize and reshape the crop rectangle as desired, but you have to move the actual photo to reposition it behind the overlay. In other words, you can grab any resize handle to change the crop rectangle, but you need to click and drag on the photo to move it to a new position. If you click and drag outside of the crop rectangle, you can rotate the photo.

Removing spots and healing blemishes

Undoubtedly, you will encounter photos that contain something you want to remove, the most common things being spots caused by dust on your sensor or blemishes in a subject's skin. (Oh, to have a perfect sensor and perfect skin!) Lightroom comes to your aid in this regard with the Spot Removal tool, as shown in Figure 7-15. You can access the Spot Removal tool by clicking its icon in the Tool Strip or by pressing N. When activated, you see the following Brush options:

On/Off button

Figure 7-15: The Spot Removal tool.

↙ **Clone/Heal:** This setting determines the behavior of the brush. The Clone brush simply takes pixels from one area and pastes them into another. The Heal brush also borrows pixels from a different area, but goes a step further by sampling the color and texture of the area you are "healing" and attempting to blend the two. The Heal brush works best in most cases, but depending on the pixels you're working with, the blend might not always be seamless, in which case you can use the Clone brush.

↙ **Size:** Adjusts the size of the brush. Use the [key to decrease the size and the] key to increase the size.

↙ **Opacity:** Controls the strength of the brush. The lower the number, the more the original spot will show through the adjustment. This feature helps when you only want to deemphasize an area instead of blocking it out completely.

↙ **On/Off button:** That little light-switchlike button in the bottom-left corner of the panel can be used to toggle the results of the tool on and off for comparison purposes.

↙ **Reset:** Clears all spot-removal points.

↙ **Close:** Click to exit the tool.

To see how powerful a tool this can be, follow along as I perform an extreme makeover to the entrance to a bluebird's house, as shown in Figure 7-16:

1. **Select the photo in Grid view and press D to jump to the Develop module — if you're not there already.**

2. **Press N to activate the Spot Removal tool.**

3. **Choose either Heal or Clone.**

4. **Size the brush as needed with the [and] keys.**

5. **Set the Opacity slider to 100.**

6. **Click and drag the affected area to the pixels you want to borrow and release when you have a good match.**

7. **Adjust source and target circles as needed for best results.**

   After you apply the brush to the area, you can click and drag either circle to reposition as needed. Use the sliders to adjust the brush size and opacity for best results. Press H to hide (or show) the circles.

8. **Press D to accept the change and exit the tool.**

   You can go back later and readjust if needed.

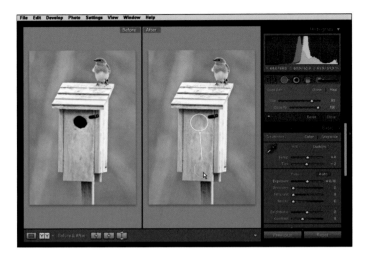

Figure 7-16: Removing a really big spot.

I chose this extreme example to illustrate the power of this tool. Just imagine what it could do with a freckle!

Correcting red-eye problems

Although the dreaded red-eye is always best avoided at the moment of capture, it's still great to remove it with minimum hassle when it's encountered. There isn't much to see with this tool until you apply it to an eye. After it's applied, the tool is in Edit mode and you have the following options:

- ✔ **Pupil Size:** Adjusts the size of the affected area inside the pupil.
- ✔ **Darken:** Darkens or lightens the affected pupil.
- ✔ **On/Off button:** That little light-switchlike button in the bottom-left corner of the panel can be used to toggle the results of the tool on and off for comparison purposes.
- ✔ **Reset:** Clears all red-eye correction spots.
- ✔ **Close:** Exits from the Red-Eye Correction tool.

Applying the correction is pretty straightforward. Here's what you do to fix the red-eyed cutie in Figure 7-17:

1. **Select the photo in Grid view and press D to jump to the Develop module.**

2. **Click the Red-Eye Correction tool icon in the Tool Strip.**

   There's no keyboard shortcut for this one.

3. **Adjust the size of the tool to exceed the size of the eye.**

   You can control the tool's size with the [and] keys or by simply clicking and dragging until you reach the desired size. It's better to be a little too big than too small.

   After you release the mouse, Lightroom moves to Edit mode, analyzing the area and finding the "red" that needs to be removed. You're just telling Lightroom where to look.

4. **In Edit mode, adjust the Pupil Size and Darken sliders as needed for best results.**

   You just have to eyeball this one (sorry!).

5. **Repeat for the other eye.**

   If the first adjustment looks good, then a single click will apply the same settings to the other eye.

6. **Click the Close button or press D to exit.**

Figure 7-17: The Red-Eye Correction tool.

In a typical workflow, you want to always perform all of your global (i.e., entire photo) adjustments first, which aside from the adjustments in the Basic panel, may also include some or all of the other adjustment panels below it, before you start using the Graduated Filter and Adjustment Brush. However, since we're already looking at the contents of the Tool Strip, I'm going to cover these two tools now. The remaining adjustment panels are all covered in Chapter 8.

Graduated Filter

If you've ever shot with a graduated neutral density filter to properly expose a photo containing a bright sky and darker land, then you'll appreciate what Lightroom's Graduated Filter is trying to do. However, unlike the actual filter that goes in front of your lens, this tool allows you to adjust exposure, brightness, contrast, saturation, clarity, sharpness, and even add a tint! You might find yourself using the real filter less and less, although to be fair, if you blow out detail because of overexposure, Lightroom can't bring back what isn't there!

Activate Graduated Filter by clicking its icon in the Tool Strip or by pressing M. When enabled you see its adjustment tools appear below the Tool Strip. The tools are divided into the following sections:

- **Mask:** Allows you to either create a new adjustment or edit an existing adjustment. You can add as many filters as you please.

- **Effect:** Contains all the settings you can use, alone or in tandem, to achieve your desired results. The drop-down menu contains existing and custom presets, which allow you to save specific settings for reuse. The toggle switch to the right of the Effect drop-down menu controls which Effect mode you're in. You have two options, as shown in Figure 7-18:

Figure 7-18: Comparison of Button mode on the left and Sliders on the right.

- *Buttons:* This is the simple mode. Chose an effect you want to use, click the negative or positive button, and then adjust the amount slider to control its strength.

- *Sliders:* This is the advanced mode. Adjust any combination of sliders with much greater control to create the desired effect.

✔ **On/Off:** Click the On/Off toggle button at the bottom to disable the results of the adjustment. This feature can be good for a quick comparison to how things looked before. Click the Reset button to clear all Graduated Filter applications.

New versus Edit

Creating a new filter is your only option when starting out. However, as soon as you click into your photo, the tool switches to Edit mode. The actual graduated filter is represented by the three lines shown in Figure 7-19. The space between the lines is where the gradual filtering takes place. The way to apply it is to click into the photo where you want the fading of the effect to begin and drag toward the area you don't want affected by the filter settings. In the test image shown in Figure 7-19, I initially clicked near the center of the image and dragged upward. The result is that the area below where I clicked got the maximum effect, the space between the filter guides was gradually faded, and the area above the filter was untouched.

When placing a filter, you can click and drag in any direction, and I encourage you to grab a photo and just play with this tool until you get a good feel for how it works. After the filter is applied, you can increase and decrease the fade area by clicking and dragging either outside guideline, or move the entire filter by clicking and dragging the Edit pin — the round icon with the black center. You can even rotate the filter by clicking and dragging the center line. Hold the Shift key when you first apply the filter to prevent any rotation and to achieve a perfectly perpendicular line.

Edit pin

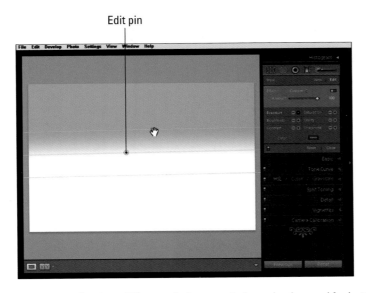

Figure 7-19: Graduated filter applied to a neutral gray background for better visibility.

Putting the tool to use

The best way to explain this tool is with an example. The subject in the Before view of the photo in Figure 7-20 is way too dark, but any adjustment to overall exposure or fill light is going to negatively impact the sky. I want to bump up the exposure of the bottom half of the photo and have it blend into the sky. Here's how:

On/Off button

Figure 7-20: The Graduated Filter in action.

1. **Select a photo in Grid view and press D to jump to the Develop module.**

2. **Press M or click the Graduated Filter icon in the Tool Strip.**

3. **Set the Exposure slider to 1.**

   I like to use the sliders, but the same can be done with the buttons.

4. **Click and drag toward the area you don't want affected by the filter.**

   This is a crucial step. In this example, I don't want to affect the sky with my exposure boost, so I click right above the horizon line and drag up into the sky. Everything below the point I click gets the maximum effect of the exposure boost. The effect is gradually faded in the space between where I start dragging and where I stop. The area above where I stop is completely unaffected by the exposure boost.

5. **Adjust filter position and size as needed.**

   Don't worry if you didn't click and drag in just the right spot the first time. You can resize, rotate, and reposition the filter as needed.

6. **Adjust effect settings as needed.**

   I usually like to start with higher-than-expected settings to help see what I am doing, and then dial it back after getting it on the image.

7. **Adjust the Recovery slider in the Basic panel to regain clipped highlights.**

   In this example, the snow on the ground was clipped when I boosted the exposure of that area. The settings in the Basic panel are still accessible while working with Graduated Filter.

I think you're going to love working with this filter and putting it through its paces. Just to show that I'm fair to all the tools on the Tool Strip, though, I'm going to highlight some of the features of the Graduated Filter's very close relative, the Adjustment Brush.

Adjustment Brush

If you thought the Graduated Filter was cool, the Adjustment Brush is going to make your jaw hit the floor. It works in essentially the same way, except that you use a brush to paint on the effects with a great deal of control as opposed to a graduated filter. The Adjustment Brush allows you to paint with any combination of exposure, brightness, contrast, saturation, clarity, sharpness, and color. This allows for an amazing level of local adjustment possibilities, which means far fewer trips to the external editor!

To activate the Adjustment Brush, you click its icon in the Tool Strip or select your photo and press K. Yes! The Adjustment Brush has its own universal shortcut, so no matter where you are in Lightroom, pressing K takes you right to the brush. When the brush is active, you see its settings appear under its icon. The settings are divided into the following four sections:

- **Mask:** Allows you to either create a new adjustment or edit an existing adjustment.

- **Effect:** Contains all the settings you can use alone or in tandem to achieve your desired results. The drop-down menu contains existing and custom presets, which allow you to save specific settings for reuse. The toggle switch to the right of the Effect drop-down menu controls which Effect mode you're in. You have two options (the same as the Graduated Filter):

  - *Buttons:* This is the simple mode. Choose an effect you want to use, click the negative or positive button, and then adjust the amount slider to control how much effect you want before you start painting.

  - *Sliders:* This is the advanced mode. Adjust any combination of sliders with much greater control to create the desired effect.

✔ **Brush:** Controls the brush settings. You can't adjust any of these settings after the effect is applied, so you want to get this right before you start. Here are the options:

- *A/B:* You can configure two different brush settings to make switching between favored settings easier.

- *Erase:* Allows you to "paint" with an eraser to clean up stray strokes. You can click the Erase button to activate or you can hold down Alt (Option on a Mac) while painting. ***Note:*** The Brush cursor switches from a + to a – when Erase is enabled.

- *Size:* Controls the size of the brush. Can also be adjusted with the [and] keys.

- *Feather:* Adjusts the softness of the edge of the brush. Can also be adjusted by holding down the Shift key in conjunction with [and] keys.

- *Flow:* A low flow amount allows you to build up the effect slowly with each stroke. A high flow amount applies more of the effect with each stroke.

- *Auto Mask:* When this box is checked, Lightroom attempts to detect the edges of the object you're painting to prevent the effect from spilling over the edge and affecting other areas. The clearer the edge, the better Auto Mask works.

- *Density:* Limits the strength of the effect.

✔ **On/Off:** Click the On/Off toggle button at the bottom to disable the results of the adjustment. This feature can be good for a quick comparison to how things looked before. Click the Reset button to clear all Adjustment Brush applications.

New versus Edit

When you first apply a brush stroke to your photo, Lightroom marks the first spot of contact with an Edit "pin," as shown in Figure 7-21. You can click and release as often as needed to continue applying the effect to other areas of your photo. All your painting continues to be associated with that original Edit pin until you click New in the Mask section. At any point, you can activate an Edit pin by clicking it once to adjust the settings applied by the associated strokes. The settings panel highlights when you're in Edit mode to show you what settings can still be adjusted.

If you place your cursor over a pin, the associated strokes glow to show you where you've painted. This is especially helpful with subtle adjustments. The glow vanishes when you move away from the pin; however, you can also enable this "stroke indicator" glow by pressing O to keep it on while you are painting (press O again to turn it off). Press Shift+O while the glow is on to cycle through white, black, red, and green highlight colors (which may help you see it better based on the colors in the photo you are adjusting). To remove a pin (and its associated effect), press Delete while in Edit mode.

Edit pin

Figure 7-21: Adjustment Brush and edit pin.

Putting the brush to use

I want to walk through one possible use of this brush to show you how it works. Figure 7-22 shows a Before and After view of a Shar-Pei I met on the street. She was very curious and a good model. I really like the shot, but one side of her face is a little too much in shadow. Before Lightroom 2, my best option would have been to take this photo into Photoshop and apply a local adjustment to open up the shadows around the one eye. Those days are gone! Here's what I can do:

1. **Select the photo in Grid view and press K.**

2. **From Button mode, click + Exposure and set the amount to 1.**

3. **Adjust the size of the brush slightly smaller than the target area.**

4. **Set the Feather to 100.**

5. **Set Flow to 50.**

   I like to set a medium flow amount to build up the effect.

6. **Uncheck Auto Mask.**

   Auto Mask is great when you have clear lines separating the area you want to adjust from the area you don't want to adjust (like the roof line of a building versus the sky above it) but in my example it's all dog hair at different brightness levels and I want to create a smooth transition between the different levels of brightness. No lines here.

7. Set Density to 100.

8. Click into the target area on the photo and paint in the effect.

I start at the eye and build up the effect with a series of clicks until I achieve the desired result. *Remember:* You can dial back the Amount slider if needed to reduce the effect, and clean up stray edges with the Erase feature.

As a finishing touch, I switched the brush to Slider mode and configured a new brush to decrease exposure and boost saturation, and then painted over the background to give it a richer look. You can see the edit pin in the upper-right corner. This tool is so much fun you're going to have a hard time stopping, too!

Figure 7-22: An example of opening shadows and boosting the background with the Adjustment Brush.

8

Taking Your Photos to the Next Level

In This Chapter

▶ Adjusting contrast and enhancing color

▶ Converting to grayscale

▶ Adding color to highlights and shadows

▶ Adding capture sharpening and reducing noise

▶ Removing purple fringe and working with vignettes

▶ Modifying the camera calibration

*F*irst things first. I say throughout this book that Lightroom is a workflow tool, and each part of the workflow consists of smaller work-flows. The process of developing a photo is no different — developing has a beginning (the import state) and an end (your vision for that photo), but you have to jump through a series of hoops (or workflows) before you get to that end. Which hoops you choose depends on which tools you rely on to get your work done, so your workflow may look quite different from mine.

I address the most common adjustments you make to most of your images in Chapter 7 (such as basic tonal adjustments, cropping, and spot removal), now it's time to explore the rest of what the Develop module has to offer (that is, all the adjustments below the Basic panel) to really set your photos apart. Keep in mind, though, that the basic tonal adjustments you've made already aren't set in stone. If you decide to work with the Tone Curve, convert to grayscale, or apply a different camera profile, for exam-ple, go back and tweak your earlier settings for better results. All these adjustments are performed on the same set of image data, which is why the Histogram panel is attached to the top of the right panel. Refer to it often, toggle your clipping indicators on and off from time to time (by pressing J) to make sure that contrast boost didn't blow out a highlight or that a creative vignette didn't clip some important detail to black. No setting is made in isolation.

Often the difference between an okay photo and a fantastic one is subtle — so subtle that the untrained eye may not even perceive what that difference is, but you know it when you see it. Typically, this difference is related to the attention to detail and finishing touches that are applied by a person skilled at his craft. The tools in this chapter focus on the techniques you can use to give each photo that "something special" that elevates it above a well-exposed capture.

Working with Contrast and Color

Being able to manipulate contrast and color digitally is very powerful and a lot of fun. Like anything else, the more you do it, the better you get at it. More importantly, the more you do it, the more you refine your eye and your own style. The adjustments you make in this area will have a dramatic effect on how people react to your work. You can easily lose a little perspective on your own work after you've looked at it, tweaked it, and changed it. To help with that problem, take advantage of the tools Lightroom offers — from creating snapshots of your progress to preserving certain settings as presets, to creating virtual copies to creating multiple versions — as a way to bring some objectivity back into the creative process. Never forget that everything you do in Lightroom can be undone! Take some time to step back and look at the history to see how far you've come, and possibly change course if things aren't going the way you'd envisioned.

Mastering the Tone Curve

The primary purpose of the Tone Curve panel, as shown in Figure 8-1, is to provide you with a set of tools you can use to adjust the amount of contrast in your photo. *Contrast* gives photos a depth and a richness that most people find pleasing. Images lacking contrast are often referred to as *flat*.

Contrast is increased or decreased by adjusting the brightness of the tones within your photo. A typical contrast adjustment might involve decreasing the brightness of the darkest tones while simultaneously increasing the brightness of the lighter tones, which creates contrast between these bright and dark regions. This type of contrast adjustment is what Lightroom applies to all raw photos by default (I tell you how you can change that below).

In the top half of the Tone Curve panel, you see a square window that contains the histogram with the active photo in the background and a diagonal line running from the lower-left corner to the upper-right corner. That diagonal line is the *curve*. By bending that line, you're in effect increasing or decreasing the brightness of all the pixels at a given point in the histogram. In

Figure 8-1, the curve represents Lightroom's default medium contrast curve. If you look very closely, you can see a slight dip at the lower-left end and a slight bump at the upper-right end. This subtle *S* shape is a classic contrast curve. The more exaggerated you make the bends (or curves) in that *S* appear, the greater amount of contrast you see in your photo.

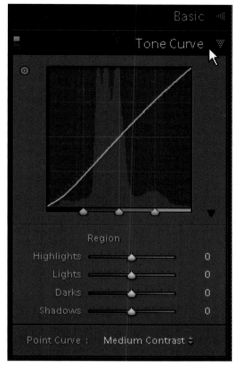

Figure 8-1: The Tone Curve panel.

Any curve adjustments you make are reflected in the *real* histogram — the one perched in the Histogram panel, sitting there on top of the Tone Curve panel. The histogram inside the Tone Curve panel, however, remains unchanged no matter how many adjustments you do as a reminder of the *before* curve state. The greater the curve adjustment you make, the more difference you see between these two histograms.

Enough of the preliminaries. Time to look at how you actually make things happen and bend that line. As is consistent with every other part of Lightroom, you have more than one way to achieve the same result. Here are the ways you can make contrast adjustments with the Tone Curve panel:

   ✔ **Apply a Point Curve preset.**
   ✔ **Click and drag points on the curve itself.**
   ✔ **Adjust the sliders below the curve.**
   ✔ **Click and drag the photo with the Target Adjustment Tool.**

Some of these methods may sound a bit techy — especially the Target Adjustment Tool — but don't let that worry you. I go over each method in detail in the next few sections.

Applying a preset

Even though you choose presets at the very bottom of the Tone Curve panel (see Figure 8-2), I give it a place of honor in my discussion because, if you're working with raw images, Lightroom has already applied the Medium

Contrast preset by default. This preset is actually a pretty subtle adjustment, and if you like it, you're done! You aren't required by law to change the contrast if you're already happy with the default state. That said, here are the two other preset options you can select in the Point Curve drop-down menu:

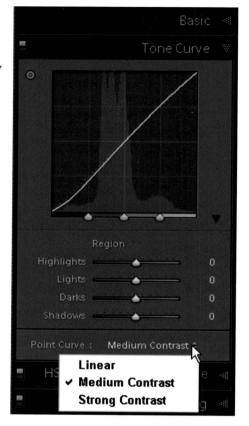

Figure 8-2: The Point Curve presets.

- **Linear:** Takes the curve out of the curve, which means no additional contrast adjustment has been made. Rendered files have this preset applied by default, or rather no additional contrast is applied to JPG, TIF, or PSD files by default.

- **Strong Contrast:** A slightly larger *S* curve than medium contrast, which means darker shadows and brighter highlights.

Interacting with the curve

With a Point Curve preset in place, you can make a custom adjustment by manually manipulating the curve. That line represents all the tones, from black to white, that could exist in your photo. The Tone Curve histogram is a graph showing you the number of pixels in your photo at each tonal level. By clicking a point on that line, you can move that point up or down to increase or decrease the brightness of all the pixels at that particular tonal level. You immediately see this adjustment reflected in the photo and the live histogram.

As an alternative, you can hover the cursor over a point in the window and use the up- and down-arrow keys to make the adjustment in + or –5 increments.

Because being able to go back is always good, you can access a helpful Reset contextual menu by right-clicking (Control-clicking on a Mac) anywhere inside the window. (See Figure 8-3.)

Sliding the sliders

Not too much to this one: The Highlights, Lights, Darks, and Shadows sliders correspond to the four regions that make up the complete tonal range of your image. Click and drag a slider to increase or decrease the brightness of the pixels in the corresponding region. Alternatively, you can place your cursor over the number field to the right of the sliders, and a small scrubby slider appears that you can click and drag to make an adjustment. (If you're a keyboard fiend, you can use your up- and down-arrow keys to make the adjustment in + or –5 increments.)

Using the Target Adjustment Tool

Pronounced *tat* for short, this is the tool for people who'd rather just work right in the photo instead of looking at sliders, numbers, or curves. After a little practice, you may just find it feels more natural and a little more intuitive.

Click the TAT icon, as shown in Figure 8-4, to activate it and then move your cursor over the photo. Notice your cursor changes to a *crosshair* (this is the working end of this tool) with the TAT icon trailing behind it (this is just a reminder that the tool is active). To make an adjustment, click a spot in the photo that represents the tonal region you want to adjust and then drag up to make the spot brighter or down to make it darker.

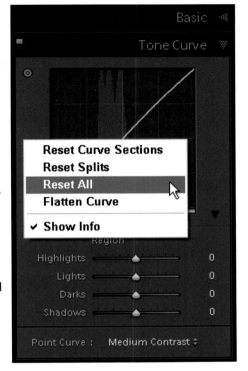

Figure 8-3: Reset options.

Enhancing and changing colors

Who doesn't like the HSL/Color/Grayscale panel? In fact, this is one of those panels where you might find yourself getting a little carried away simply because it *is* so much fun. My advice to you: Gather some practice images and get all that wild colorizing out of your system. That way, when you really need to use this panel, you can be a little more subtle.

Unless you've selected a true *monochrome* image (a photo that really has only one channel), the photos you work with in Lightroom will be RGB (Red, Green, Blue) images, which means you'll always have the information contained in each of the three RGB channels to work with, even when you're looking at a grayscale image.

TAT icon

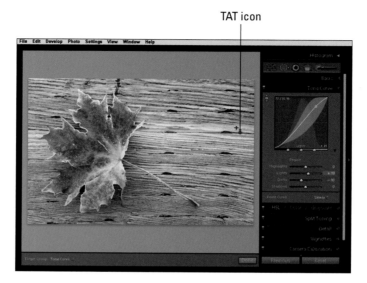

Figure 8-4: The Target Adjustment Tool icon.

The HSL/Color/Grayscale panel, as shown in Figure 8-5, is actually three panels in one. The HSL and Color options are essentially variations on the same set of controls, which allow you to adjust the hue, saturation, and luminance values in your photo. The Grayscale options are for converting a color photo to grayscale. Because grayscale conversion is a topic unto itself, I cover it in great detail in the next section. For now, though, I want to call your attention to a unique aspect of this panel — the HSL/Color/Grayscale labels in the panel's header are also the buttons used to switch between each option. While you move your cursor over each label, the label lights up. The label you select remains highlighted to indicate which option is active.

Figure 8-5 shows the Color face of the HSL/Color/Grayscale panel — the Reds section, to be more precise. Along the top of the panel is a row of color swatches that represents each of the colors you can adjust. Click any swatch to activate the controls for that color or click the All button to see all the controls at once. Each color has three possible adjustments:

- **Hue:** This adjustment shifts the color between all its possible hues.

- **Saturation:** Use this slider to change the intensity of the hue.

- **Luminance:** This slider changes the brightness level of the hue.

The HSL options, as shown in Figure 8-6, group the adjustments by hue, saturation, and luminance instead of by color. You can see the labels for each grouping across the top of the panel. Click each label to activate the controls for that group or click All to see the controls for all three groups at once.

I think you'll find that using the HSL face of the panel is a more intuitive way to work, mainly because of the way the Target Adjustment Tool has been integrated for each group of adjustments. The Target Adjustment Tool functions just like it did in the Tone Curve panel, except it controls the adjustment of sliders in your chosen group: Hue, Saturation, or Luminance.

Figure 8-5: The HSL/Color/Grayscale panel set to Color.

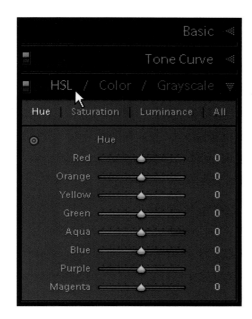

Figure 8-6: The HSL section of the panel set to Hue.

Creating black and white images

In the absence of color, an image becomes a study in light and shadow, texture and detail in a very different way than would be the case with color photos. Because of this, black and white photos can often achieve a visual impact that color photos can't. When converting a color photo to black and white, the process starts with a conversion to grayscale but the process doesn't end there. To see all that's involved, start by taking a look at the Grayscale face of the HSL/Color/Grayscale panel and then follow along as I address how you can call on a few other Lightroom panels to enhance the final result.

To initiate a grayscale conversion on the active photo, try one of the following methods:

- **Press V.**
- **Click the Grayscale button in the Treatment section of the Basic panel.**
- **Click the Grayscale label of the HSL/Color/Grayscale panel.**

Note: The General – Grayscale preset — part of the Presets panel on the left side if the interface — *does* convert a photo to grayscale, but the preset also includes an auto white balance and an auto tone function as well. (Give this preset a try to see whether you like it.)

To see how this whole grayscale conversion process works with the HSL/Color/ Grayscale Panel method, follow along as I recount the steps I take to move a photo from its Color state to its Grayscale state:

1. **Select the photo in the Filmstrip and press V.**

2. **Adjust white balance settings in the Basic panel as needed.**

   Keep in mind that, even though you see a grayscale image, all the color data in the original image is still at your disposal. Adjusting the Temp and Tint sliders while in Grayscale mode can bring out additional detail and texture.

3. **Readjust basic tonal settings in the Basic panel as needed.**

   Similar to white balance, now that you're working with a range of grayscale values, you might find that an adjustment to exposure or to the black clipping level is required to achieve your desired result.

4. **Expand the HSL/Color/Grayscale panel, as shown in Figure 8-7.**

   This is your opportunity to pick up where Lightroom left off and adjust the mix of color data to bring out the tonal qualities of the image you're after.

5. **(Optional) Click the Target Adjustment Tool (TAT) inside the Grayscale Mix panel.**

   Although you can certainly adjust individual color sliders in the panel, you'll find that working right inside the photo with the TAT is a much more intuitive and satisfying process.

6. **If you decide to use the TAT, click a tone in the photo and drag the tone down to darken or drag up to brighten.**

   This is where your creativity and vision come together! While you click and drag the TAT, the corresponding Grayscale Mix sliders move within the panel. You can always undo an adjustment by pressing Ctrl+Z (⌘+Z on a Mac) or by stepping back to an earlier history state. This exploration process is also a good time to make use of the Snapshots panel if you want to preserve a particular state. (For more on the Snapshots panel, see Chapter 7.)

7. **If you chose the TAT route, click the Done button in the Toolbar to quit the TAT after you complete your mix adjustments.**

   Figure 8-8 shows you the kinds of transformations you can achieve with the Grayscale face of the HSL/Color/Grayscale panel.

Figure 8-7: The Grayscale Mix controls.

Just because you've completed the grayscale mix doesn't mean the photo is finished. Depending on the photo and the result in your mind's eye, you may go on to do any (or all) of the following to finish the job:

- Use the Adjustment Brush in the Toolstrip to make Dodge and Burn local adjustments.
- Use the Tone Curve panel to increase contrast.
- Use the Split Toning panel to add color to the highlights and shadows.
- Use the Vignettes panel to darken or lighten the edges.

Figure 8-8: A Before and After example of a grayscale conversion.

The best way to know when done is actually done is to roll up your sleeves and experiment. The wonderful thing about Lightroom is that none of these adjustments will alter the pixels in your original images. You can always go back. Making use of the Snapshots panel to preserve key states in the development process or even virtual copies to branch out into multiple versions gives you a lot of room to move.

Adding color to shadows and highlights

The most common use of the Split Toning panel — the panel stuck right under the HSL/Color/Grayscale panel — is to add a hint of a color tint to grayscale images. That doesn't mean you can't use it with color images, too. Split toning actually allows you to add one color tint to the highlights and a second color tint to the shadows, with the Hue and Saturation sliders for each region. (See Figure 8-9.)

In Lightroom 1, you could either adjust the Hue slider or enter numerical values directly into each field. Now, in Lightroom 2, you can also click the color swatch to access a popup color palette, which makes the process much more interactive. Moving your cursor over the color palette changes the cursor to an eyedropper tool.

Click any color to apply that Hue and Saturation settings and get a live preview of your photo. Click and drag left or right to change the hue or up and down to change the saturation. As an alternative, click a point to select a color and then use the left and right arrow keys to change the hue, or the up- and down-arrow keys to adjust saturation.

You have one last adjustment to make (or not — the choice is yours) after you select your Highlight and Shadow colors, and that adjustment involves the panel's Balance slider. By default, the panel gives equal weight to the highlight and shadow tints. If you move the Balance slider to the left, you shift the balance toward the Shadow tint, whereas an adjustment to the right favors the Highlight tint. If taken to either extreme, the Balance slider gives the effect of applying a single tint.

Figure 8-9: Splitting your tones with the Split Toning panel.

The Devil's in the Details

Working your way down the right side of the Lightroom interface, your next stop is the Detail panel, which is your place for getting up close and personal with your photos. I think you'll agree with me that, sometimes, you need to zoom to the 1:1 view to see what's happening in your photo. In fact, the only way you can really see the adjustments made in the Detail panel is when you're in at least 1:1 zoom level (or greater). To make that easier, the folks at Adobe added a nice little 1:1 Preview window to the Detail panel in Lightroom. (See Figure 8-10.) You can click and drag inside the Preview window to view different areas of the photo or click the squarish crosshair to the left of the window to focus on a different area of the photo. If you want to zoom closer, you can right-click (Control+click on a Mac) inside the window to choose either the 1:1 or 2:1 zoom level from the contextual menu that appears.

Now that I'm sure you can see what you're doing, I feel comfortable pointing out how you can put the Detail panel to good use in your never-ending struggle to produce the perfect photo. The next few sections give you the details.

Applying capture sharpening

Sharpening can't correct an out-of-focus image, but sharpening can increase the perception of detail in a properly focused image. Lightroom 2 has come a long way in regard to sharpening. You can now put sharpening to use in both Print and Web modules, as well as in the Export dialog box. In addition, you can *paint* with sharpness by using the Toolstrip's Adjustment Brush for more creative and localized sharpening applications. When put together in a sharpening workflow, you can now apply the sharpening in the Detail panel as it was originally intended, which is simply to compensate for the inherent softness in raw captures.

Sharpening is a very powerful adjustment, and as with most powerful things, you should never use more than the minimum required to get the job done. Increasing sharpness can bring details to life, which can translate into a greater visual impact. Increasing sharpness too much can make a photo appear crunchy and overprocessed and cause a negative reaction to the image. You always want your sharpness setting to be *just right* — if anything, you might want to err on the softer side.

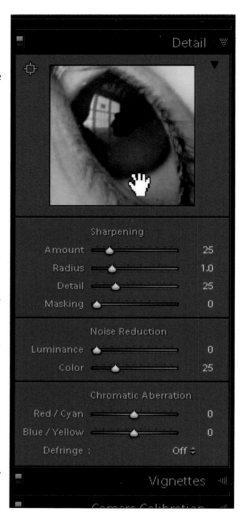

Figure 8-10: The 1:1 Preview window.

One of the key traits that humans find pleasing to the eye is the separation of edges around certain details (sharpening). The human eye is drawn to this edge detail and sharpening can be used to bring a viewer in closer. Lightroom's sharpening controls are all about edge detection and enhancement. If you look at Figure 8-10, you see the following Sharpening controls at your disposal:

✓ **Amount:** This is simply the amount of sharpening being applied. An increase in the amount translates to an increase in sharpening.

✓ **Radius:** This determines how far that sharpening amount extends from the edges being sharpened. The higher the radius, the farther the reach from the edges.

✓ **Detail:** This determines how much of the finer detail between the prominent edges has sharpening applied to it. The higher the setting, the more the finer detail edges are sharpened.

✓ **Masking:** Provides a means to protect areas of the image from having sharpening applied. No mask means all areas have sharpening applied to them. A high mask means only the most defined edges have sharpening applied.

By default, all raw photos have a moderate amount of sharpening applied. However, you may want to move beyond the defaults, depending upon the subject matter of your photos. One of the best ways to understand how this panel was intended to be used is to examine the settings contained in the two sharpening presets against the default sharpening settings. The chart in Table 8-1 compares the default values against the values found in the presets Sharpen – Landscapes and Sharpen – Portraits (found in the Presets panel on the left side of the Lightroom interface).

Table 8-1	Comparison of Preset Sharpening Settings		
Settings	*Default*	*Landscapes*	*Portraits*
Amount	25	40	35
Radius	1.0	0.8	1.2
Detail	25	50	20
Masking	0	0	70

Here's what the Adobe folks were thinking when they came up with a Landscapes preset and a Portraits preset. In a typical landscape photo, you see a lot of details. In fact, overall detail is a favored trait. You *want* to see details. Detail draws in the eye. Now think about a portrait. Detail is certainly important, but only in certain places. Sharpness of the eyes is very important. Showing every pore and wrinkle in sharp relief is not important.

Looking at the settings of the Landscapes preset, you see the amount is set to 40, compared to 35 in Portraits. Not a huge difference, but it's not surprising that Landscapes would get a greater amount of sharpening. I come back to Radius at the end, but for now, I want to move on to the Detail setting. The

Landscapes Detail setting is twice the default, whereas the Portraits setting is lower than the default. This too makes sense because you definitely want to bring out the finer detail in a landscape, but not in a person's skin. Now, as you compare the Masking setting of 0 for Landscapes versus 70 for Portraits, you can see that sharpening is being applied to all areas of the landscape image, but only on the most defined edges of the portrait. This high Masking value also explains why the radius (or *reach*) was slightly bumped up in the portrait image to thicken the edges of the most defined features, knowing that the finer detail was going to be left unsharpened.

So, ask yourself the following question: Is your photo more like a portrait, where only the most defined edges should be sharpened, or is your photo more like a landscape, where even the finest detail needs a boost? With that determination in mind, I suggest applying the appropriate preset even if you just use it as a new starting point over the default.

To see how all this works in tandem with the Detail panel, follow along as I walk through one example. Figure 8-11 shows a Before and After version of a photo that clearly falls into the Portraits category. The Before version has all the Sharpening settings zeroed out for the sake of comparison.

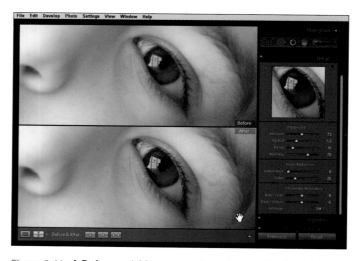

Figure 8-11: A Before and After comparison of an application of capture sharpening.

1. **Click the eye (or an equally important detail) to zoom into 1:1 view.**

   You can only see the effects of the sharpening when you're zoomed to 1:1 in the content area or are looking at the 1:1 Preview in the Detail panel.

2. **In the Presets panel on the left side of the Lightroom interface, apply the Sharpen – Portraits preset.**

   In many cases, you can stop right there, but for the sake of explaining the process, I want you to see if you can finesse this starting point.

3. **Increase the Amount setting and then dial the setting back until you see nice edges without any jagged pixels or white haloing along those edges.**

   Hold the Alt key (Option on a Mac) while dragging the slider to see your photo in grayscale. Sharpening is applied only to the luminance (brightness data), not to the color data, so seeing the photo in grayscale provides another way to see what exactly is happening to the photo.

4. **Leave the Radius at its default.**

   By making the decision about what preset to apply, you're already in the ballpark. If anything, you may want to dial back Radius, but in reality, your energy is better spent on the other three adjustments.

5. **Hold the Alt key (Option on a Mac) and increase the Detail slider until you can see unwanted detail appear and then dial the slider back until only your key edges are visible.**

   By using the Alt (Option) modifier with this adjustment right from the start, you can really focus on just the detail. In this example, I dialed up Detail until I could see pores on the skin and then dialed it back until those pores were diminished. Keep in mind that by applying the Portrait preset, you already have a high-level mask being applied, which limits the areas being sharpened.

6. **Increase the Masking amount if necessary to compensate for increases made to the Detail setting.**

   The Alt (Option) modifier works with this slider too! In this case, you see the mask itself. Areas of white in the mask are the areas where sharpening will be applied. Black areas will have no sharpening.

7. **Check other areas of the photo at 1:1 to evaluate the level of sharpening applied.**

At the end of that process, the settings I preferred were not very far from the Portraits preset. Would anyone notice that difference in a normal viewing environment? Not likely. When you're processing tens, hundreds, or thousands of photos, you don't want to spend this kind of time finessing the capture sharpening on a photo-by-photo basis. Get a good feel for what the sliders can do, create your own presets (or use the existing ones) that suit your needs/tastes, and apply those presets in batches to your photos.

Dealing with noise

The middle section of the Detail panel deals with noise reduction — no, not that acoustic paneling stuff. In terms of digital photography, *noise* is simply random electrical signals recorded by the camera's sensor that can degrade the quality of the photo. In the absence of light, these random signals are more visible because the sensor records less actual data, which is why noise issues are common in underexposed photos.

Lightroom's noise-reduction options are pretty simple (refer to Figure 8-10), but they can be effective when it comes to reducing minor noise issues. You have one slider for increasing the amount of luminance noise reduction, and another slider for reducing the effects of color noise. After you figure out how to differentiate between the two, it's simply a matter of adjusting the respective slider just enough (and no more) to solve the problem. Here's my handy guide to telling luminance noise from color noise apart:

- **Luminance noise tends to look like the more familiar *grain* you see in film.** You have fluctuations in brightness levels whereas color remains essentially consistent — common in areas of blue sky.

- **Color noise can be recognized by the presence of multicolored pixels (like Christmas tree lights).** Typically present in the shadow areas of your photos.

Figure 8-12 shows a Before and After example of a color noise reduction. Continue to increase the Color slider until you've neutralized as much of the random multicolored pixels as you can.

As for luminance noise, the most likely place you'll encounter that headache is in blue skies. Figure 8-13 shows a Before and After example of a blue sky with the typical grainy signs of luminance noise. To counteract the noise level seen in the Before image, I adjusted the Luminance slider until the tones in the sky smoothed out.

The main issue to watch for with any type of noise reduction is the loss of detail. Too much noise reduction can turn your photo into a mush of pixels resembling a watercolor painting. Having a little noise and more detail rather than less noise and pixel mush is usually better.

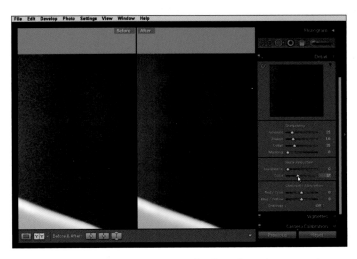

Figure 8-12: A Before and After example of a color noise correction.

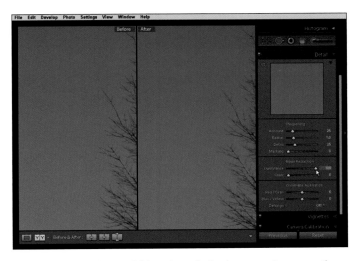

Figure 8-13: A Before and After view of a luminance noise correction.

Reducing chromatic aberration

If you ever notice a purplish fringe along an edge of high contrast in your photos, you're looking at a case of *chromatic aberration*. The problem results when your lens can't focus all wavelengths of light at that particular point, and this problem is most commonly seen with wide-angle lenses. Luckily for you, you can usually correct it pretty easily with the Detail panel's very own Chromatic Aberration controls, as shown in Figure 8-14.

The adjustment works by reducing the size of one of the three RGB color channels relative to the other two — by adjusting either the Red/Cyan or Blue/Yellow sliders. You have to play it a bit by ear (or by eye), but holding down the Alt key (Option on a Mac) while adjusting each slider can make eyeballing the adjustment a bit easier. (Holding the Alt modifier key reduces the color in all but the area of the color fringe, making the changes easier to see during the correction.)

If the slider adjustments aren't completely removing the fringe, choose Highlight Edges from the Defringe drop-down menu. This setting is usually just enough to get you in the ballpark. Figure 8-15 shows a Before and After example of a combination Blue/Yellow slider adjustment coupled with the Highlight Edges Defringe option. The purple fringe is scaled back considerably.

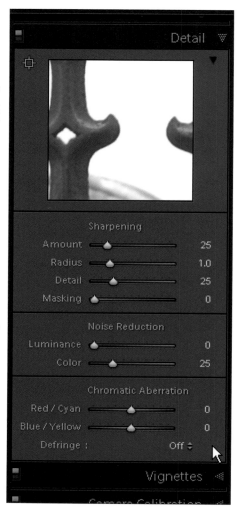

Figure 8-14: The Chromatic Aberration controls.

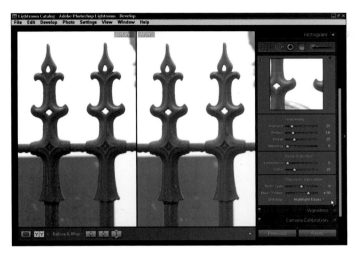

Figure 8-15: A Before and After view of a chromatic aberration correction.

Working with Vignetting

Although originally intended as a correction tool, the Vignettes panel is more often used these days for the creative effects it can produce. A *bad* vignette happens when you have unwanted darkening around the edge of a photo, usually caused by the reduction of light entering the lens (such as interference from stacked filters). Proving the old adage of *when life gives you lemons, make lemonade,* some folks decided they kind of liked that darkening around the image because it almost acted as a matte or a framing device.

This phenomenon of the Good versus Bad vignette led to the rather schizophrenic makeup of the Vignettes panel, as shown in Figure 8-16. The panel has two distinct sections, each with its own definite agenda:

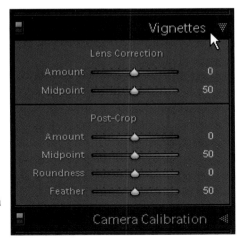

Figure 8-16: The Vignettes panel.

✓ **Lens Correction:** Allows for the correction or the application of a vignette from the outer edge of the photo toward the center. Because this is intended as a correction tool, it only works on an uncropped version of the photo.

✔ **Post-Crop:** Reach for this tool when you want to add a vignette for creative effect. Not only do you have more adjustments to refine the effect, but it works equally on the cropped and uncropped versions as well.

Two sections, two agendas. The next two sections take a stab at each one.

Correcting a photo with a vignette

Although you're better off making sure your lens configuration doesn't create a vignette in the first place, if the unfortunate event does occur, you can use the Lens Correction section of Lightroom's Vignettes panel to help reduce the effects of an unwanted vignette. The section has two controls:

✔ **Amount:** Moving the Amount slider in a positive direction (to the right) brightens the edges of your uncropped photo. The Amount slider essentially helps you recover any data that may still exist in that darkened area around the edge and blend it with the rest of the photo. Keep in mind that, if the vignette is extreme (fades all the way to black), this adjustment won't bring back detail that isn't there to begin with.

✔ **Midpoint:** If the Amount slider alone isn't completely removing the vignette, a slight adjustment of the Midpoint can provide a little boost. Adjust to the left to brighten and adjust to the right to darken the center of the photo.

This Lens Correction tool only helps with the mildest of vignette problems. If you can't completely remove the darkened edge with the Lens Correction sliders, your best bet may be to crop inside the vignette to remove the outside edge.

Creative vignette applications

The Post-Crop vignette controls were added in Lightroom 2 after the explosion in popularity of adding a vignette as a creative effect. The goal here isn't to remove a vignette but to apply one! Applying a vignette is a simple way to create a framing effect that draws the eye into the photo. Like any creative effect, you can easily overdo it, but I really enjoy the effect all the same. Another great thing about the Post-Crop vignette is that it reapplies the vignette settings to the cropped version of the photo should you use Lightroom's Crop tool (located in the Tool Strip) after having already applied a creative vignette.

You can play around with four separate sliders in the Post-Crop section:

✓ **Amount:** As you might expect, this slider controls the amount of the added vignette. Move to the left to darken and to the right to brighten. Unlike the Amount slider in the Lens Correction section, this Amount slider doesn't attempt to brighten the edge of the vignette that bleeds into the photo, but rather it adds black or white to the edge from the outside in.

✓ **Midpoint:** This increases or decreases the area at the center unaffected by the vignette. Moving the slider all the way to the left reduces the midpoint and by extension, maximizes the range the vignette can extend into the center of the photo. Moving the slider to the right has the opposite effect.

✓ **Roundness:** Increasing the Roundness value results in a more circular vignette, whereas decreasing roundness results in a more elliptical result.

✓ **Feather:** This controls the amount of fade applied to the edge of the vignette into the midpoint. A feather setting of 0 results in a hard-edged solid border, whereas a feather setting of 100 results in the most gradual transition from the midpoint to the edge of the photo.

There's no right or wrong way to apply a vignette; it's completely a matter of personal taste. To see what *I* like in a vignette, check out Figure 8-17, which shows the kind of drama you can achieve when you add a darkened vignette to a photo.

Figure 8-17: An example of a creative vignette.

Modifying the Camera Calibration Settings

The Camera Calibration panel, the last panel for this chapter, provides the ability to customize the default rendering of your raw photos. Adobe creates a profile for each camera it supports, and this is what is used as the default rendering for raw photos from your camera. If you see a consistent rendering issue with your raw photos, you can tweak the default rendering to your liking. Here's what this panel has to offer:

- **Profile:** This drop-down menu shows the version of the profile being used with your camera. In most cases, you have only one profile, but Adobe has revised the profiles for some cameras in the past, so depending upon your camera model, you may see more than one. (Figure 8-18 shows the ACR [*Adobe Camera Raw*] 4.4 profile.)

- **Shadows:** Allows for the correction of a tint in the shadow areas.

- **Red, Green, and Blue primaries:** Lets you adjust the hue and/or saturation of each of the primary colors used to render the color in your photos.

Each slider is color-coded to indicate which direction to move to create the desired adjustment. I don't recommend making a correction just by eye-balling the colors in your photos, though. The actual calibration process isn't for the beginner, but if you're interested in reading more about how it's done and what tools you need, Ian Lyons put together an excellent resource to get you started. Check out this resource at www.computer-darkroom.com/lr_camera/camera-defaults.htm.

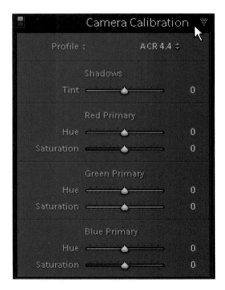

Figure 8-18: The Camera Calibration panel.

9

Using an External Editor

*L*ightroom's Develop module contains an array of powerful editing tools and can accomplish many tasks that were previously performed in an image editor, such as Photoshop. However, at times, you have to move beyond Lightroom to achieve certain results (such as creating image collages, performing selection based editing, using Photoshop plugins, and so on). The important distinction to make between editing in Lightroom and editing in an external editor is that Lightroom never alters the original pixels in your source photos. Instead, Lightroom records the adjustments you make inside the catalog file as a set of instructions to be applied to copies of the original photos during output. By writing your changes as a set of instructions, you up Lightroom's speed when processing large numbers of files and you enable its unlimited *undo* functionality (because you can always step back through that set of instructions).

On the other hand, most image editors are pixel editors at heart, which is a good thing! Pixel-level editing is extremely powerful, and Photoshop's the best tool for the job. When you want to combine the pixels in one image with the pixels in another image, create detailed selection around an object, or take advantage of layer-blending modes to get a specific result (just to name a few examples), call on a pixel editor. The external editor function comes into play any time you need to send photos out of Lightroom to leverage the power of a pixel editor.

Configuring Your External Editors

I go over the External Editor settings back in Chapter 1 — along with all the other preference settings — but I want to remind you of them since this is where you actually use them. Because Lightroom is an Adobe product, it does play favorites with Photoshop and Photoshop Elements. Lightroom reserves the primary (default) external editor slot for either Photoshop or Elements and will automatically recognize them if they're installed. If you have both Photoshop and Elements installed, Lightroom defers to Photoshop as the default editor. Although it's not possible to manually configure the default editor, you can choose any other image-editing application as the secondary editor (and save the settings as a custom preset). Here's how to set up your primary external editor settings, as shown in Figure 9-1:

Figure 9-1: External Editing preference settings.

1. **Choose Edit➪Preferences (Lightroom➪Preferences on a Mac) from the main menu.**

   The Preferences window displays.

2. **In the Preferences window, click the External Editing tab.**

3. **Choose your default file type from the File Format drop-down list.**

   PSD and TIFF file formats are, for all intents and purposes, equal to the task of supporting anything you can imagine doing in Photoshop. TIFF is a more widely supported format outside of the Adobe family whereas PSD is Photoshop's native file format. I tend to lean toward TIFF, but you really can't go wrong either way. Refer to Chapter 3 for a more in-depth look at file formats.

4. **Choose your default color space from the Color Space drop-down list.**

   Your choices here are ProPhoto RGB, Adobe RGB, and sRGB. If you've configured your camera to save photos in raw format and want to maintain as much of the original color as possible throughout the editing process, choose ProPhoto RGB. If you've configured your camera to save photos in JPG format, you've already made a color space choice in your camera settings, so you may as well choose that same color space here to be consistent.

5. **From the Bit Depth drop-down list, choose your default bit depth.**

   This option goes hand in hand with color space. If you chose ProPhoto as your color space, choose 16 Bits/Component. (ProPhoto is a 16-bit color space.) If you didn't choose ProPhoto, choose 8 Bits/Component. The important difference is that a 16-bit file contains much more data than an 8-bit file, which is great for editing but does come with a greatly increased file size.

6. **(Optional) If you selected the TIFF file format, you can also choose either Compressed or Uncompressed TIFF.**

   You get the same data either way, but compressed TIFF takes longer to open and save, whereas uncompressed TIFF files have a larger file size. I favor uncompressed because I prefer the speed benefit over the file size cost.

With your primary external editor configured, you can move on to setting up an additional external editor. Do you need one though? Well, whether you need one or not is entirely up to you and your workflow. You may not have Photoshop or Elements, or perhaps you prefer another image editor for certain tasks. Lightroom just provides you with the option. Here's how to set up an additional external editor:

1. **Click the Choose button in the Additional External Editor section of the External Editing preferences dialog box (refer to Figure 9-1).**

2. **In the dialog box that appears, navigate to the application file you want to use, and then select it and click Choose.**

On a PC, you find the application files in the Program Files folder. On a Mac, you want to look in the Applications folder. In both cases, Lightroom should open the correct folder by default, but if it doesn't you'll have to navigate to the right place. After you've selected the application and clicked Choose, you're brought back to the External Editing dialog box with your application choice displayed.

3. **Configure File Format, Color Space, and Bit Depth as desired.**

The choices you make here depend on the image editor you choose (not every application supports 16-bit files, for example), but be consistent with the settings you choose for your primary editor.

4. **Choose Save Current Settings as New Preset from the Preset drop-down menu.**

Doing so launches the New Preset dialog box. This is an optional — but recommended — step which is new to Lightroom 2. By saving your Additional Editor settings as a preset you can actually configure more than one additional editor, which simply gives you more options for how you want to edit your photos. You could even save different configuration settings for the same application. (Perhaps you want a 16-bit preset as well as an 8-bit, whatever fits your needs.)

5. **Give the preset a descriptive name and click Create.**

The preset names will display in the External Editor menu when you choose to send a photo out for additional work, so give it a name that tells you the name of the application and possibly hints at the settings used. This will only make life easier for you when you want to use the preset.

After you've created that preset you can go back to Step 1 and repeat the process to configure additional applications if you wish. At any point in the future, you can return to this dialog box and add new editors. Figure 9-2 shows the Preset drop-down menu extended to reveal two different presets I created for two different image editors (LightZone and NeatImage).

6. **Click OK to close the Preferences dialog box.**

When Lightroom creates a copy of your source photo to send to an external editor, it needs to give that copy a new name — technically, just a variation on the source photo's name. The naming convention you want Lightroom to use when it creates these copies is the last option in the External Editing preference dialog box (refer to Figure 9-1). By default, Lightroom appends `-Edit` to the end of the filename. (You can see an example of this to the right of Edit Externally File Naming heading.) If that works for you, you don't need to do anything else. If you want to customize how edited files are named, you can choose Edit from the Template drop-down menu and configure a naming convention of your choice in the same Filename Template Editor I cover in Chapters 4 and 6.

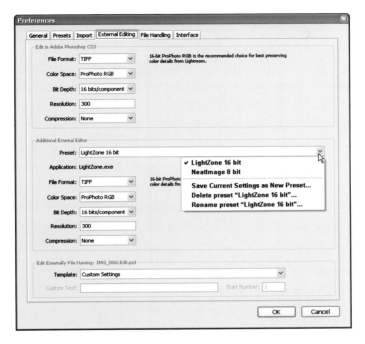

Figure 9-2: Preset menu showing multiple additional editor presets.

If you choose to work with the PSD format, open Photoshop's preferences and turn on Maximize Compatibility. Choose Edit⇨Preferences⇨File Handling from the main menu (Photoshop⇨Preferences⇨File Handling on a Mac) and set Maximize PSD and PSB File Compatibility to Always. This enables Lightroom to import your layered PSD files without any problems.

Basic Editing in an External Editor

The most common reason to send a photo from Lightroom to an external editor is when you simply need to do something with a photo that Lightroom cannot do (or doesn't do as well as some other editor). This typically comes after you make all the Lightroom adjustments your photo requires and before you're ready to move to some form of output (print, slideshow, Web, file export). Here's how to send photos to an external editor from Grid view in the Library module:

1. **Select your photo(s) in either the Filmstrip or Grid view.**

   Technically, you can access the External Editor menu from just about anywhere you can see a photo inside of Lightroom, but the most likely place will be from either Grid view in the Library module or the Filmstrip in any module. (Refer to Chapter 1 for an overview of the interface components.)

You can send more than one image to your external editor just be aware that the more files you send, the more computer resources are required to process that much data.

2. **Right-click (Control+click on a Mac) the photo and choose your external editor from the contextual pop-up menu that appears by choosing Edit in⇨Edit in (*your editor*).**

Figure 9-3 shows the menu options if you have Photoshop CS3 as your primary editor. In this example, I sent my selected photo to Photoshop, but the process works the same for all editors. You can see the additional editor presets I made earlier in the chapter are listed there as well.

Figure 9-3: The Edit in External Editor contextual menu.

After you select your editor, Lightroom does a few things, such as

- **Rendering a copy of the selected photo based on your external editor default settings.**
- **Opening that photo in your external editor.**

Note: What's really happening here is a file hand-off between Lightroom and your external editor. If you're working with raw files in Lightroom, a rendered copy of the raw file always has to be created before it can be sent to your external editor. However, if you're sending a rendered file (PSD, TIF, or JPEG) to your external editor, you have some choices, as shown in Figure 9-4, such as

- **Edit a Copy with Lightroom Adjustments:** This is the only option that enables you to incorporate your Lightroom adjustments into the file you edit in the external editor. If you're sending a layered PSD or TIF file and you choose this option, the layers will be flattened so that the Lightroom adjustments can be applied to the image.

- **Edit a Copy:** This option simply creates an exact copy of the selected photo and opens it in your editor. Any layers in the original image remain intact. No Lightroom adjustments are applied.

- **Edit Original:** Your original image is opened in the editor as it was the last time you saved and closed it in an external editor.

3. **Perform desired edits in the external editor.**

4. **Save and then close the photo in the external editor.**

   Don't choose Save As in this step because you'd be making a new copy of that file that Lightroom doesn't know anything about. By saving and then closing the file, you're telling Lightroom you're done working on it, and Lightroom will update its preview of that photo to reflect the changes you made.

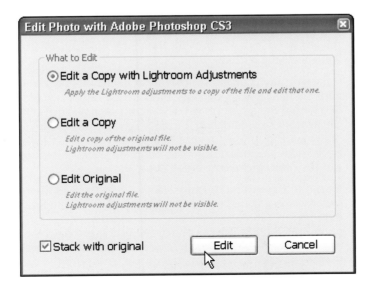

Figure 9-4: The Edit Photo with External Editor options.

You may have noticed the other options listed in the submenu in Figure 9-3. You need Photoshop CS3 to take advantage of Lightroom's ability to send multiple photos directly to Photoshop CS3 as a panorama, HDR (high dynamic range), smart object, or layers. If you don't have Photoshop CS3, this may just be enough to change your mind. To see what you're missing, check out my discussion of each of those options in the following section.

Advanced Editing Options with Photoshop CS3

New to Lightroom 2 are some advanced external-editing options that leverage powerful functionality built into Photoshop CS3 (and only CS3). This integration creates a direct path from inside Lightroom right into the chosen Photoshop option, so it's a real timesaver for those who were using these options previously. For this to work, you'll need to make sure you have the latest version of Photoshop CS3 installed (go to Help➪Updates in the Photoshop menu to check). Since this is a Lightroom book, I'll just highlight what you need to know on the Lightroom side of the equation, but if you want to learn more about Photoshop CS3 specifically, I highly recommend picking up a copy of Peter Bauer's *Photoshop CS3 For Dummies* (Wiley)!

There are four menu options, as shown in Figure 9-5, which only appear if you have Photoshop CS3 installed:

- **Open as Smart Object in Photoshop:** A *smart object* is a special kind of Photoshop layer that embeds a copy of the photo you select in Lightroom inside the layer. The benefit of this option is that you retain the ability to go back and edit the embedded source file at any time while working in Photoshop.

  Going the smart object route is most useful when your source photo happens to be a raw file, because then a copy of the raw file itself is embedded within the smart object. If you wish to make further adjustments to the raw file, you can open it from the smart object into Photoshop's raw editor plug-in Adobe Camera Raw, make your adjustments, and put it back inside the smart object to continue your Photoshop editing. This can be a very powerful editing combination.

- **Merge to Panorama in Photoshop:** A panorama is a photo that encompasses a very wide field of view (sometimes as much as a full 360 degrees). While there are some cameras that can capture a single panoramic photo, it is far more common these days for a photographer to create a panorama from a series of photos which, although taken from the same point, manage to cover a wide range of the scene. Photoshop has a powerful feature called *Photomerge* that can take a series of these photographs and seamlessly combine them into a single merged photo. It is really very impressive technology! This Lightroom function allows you to select your series of photos in Lightroom and send them directly to Photomerge inside of Photoshop.

✔ **Merge to HDR in Photoshop:** HDR stands for *H*igh *D*ynamic *R*ange, which means a photo that contains detail all the way from the brightest highlights to the darkest shadows. Our eyes (and brain) are quite good at this by design; just imagine standing in your house looking out at a bright sunny day. You can see detail in the shadows of the room you are in as well as the white puffy clouds in the sky outside the window. Now, try to take a photo of that same view that captures the shadow detail of the interior as well as the highlight detail of the clouds — you can't! Your camera just can't capture detail across that wide of a range of brightness levels, at least not in a single photo.

It is possible to take a series of photos of the same scene while changing the exposure with each photo to capture a different range of brightness values (from dark shadows to bright highlights) and then combine them all into a single photo that does contain the full high dynamic range of brightness levels. This is where the Merge to HDR function comes into play. If you have such a series of photos, you can select them in Lightroom and then use this menu command to send them directly to Photoshop's Merge to HDR function, which then does the work of combining them into a single image. Head over to the HDR group on Flickr (`www.flickr.com/groups/hdr`) to get a taste of what HDR images look like.

✔ **Open as Layers in Photoshop:** This option is not as fancy as the other three, but it may be the one you use most often. What it does is allow you to select multiple photos in Lightroom and send them all to a single new document in Photoshop with each photo being placed on its own separate layer. This is extremely handy when you have two or more photos that you'd like to combine into a single composite photo, such as taking multiple photos of the same group of people and creating a composite that shows a final version where everyone's eyes are open and mouths are shut.

The workflow with these advanced options is essentially the same as the basic editing in that you still

1. **Select the photos you want to send to Photoshop from within Lightroom.**

2. **Choose the type of editing option you want to use from the Edit In menu.**

3. **Perform the work inside of Photoshop.**

4. **Save and close the file in Photoshop and return to Lightroom.**

If you only have a single photo selected, the only Photoshop CS3 option that will be enabled is Open as Smart Object in Photoshop, as the other three options all require multiple photos to be selected.

Figure 9-5: Edit in Photoshop CS3 menu commands.

Part IV
Sharing Your Work with the World

The 5th Wave   By Rich Tennant

"Hey— let's put scanned photos of ourselves through a ripple filter and see if we can make ourselves look wierd."

In this part . . .

You've come this far, and now it's time to lift the curtain and put your work in front of your audience, whether it's a client, an art buyer, a colleague, or friend. Lightroom provides a variety of output options, so if you're curious about how you can produce copies of your source files for a wide range of end uses, Chapter 10 should be your first stop.

From there, I introduce you to the Slideshow module in Chapter 11, and walk you through the process of creating your own custom slideshows.

Chapter 12 is all about getting your photos into a Web gallery, customizing it to fit your style, and then putting it online for the world to see.

I wrap up Part IV with Chapter 13, an in-depth look at the Print module. I cover all the steps in the process for producing the best possible output, whether you're sending it to a locally connected printer or to a print service.

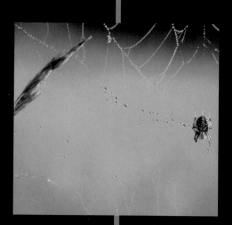

Exporting Photos

In This Chapter

▶ Understanding the export concept

▶ Getting to know the export dialog box

▶ Using an export workflow

▶ Saving time with presets

▶ Extending export options

*T*hose in the know about Lightroom will tell you that your photos are never actually inside Lightroom. (I'm in the know, and I make that exact same point in Chapter 4.) Such a We're-So-Lightroom-Hip-We-Can-Make-Seemingly-Off-The-Wall-Claims kind of statement does beg the question that if the photos are never in Lightroom, why does exporting sound an awful lot like you're getting them out? Good question! "It depends on what the meaning of the word 'is' is . . ."

Oops, sorry about that — wrong question. Nevertheless, it does depend on how you define "export." In Lightroom, the export process could be called "creating copies of your photos while applying your Lightroom adjustments" but it doesn't quite roll off the tongue the same way as "exporting" does. However, that is what's really happening here. If you're familiar with Photoshop or Elements, then you can think of exporting as a Save As command on steroids. No matter how you think about it, the essential point you need to keep in mind is that this is how you apply your Lightroom edits to copies of your source files.

You export images for many reasons, and here are a few of the most common:

- You want to e-mail photos to someone.
- You want to burn a group of images to DVD/CD.
- You want to upload to a photo-sharing site, an online print service, or your Web server.

In each case, you're going to have a specific output destination with specific file requirements, which is what will drive the choices you make when configuring the export settings. Take a closer look at what is involved.

Exploring the Export Dialog Box

Before I get into all the ways to access the Export dialog box, shown in Figure 10-1, and the overall workflow involved with the export process, I'd like to introduce you to what you'll find there so that you have a sense of what's involved as you move forward:

- **Preset section:** A consistent Lightroom feature is the ability to save a collection of settings as a preset to make it faster and easier to use those same settings again in the future. The left side of the dialog box is reserved for the creation and management of export presets.

- **Plug-in Manager:** *Export plugins* are third-party scripts that extend Lightroom export functionality by allowing you to perform additional tasks, such as applying a watermark or uploading files to photo-sharing sites, as part of the export process. You'll use the Plug-in Manager to find and install new export plugins.

- **Export [*some number of*] Selected Photos To:** The topmost section in the main part of the dialog box is used to choose where you are going to export your photos to. Assuming you have a CD and/or DVD burner installed, you'll have two default options — Files on Disk or Files on CD/DVD, which are accessible via the drop-down menu. If you've installed any export plugins they'll also appear in the drop-down menu.

- **Export Location panel:** Continuing through the panels, the Export Location panel is for choosing where you want the exported copies saved. No matter what may happen with the photos after the export is complete, they first need to be saved to a location on your disk.

- **File Naming panel:** As exporting always involves creating copies, Lightroom provides you with the opportunity to decide how those copies are to be named. The File Naming panel displays all the filename templates you may have created earlier (during import or while working in the Library module) as well as providing access to the Filename Template Editor used to create new templates.

✔ **File Settings panel:** Here you choose which file format (JPG, PSD, TIFF, DNG or same as the source file) you want the copies saved as; you can also configure any file specific settings here, such as color space (the gamut of colors it contains) and bit depth (the amount of data it contains).

✔ **Image Sizing panel:** This panel provides the ability to resize JPG, PSD, or TIFF files created during export.

✔ **Output Sharpening:** Provides the option of applying additional sharpening to the copies based on where these they are going to be viewed (either on screen or in print).

✔ **Metadata panel:** Control how much metadata (ranging from camera-generated shooting information to keywords) is included with the exported copies. There is also the option to add a small textual watermark on JPEG, PSD, and TIFF files.

✔ **Post-Processing panel:** When using the Files on Disk option, you can have Lightroom open your exported copies in another application (like a file browser or another image editor) to facilitate moving to the next stage of your workflow.

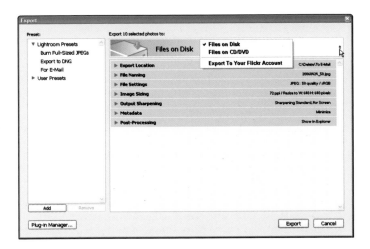

Figure 10-1: The Export dialog box.

I highly recommend confirming the number of files to be exported before you click the Export button. The number is displayed right above the configuration panels. (In Figure 10-1, for example, it reads *Export 10 selected photos to.*) I have discovered on more than one occasion that I accidentally selected more photos than I intended to export. Believe me, the last thing you want is to find that you just exported several thousand more images than you needed! Thankfully, a Cancel button is included, too.

Panels are collapsible and expandable. Click a panel label to collapse or expand that panel. Ctrl+click (⌘+click on a Mac) any panel label to collapse or expand all panels. Alt+click (Option+click on a Mac) any panel label to enable or disable Solo mode (meaning only one panel can be expanded at a time). When a panel is collapsed, you see a summary of its settings displayed in the header. When you eventually install export plugins (and I suggest that you do so), you'll find that they add several configuration panels to the dialog; therefore, using Solo mode reduces the need to scroll and allows you to see all settings at a glance. Nice!

Okay, enough of the introduction. Time to take a step back and look at all the steps involved in the export process and then I'll drill down deeper into the settings used in each export panel.

Creating Copies of Processed Photos

You've processed your photos like a pro, and now its time to send them out into the world. That means it's export time! There's a lot of power behind the humble Export dialog box, and with a little practice, you can harness all it has to offer.

Employing an export workflow

Lightroom (as you've probably figured out by now) is a workflow application, and within the larger workflow of taking your photos from input to output, there exists many smaller workflows within workflows. Export is no exception. Here are the basic steps:

1. **Select the images you want to export.**
2. **Initiate the export command.**
3. **Configure settings as needed to meet your output needs.**
4. **(Optional) Save settings as a preset for reuse.**

   In some cases you may not need, or want, to create a preset for every export. Additionally, after you create a preset, you don't need to create it again.

Here's a closer look at each step in the workflow, and a follow up with a real world example.

Step 1: Selecting the images you want to export

Your output needs determine which files you export. You can export images from within any Lightroom module, but you'll soon find that the Library module gives you the greatest access to your entire portfolio and exporting from there makes a lot of sense. So, if you're not there already, press G to jump to the Library's Grid view. From here, you have access to all your folders and collections, as well as the Browse bar, meaning you can go ahead and track down the images you want. (Go ahead, take your time.)

After you locate the images you want to export, you can select them by any of the following methods:

- Pressing Ctrl+A (⌘+A on a Mac) to select all photos within a folder or other grouping of photos.

- Clicking the first image in a series, holding the Shift key, and clicking the last image in the series to select all images in between.

- Holding the Ctrl key (⌘ on a Mac) and clicking each image individually to make a noncontiguous selection.

Step 2: Initiating the export command

After you select the images, you can initiate an export from any module (except where noted) through the following means:

- **Choose File⇨Export.** Launches the Export dialog box.

- **Choose File⇨Export with Previous.** Skips the Export dialog box and simply exports selected files by using the settings from the last export.

- **Choose File⇨Export with Preset⇨Select Preset.** Allows you to select a preset and export without additional configuration of the Export dialog box.

- **Press Ctrl+Shift+E (⌘+Shift+E on a Mac).** Keyboard shortcut that launches the Export dialog box.

- **Press Ctrl+Alt+Shift+E (⌘+Option+Shift+E on a Mac).** Keyboard shortcut for Export with Previous.

- **Right-click (Control+click on a Mac) a selected photo and choose one of the previously mentioned export options from the contextual menu that appears.**

- **Click the Export button at the bottom of the left panel in the Library module.** Only visible in the Library module, but comes in handy.

Can't say Adobe didn't give you enough choices! I would encourage you to use the keyboard shortcuts in your workflow as soon and as often as possible. They'll be second nature before you know it and they're great timesavers.

Step 3: Configuring settings as needed to meet your output needs

Okay, okay, I admit it. The broad overview of the export dialog box's panels I provide earlier in the chapter is fine, but we're going to need to drill deeper to understand how each panel works. So get ready for the gory details.

The first choice you're going to make is if you plan to export Files to Disk, Files on CD/DVD, or some export plugin (which I'll cover at the end of the chapter). Your most common choice will be Files to Disk. Refer to Figure 10-1 to see the drop-down menu expanded. From there, you configure all the panels relating to the choice you made. While additional panels will appear with different export plugins, they are too specific and varied to be covered here. I'll only focus on the panels that come with the two installed options (Disk or CD/DVD).

The Export Location panel

The Export Location panel, shown in Figure 10-2, is used to configure where you want to save a batch of copies on your hard drive. Even if you ultimately burn these copies to DVD or hand them off to another application, Lightroom first needs to save the copies to your hard drive.

Where you choose to save the files is driven by two factors: how you manage your files and what you determine your output needs to be. The Export To drop-down menu provides two options for designating a location:

- **Specific Folder:** When selected, you can point Lightroom to any folder on your disk. Just make sure it has enough free space to hold all the new copies. Click the Choose button and navigate to the folder you want to use.

- **Same Folder as Original Photo:** This option does exactly what it describes, which is to put your exported copies back into the same folder the original is found.

If you're exporting copies because you decided you want to e-mail them, you might not have any need for those copies after the e-mail is sent (since you can always re-export new copies). For this type of transitional export, I have created a special folder on my main disk named *Delete* that I choose as the Export To folder in those situations. Just remember to periodically go into that folder and send those files to the Recycle Bin (Trash on a Mac).

After you choose the location for the export, you have a few additional options to consider:

- **Put in Subfolder:** This option allows you to create a subfolder within the designated export location. Check the box and enter a name for the subfolder in the corresponding text field.

- **Add to This Catalog:** Think of this as an Automatic Import option. After your copies are exported, they'll appear inside Lightroom without having to go through the Import dialog box.

✓ **Stack with Original:** Stacking is a folder-specific function that allows you to arrange groups of photos within a given folder under a single thumbnail for organizational purposes. This option is only available when you're exporting copies back to the same exact folder as the originals (and not putting them in a subfolder). When checked, the exported photos appear *stacked* with the source photos when you view that folder in Lightroom.

Since it's possible that you may be exporting photos into a folder that already contains other photos, Lightroom needs you to tell it how to handle situations where your exported copies have the same name and are the same file type as the existing photos. You have four options:

✓ **Ask What to Do:** This is the safest option, and the one I recommend using. If such a situation occurred, Lightroom would prompt you for further instructions, where you would choose one of the other three options. I like having the reminder.

✓ **Choose a New Name for the Exported File:** In this case, Lightroom would simply append a new sequence number to the end of the exported file, so you would end up with two copies of the same file but with unique names.

✓ **Overwrite WITHOUT WARNING:** Does what it says (and it even uses all caps in the drop-down menu! Only choose this option if you are really sure it is what you want to do. *Note:* Lightroom will not allow you to overwrite the source photos, so don't choose this option thinking you can export copies with Lightroom adjustments and save over the existing source files — it won't work.

✓ **Skip:** If an existing file is encountered, no new copy will be created (i.e. it will be skipped).

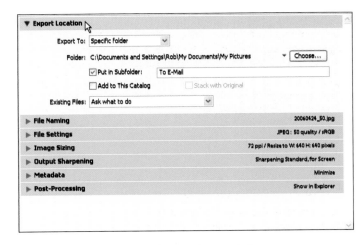

Figure 10-2: The Export Location panel expanded.

The File Naming panel

In many cases, you'll want to maintain name consistency between your source files and your exported copies. By simply choosing the Filename template, you can achieve just that. Other times, you may want to use custom names that are completely different or perhaps some variation of the original name. In any case, since you're always creating copies, you have to tell Lightroom how you want them named, and just like during Import or renaming in the Library module, Lightroom uses filename templates to do it.

Click the Template drop-down list, as shown in Figure 10-3, and choose one of the installed templates, or you can click Edit and create a custom filename template using the good old Filename Template Editor. See Chapter 4 for more information about creating filename templates.

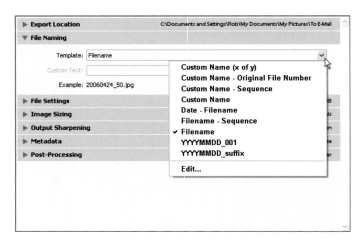

Figure 10-3: The File Naming panel expanded to show the Template drop-down list.

The File Settings panel

Choose your file format based on your output needs (such as choosing JPEG for photos going on a Web site). Some formats might require additional settings. Here's a list of the formats and their options:

- **JPEG:** When choosing the JPEG (or JPG) format you also need to choose the level of compression to be applied to each JPEG file. This is done with the Quality slider, as shown in Figure 10-4. The higher the quality value, the less compression — and the larger the file size. JPEG compression is always a tradeoff between file size and image quality. If you're not too concerned about file size, then leave it set to 100.

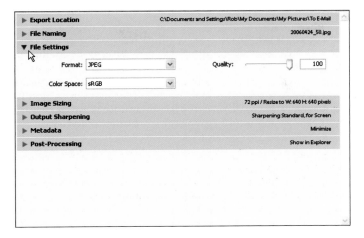

Figure 10-4: The File Settings panel expanded to show JPEG format and Quality slider.

- **PSD:** Photoshop's native file format. There are no additional settings with the PSD option.

- **TIFF:** TIFF is a widely supported format. Use the panel's Compression drop-down list to pick one of the lossless compression options, as shown in Figure 10-5. ("None" is pretty straightforward; ZIP and LZW means the file size will be reduced, but the length of time to open and close the file will increase, plus not all image editors can open compressed TIFF files.) *Note:* Only the ZIP compression option is available with 16-bit files.

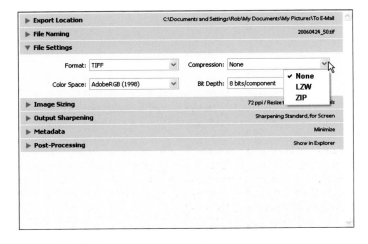

Figure 10-5: TIFF format and compression options.

✔ **DNG:** This is Adobe's open format for raw (unprocessed by the camera) photos. Figure 10-6 shows the configuration options available with DNG. The lowercase file extension is the norm, so there's no reason to change it. The medium-size JPEG preview is a good compromise on file size. The default conversion method settings are great because they preserve the raw data and create a smaller file using lossless compression. The big choice is if you want to embed the original raw file or not. You would want to embed the original raw file if you felt there may come a point in time where you might want to extract the original raw file so that you could process it in software that doesn't work with DNG. The downside to embedding the original raw file is that you double the file's size because you'll have the converted raw data and then add the entire original unaltered file as well (which just sits untouched in case some day it is needed). I prefer to leave this unchecked.

✔ **Original:** Selecting Original from the drop-down list results in the creation of an exact copy of your source image. There are no additional file settings.

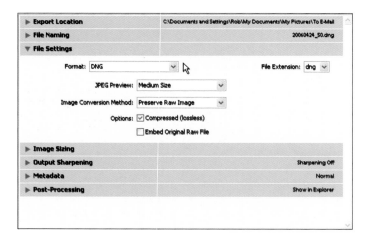

Figure 10-6: DNG configuration options.

There are two additional options that only appear when JPEG, TIFF, and PSD formats are chosen that warrant a separate discussion (raw files are always 16 bit and don't have a color space):

✔ **Color Space:** A photo's color space is what determines the range of possible colors it can contain. You need to decide what color space you want these copies converted into during the export process. Your choice of color space is completely determined by the reason you are exporting these copies to begin with. You'll find a more in-depth look at color spaces in Chapter 3, but here's a look at your choices:

- *sRG:* This color space contains the narrowest range of colors and is the standard for exporting photos destined for the Web, but is also used by some print services.

- *AdobeRGB (1998):* Contains a wider range of colors than sRGB and is most often used when additional editing or printing is the next destination for your files.

- *ProPhoto RGB:* Contains the widest range of colors and should only be used with 16-bit files. (I'll discuss bit depth next.) This is the best option when you want to retain all the color information that was in your source files. Not recommended when delivering copies destined for the Web or anyone not used to working with ProPhoto color space.

- *Other:* While the previous three options are the most common, there may also be advanced situations where you need to convert your files to a custom color space for printing purposes. Consult with your print service to see if it provides or requires custom profiles and it will help you get them installed. By choosing Other, you'll be taken to the Choose Profiles dialog box, where you can select the desired color profile.

✓ **Bit Depth:** Bit depth determines the amount of data a file contains. The higher the bit depth, the more data is contained in the file (which also means its file size is going to be larger too). If you're working with raw files, then you're working with 16-bit files. If you're working with JPEG files then you're working with 8-bit files. During export, you have the option of saving PSD and TIFF files in 16 bit. If you choose JPG, you will see that bit depth is grayed out, but know that JPEGs are all 8 bit by default. It only makes sense to save files in 16 bit when both the source files were originally 16 bit and when the output needs require this original data (such as if you are going to be archiving the exported copies to DVD or are going to be editing them in some other image editor). In all other situations, 8 bit will be the more common choice.

The Image Sizing panel

There are circumstances where you might need to save your exported copies at a different size from the source photos, such as when e-mailing them or putting them in a Web page, and this is where the Image Sizing panel comes into play (see Figure 10-7). Lightroom can make the exported images smaller or larger than the original images — a process known as *resampling*. The four different options for resizing your exports are

✏ *Width & Height:* The values entered for width and height define the maximum amount each side can be resized to fit while maintaining original aspect ratio.

✏ *Dimensions:* This option resizes exported images to fit within the entered dimensions while maintaining aspect ratio. When this option is selected, height and width are no longer associated with the values fields. You just enter the maximum dimensions you want the images resized to fit and Lightroom does the rest regardless of orientation.

✏ *Long Edge* and *Shortest Edge:* These both function in the same manner. You set the maximum value for the edge in question and Lightroom resizes all images to fit accordingly.

Check the Don't Enlarge box to prevent an image from being resampled larger than its original pixel dimensions. (This option is grayed out when Resize to Fit is unchecked.)

If your output needs require your photos to print at a specific size and at a specific number of pixels per inch (PPI), you can set its *resolution* value — the metadata tag used by software to determine how big the printed file should be. For example, the value of 300 PPI is commonly requested by print services, in which case you would enter 300 and choose pixels per inch. 300 PPI is always a safe choice, but if your photos are destined for the Web only, this value is meaningless and can be ignored.

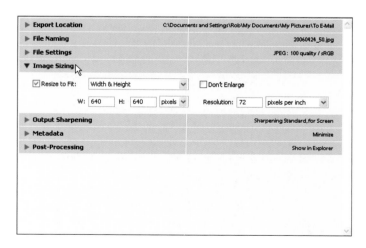

Figure 10-7: The Image Sizing panel.

The Output Sharpening panel

A new feature in Lightroom 2 is the ability to add sharpening tailored for the specific output destination as part of the export process. The Output Sharpening panel, as shown in Figure 10-8, is where you choose and configure your output sharpening settings. The possible output settings are defined as

- ✓ **Screen:** This is used when your photo's final viewing destination will be on a computer screen (i.e. on a Web page).

- ✓ **Matte Paper:** This is for when you are sending your photos to be printed on a type of photo paper that has a matte (nonshiny) finish.

- ✓ **Glossy Paper:** This is for when you are sending your photos to be printed on a type of photo paper that has a glossy (shiny) finish.

After you've identified what output you are sharpening for, you can set the amount of sharpening to apply; your choices here range from Low (almost none) to High (often too much), with Standard in the middle (which is a good default choice).

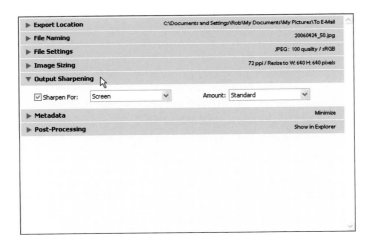

Figure 10-8: The Output Sharpening panel.

The Metadata panel

The Metadata panel, shown in Figure 10-9, offers the following settings:

- ✓ **Minimize Embedded Metadata:** Although this option isn't grayed out for TIFF and PSD files, it really only works on JPG files. It's intended to be used in those situations where you want to deliver a JPG with all metadata removed except for your copyright information.

🖌 **Write Keywords as Lightroom Hierarchy:** Keywords are the descriptive terms you assigned to your photos in the Library module. When this option is enabled, and if you're using keywords with parent/child relationships (meaning the keywords are in a hierarchical structure), then the exported copies will retain that same keyword structure. This is useful for photos that will be imported into another Lightroom catalog or managed with Adobe Bridge. Lightroom's use of keywords is explained in Chapter 6.

🖌 **Add Copyright Watermark:** When this box is checked, Lightroom pulls the information from the Copyright field of each file's metadata and renders it as a watermark in the lower-left corner of each exported copy. There are no configuration options for the watermark.

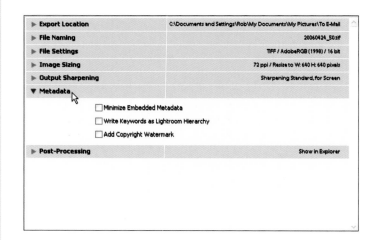

Figure 10-9: The Metadata panel expanded.

The Post-Processing panel

This is an optional setting that only appears when using the Files on Disk export option, but it can provide a nice productivity boost to your output when you know your photos are going to be opened in some other application after they have been created (such as for e-mailing or additional image editing). The Post-Processing panel (with the After Export drop-down list expanded) is shown in Figure 10-10. With the help of this panel, you can tell Lightroom to hand off your exported images to another application — in effect, having Lightroom perform what is commonly referred to as an "export action" on your stuff.

The After Export drop-down list includes the following preinstalled options:

- ✔ **Show in Explorer (Show in Finder on a Mac):** Automatically opens the folder containing the exported images in your file browser.

- ✔ **Open in Photoshop:** If you have Photoshop installed, then you have the option to open the exported images in Photoshop after they're saved to the export location.

- ✔ **Open in Additional editor:** If you've configured an additional external editor (refer to Chapter 9) you'll see it listed here as an option.

- ✔ **Open in Other Application:** Selecting this option gives you the opportunity to designate another application (such as an e-mail client, an alternative image editor, or an FTP client) that will be invoked at the end of the export. Lightroom will attempt to open the exported photos in that application; just keep in mind that not every application can accept images this way. Click the Choose button and navigate to the application that you want to send your photos to.

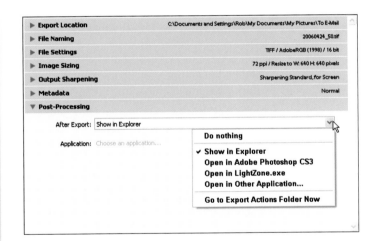

Figure 10-10: Post-Processing panel expanded to show After Export options.

At the bottom of the After Export drop-down list is the Go to Export Actions Folder Now command. Selecting this option opens Windows Explorer (Finder on a Mac) with Lightroom's Export Actions folder selected. You can place either an executable file or a shortcut (alias on a Mac) to an executable file in the Export Actions folder to include it as an option in the After Export drop-down list the next time you start Lightroom. This is another way to set things up so you can send your photos to a specific program or a Photoshop droplet with one quick command.

"What's a droplet?" you say. A *droplet* is a Photoshop action that you manage to turn (with Photoshop's help) into a tiny executable file. After you create a droplet, you can literally drag and drop photos on top of it to run the photos through the action automatically — a really powerful way to run a batch of images through a favorite action — applying a specific Photoshop filter, say, or converting to an alternative color space, or applying a custom watermark. By including the droplet as an export action Lightroom automatically runs the exported copies through the droplet after they have all been created.

Saving settings as a preset for reuse

Presets are such an awesome timesaver! Just think about it — you get to save scads of commonly used settings and then access them any time you want directly from the File⇨Export with Preset menu. Sweet!

Figure 10-11 shows the Presets panel — it's there on the left side. You get three preinstalled presets to start you off, right under the Lightroom Presets heading — presets that can't be ditched or updated, by the way. They are

- **Burn Full-Sized JPEGs:** Sets JPG as the file format with the least compression and no resizing and then adds burning the exported images to a disc as an After Export step.

- **Export to DNG:** Sets DNG as the file format, which essentially means you're set to convert to DNG on export. *Note:* Using this preset only makes sense when your source files are raw format.

- **For E-Mail:** Sets JPG as the file format with 50 percent JPG compression and resizes all images to fit within 640 x 640 pixels. *Note:* This preset doesn't actually pass files to your e-mail client; it just configures the export to an e-mail–friendly size.

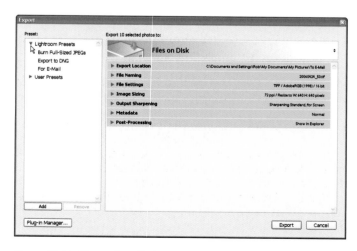

Figure 10-11: The preinstalled export presets.

I'm the first to admit that the preinstalled presets aren't incredibly sophisticated, but they do make good starting points and can help you see the possibilities. I often create DVDs of full-sized JPG copies that I give to friends and family so I took the Burn Full-Sized JPEGs preset as a starting point and customized it to my liking. Here's how I did that:

1. **Click the Burn Full-Sized JPEGs preset to load its settings into the dialog box.**

2. **Expand the Export Location panel.**

   When I create these JPEG copies, I'm not interested in keeping them after burning to disk, so I want to change the export location to a different folder.

3. **Click the Export To drop-down menu and choose Specific folder.**

4. **Click the Choose button and navigate to the desired folder.**

   Again, in my case I called upon my special Delete folder so I can easily get rid of these copies after the disk has been created.

5. **Leave the settings in the remaining panels as they are.**

   This is up to you of course, but the remaining settings work great for me so there was no need to change them.

6. **Click the Add button at the bottom left of the Lightroom Presets panel.**

   This opens the New Preset dialog box.

7. **Enter a descriptive name in the Preset Name field.**

8. **(Optional) Create a new folder in the process of saving your preset.**

   You can click the Folder drop-down list and choose an existing preset folder or create a new one. I find keeping presets organized in folders makes it easier to find the one I'm looking for.

9. **Click the Create button to complete the process and have the preset added to the Preset panel.**

You can delete custom presets and folders by highlighting them and clicking the Remove button. _**Note:**_ Removing a folder deletes any presets inside of it!

You can share presets among other workstations by right-clicking (Control+ click on a Mac) the preset and choosing Export from the contextual menu that appears. Copy the preset to the destination workstation and right-click (Control+click on a Mac) the folder you want to keep it in and choose Import. Presets can be updated with new settings by adjusting the settings as desired, right-clicking (Control+click on a Mac) the preset, and then choosing Update with Current Settings.

You can't update the preinstalled Lightroom presets with new settings.

Putting it all together

Time for a walk through the export process from start to finish. I love making photographs of the New England landscape as it transforms from one season to the next. It's such a visually rich area to live in! Awhile back, I came across a program called Helicon Focus, which can combine multiple shots of the same scene with different focus points into a single photo that's in complete focus from foreground to background. The effect is just stunning, displaying an incredible amount of detail and depth.

Because I'm a workflow kind of guy, I immediately play out the process from (raw) start to (stunning) finish. I shoot raw, so first I must process my image series in Lightroom. When my adjustments are complete, I can export full-sized TIFF copies straight to Helicon Focus.

And here's where the light bulb came on. If I set it so that Helicon Focus is ready, willing, and able to accept my images as part of an After Export step, it would create a seamless workflow. Here's how I'd accomplish just that:

1. **Press G to jump to Grid view in the Library module and choose the folder containing the photos you want to select for export.**

    I'm thinking five photos of pristine New England wilderness should do fine. In my case I used the Ctrl+A option to select all photos in that folder, but how you select them is not as important as making sure they are selected. You could just as easily have conducted a keyword search or chosen one of your collections to gather the photos you wanted to export.

2. **Press Ctrl+Shift+E (⌘+Shift+E on a Mac) to launch the Export dialog.**

    Alternatively, File➪Export works, too.

3. **Expand the Export Location panel and then select a specific folder to save the files to.**

    After I've combined these photos into a single photo, I want to save the final version back to my source folder, but I'll no longer need the exported copies used in the process. For this reason, I'm going to choose my Delete folder as the destination for these copies. I periodically clear out the files in this folder to conserve disk space.

4. **Expand the File Naming panel and then select the Filename template.**

    No reason to change the filename in this instance.

5. **Expand the File Settings Panel and then select TIFF format with no compression.**

    No need to apply compression because these files aren't keepers anyway.

6. **Choose ProPhoto RGB for Color Space and 16 bits for Bit Depth.**

    I want to minimize conversion of color spaces and take advantage of all the data contained in my original raw file. This option creates the largest file size, but provides as much of my original data as possible.

7. **Expand the Image Sizing panel and uncheck Resize to Fit so that no resizing takes place.**

8. **Expand the Output Sharpening panel and uncheck the Sharpen For box.**

    This is not the final output stage for these photos, so no need to apply output sharpening yet.

9. **Expand the Metadata panel and uncheck all options.**

10. **Expand the Post-Processing panel.**

11. **In the After Export drop-down list, choose Open in Other Application.**

12. **Click the Choose button and navigate to the program file.**

    In my case, I'd navigate to the Helicon Focus executable file. (This would be located in the Program Files on Windows or the Applications folder on a Mac.) The same process is used to assign any other application as an export action.

13. **(Optional) Click the Add button to save settings as a preset.**

    You've gone through the trouble of configuring the dialog how you want it, so you might as well benefit from your labor and save it for reuse.

14. **Click the Export button to start the process.**

    Figure 10-12 shows the completed Export dialog box.

After clicking Export, the dialog box goes away and you'll see Lightroom's progress meter start advancing as each copy is saved to the export location. After all copies have been created, the application designated in the Post-Processing panel opens, displaying the exported copies. Everything's ready for you to begin the next stage in your workflow.

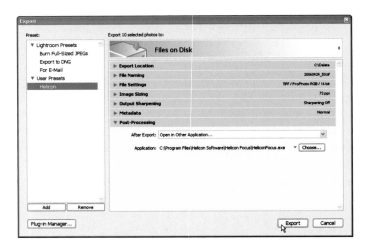

Figure 10-12: Completed Export dialog box.

Extending Possibilities with Export Plugins

Along with the release of Lightroom 1.3 came the Export Software Development Kit (SDK). The Export SDK opened the door for third-party developers to extend Lightroom's export functionality in an almost limitless number of ways. That is, by installing specific export plugins, you're no longer limited to simply exporting files to disk and then uploading them to your online print service, photo-sharing site, or Web server. Say you want to perform additional image manipulation that isn't possible in Lightroom, for example. Well, with the right export plugin, you can interact with external programs in a number of new ways. Here are some examples of the available export plugins:

- **Export to Flickr:** Sends your photos right to your Flickr account.
- **Export to Zenfolio:** Sends your photos right to your Zenfolio account.
- **Export to SmugMug:** Sends your photos right to your SmugMug account.
- **Export to PicasaWeb:** Sends your photos right to your PicasaWeb account.

Flickr, Zenfolio, SmugMug, and PicasaWeb are all online photo-sharing sites. You need to have an account to connect with any of the services. In each case, the export plugin interfaces directly with the service right in the Export dialog box. Figure 10-13 shows the Flickr export plugin interface.

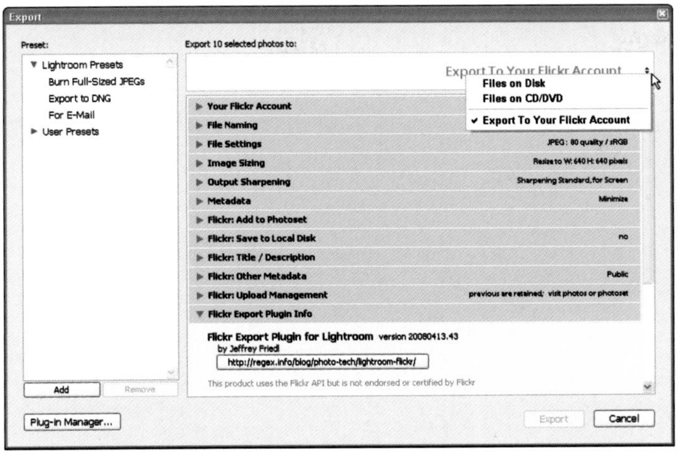

Figure 10-13: Flickr Export Plugin info expanded.

That's all fine and dandy, but you're probably wondering how to get your hands on some of these plugins. Thankfully Lightroom 2 makes it a little easier to find some, but first we're going to click the Plug-in Manager button (refer to Figure 10-1) on the bottom of the Export dialog box to open the Lightroom Plug-in Manager dialog box shown in Figure 10-14. **Note:** You can also access the Plug-in Manager at any time from the File⇨Plug-in Manager menu.

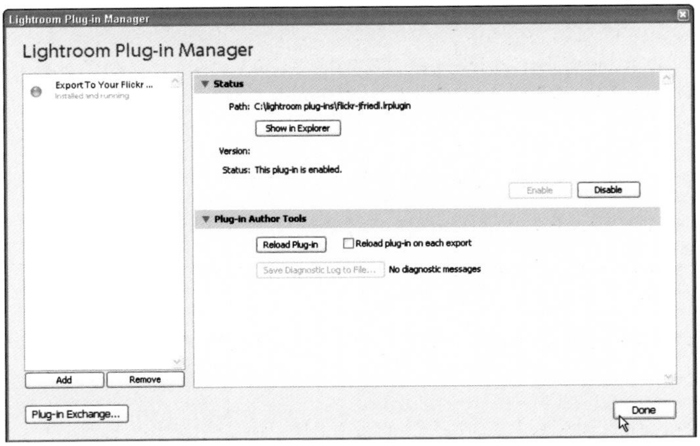

Figure 10-14: The Lightroom Plug-in Manager dialog box.

From there you can click the Plug-in Exchange button on the bottom of the dialog box. This opens your Web browser to Adobe's Lightroom Exchange service, which is a centralized clearinghouse for all known export plugins. Here you can find out a bit about each plugin and go directly to the Web site for each plugin developer to download the required plugin files. Read the installation instructions provided by the plugin developers to ensure you have all the required files and put them in the right location.

While some plugins are free, others may require a fee. These are all developed by parties outside of Adobe so there will be some variation in both cost and functionality. Read the developer's instructions carefully.

After you've downloaded a plugin or two you can return to the Plug-in Manager dialog box to enable the plugins to work with Lightroom. Here are the steps to add the Export to Flickr plugin I mentioned earlier:

1. **In the Plug-in Manager dialog box, click the Add button.**

   This launches the Add Lightroom Plug-in dialog box.

2. **Using the Add Lightroom Plugin dialog box, navigate to the folder where you saved the plugins you downloaded.**

   In the case of the Flickr plugin (and many others) you will be instructed to save them to the following location (depending upon your operating system):

   Mac
   ```
   /Library/Application Support/Adobe/
   Lightroom/Modules
   ```

   XP
   ```
   \Documents and Settings\username\Application
   Data\Adobe\Lightroom\Modules
   ```

   Vista
   ```
   \Users\username\AppData\Roaming\Adobe\Lightroom\
   Modules
   ```

3. **Select the plugin.**

   Lightroom plugins have a `.lrplugin` file extension.

4. **Click the Add Plug-in button on the Add Lightroom Plug-in dialog box.**

   Doing so returns you to the Plug-in Manager where you will see that your plugin has been added successfully (refer to Figure 10-14).

5. **Repeat the steps if you have additional plugins to add and click the Done button when finished to close the Plugin Manager.**

After you've added all your plugins, you'll be able to access your installed plugins from the Export Selected Photos To drop-down menu. Enjoy!

Producing a Slideshow

The Slideshow module offers a flexible interface for creating simple, yet professional, presentations of your photos. Slideshows aren't only useful for sharing your images with clients, peers, family, and friends, but they can also be a practical tool for reviewing your own work. You have relatively few settings to configure, and the changes update in the main workspace area while you work, so you'll be displaying your images in no time at all!

You can create a slideshow from any grouping of images you can dream of pulling together. Whether it's a folder, a collection, or an on-the-fly assemblage of images based on dates, keywords, and/or metadata, if you can group them, you can show them. You don't need to be in the Slideshow module to play a slideshow either. Press Ctrl+Enter (⌘+Enter on a Mac) from within any module to run an *impromptu slideshow,* which uses the last configured settings from the Slideshow module to run a show with the active images.

Exploring the Slideshow Module

An important point that bears repeating: The consistency of Lightroom's interface across modules is a key strength as a workflow tool. That's true as far as it goes — otherwise, I wouldn't say it — but be aware that each module performs a unique set of tasks, which means that each module requires a specialized set of panels, tools, and menus. You have to be acquainted with each set. (Don't worry too much — I help acquaint you to the Slideshow module's particular set in the next few sections.)

Getting to know the panels and tools

Before showing you around the Slideshow module, I want to remind you that you can show/hide and collapse/expand panels as needed to maximize your work area and display only the controls you need. Refer back to Chapter 1 for a complete rundown of the interface controls.

Okay, time to dive in! The left panel contains the organizational and preview panels; whereas, the right panel is where the adjusting, tweaking, and modification panels are found. Each module has its own specialized toolbar, but the images always take center stage. Here's a brief introduction to the Slideshow interface, as shown in Figure 11-1:

- **Menu bar:** Contains both the applicationwide commands as well as module-specific menu options.

- **Preview panel:** Displays a preview of each slideshow's layout while you move your cursor over the templates listed in the Template Browser.

- **Template Browser:** This Template Browser (or template organizer) is where you find the preinstalled templates as well as all your saved templates.

- **Collections panel:** Provides access to all the collections (think of them as virtual folders) you've created in the past as well as the controls to add new ones that retain the slideshow settings. Refer to Chapter 5 for a Collections refresher, if needed.

- **Export JPEG and Export PDF buttons:** These buttons provide an alternate output option for your slideshow. The JPEG button saves your slideshow as a series of JPEG images, while the PDF button creates a single PDF document. Neither option includes Intro Screen, Ending Screen, or music.

- **Filmstrip:** Shows the thumbnails of the image grouping you're working with. Can be used to choose which images appear in the slideshow, and in certain cases, you can use it to rearrange their order of appearance. (I discuss the specifics of reordering in the section "Creating a Slideshow.")

- **Options panel:** Controls the look of the photo's border and drop shadow, and how the photo appears within the layout guides.

- **Layout panel:** The settings in this panel determine the size and location of the photos on the slide.

- **Overlays panel:** Controls the look of the overlay elements (such as identity plate, text, and ratings) that you can add to enhance a slideshow.

- **Backdrop panel:** This is where you configure the look of the *backdrop,* which is the part of the slide not covered by the photos.

✓ **Titles panel:** Allows you to add optional intro and/or ending slides to your slideshow. This provides a nice finishing touch to any slideshow.

✓ **Playback panel:** The place where you add music, configure slide timing, and can randomize playback order.

✓ **Preview and Play buttons:** The Preview button plays the slideshow within the Content area, while the Play button controls the start of the full screen show.

✓ **Content area:** Displays a live preview of the active image (or the *most selected* image) within the slide layout. I'm first to admit that "most selected image" sounds rather odd at first, but in Lightroom parlance, it means that if you have multiple images selected (or highlighted) in the Filmstrip, you still need to select one of them to display in the content area. This most selected image is highlighted more brightly than the other less-selected images, as you can see in Figure 11-1.

✓ **Toolbar:** Contains the controls for navigation, designating which photos to use in the show, playback, rotating the overlay elements, and the addition of text overlays.

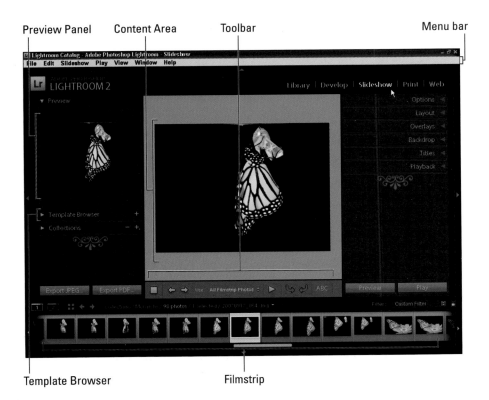

Figure 11-1: The Slideshow interface.

Becoming familiar with the menu options

The File, Edit, View, Window, and Help menus remain largely consistent throughout Lightroom. The menu commands unique to the Slideshow module are related to creation and playback:

- **Slideshow menu:** Here you find the commands for creating new templates and template folders, exporting a slideshow to PDF or JPEG, adding text overlays, and rotating an image within the slide. The Save Slideshow Settings allows you to save the current settings temporarily without having to create a template. You can then select a template or change settings, and use the Revert Slideshow Settings command to return to your saved state.

- **Play menu:** Contains commands for playing, ending, and navigating within a slideshow. The Content command provides the option to choose which photos within the active image grouping end up being displayed in the show.

Creating a Slideshow

Your photos, your intended audience, your reason for showing these images, and your own creativity drive the look of your slideshow. Some questions you want to think about before you begin are

- Who is my intended audience?
- What image order will make the most sense and impact?
- Is there any supporting information (such as captions, titles, camera-generated data like f-stop and shutter speed, and so on) that will make this presentation stronger or more targeted to this audience?
- How much time do I have?
- Would the addition of an audio component make this slideshow stronger?

With that in mind and knowing that new questions will emerge, you can enter your slideshow workflow on the right footing.

Employing a slideshow workflow

Lightroom is all about workflows. To me, *workflows* are ways to build efficiencies into the repetitive tasks required to reach a desired outcome. Creating a slideshow presentation is no different. The creation of every slideshow follows the same basic steps. Here's an overview of the process:

1. **Bring your photos to the Slideshow module.**

2. **Select a template for your starting point.**

3. **Customize the slideshow as desired.**

4. **(Optional) Save your settings as a template for reuse.**

5. **(Optional) Save your settings and photos as a special slideshow collection.**

   I'll cover this Saving as a Collection business in great detail later in the chapter, but for now I just want to say that this is a new feature in Lightroom 2 that allows you to bundle photos and settings in a special type of module-specific collection. This is great if you want to save multiple slideshow versions for a given group of photos with the bonus of having quick access from the Collections panel.

The next few sections take a closer look at each of these steps in the process. I bring it home at the end with a *soup to nuts* example of how I built a slideshow layout I use all the time.

Step 1: Bring your photos to the Slideshow module

The Library module is your organizational hub. You've already spent time putting photos into a folder structure, embedding them with keywords, and organizing them into collections. (Check out Chapter 5 for a refresher on these special virtual folders.) You have an array of camera-generated metadata that can also be used to refine your image groupings further. Figure 11-2 shows how photos can be assembled from many places. All these options are accessible from the Library module, and that's why the first step in slideshow creation starts there.

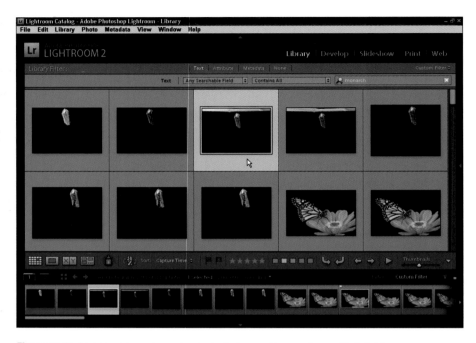

Figure 11-2: An image grouping using a single keyword spanning multiple folders.

One of the best ways to begin the slideshow process is to use (or create) a collection because it can contain photos from every corner of your portfolio. A *collection* is Lightroom's way of providing an alternate method to group photos, regardless of what folder the original photo resides in, which means you can think of them as a kind of virtual folder. Any single photo can be placed into an infinite number of collections, but the original photo can only be in a single folder. The other benefits of using a collection are

✔ You can manually control the order the images appear in the slideshow.

You can only do a manual sort when you're working within either a single folder or a single collection. So, if you manually want to sort images that are across a range of folders (or collections), you first need to put them into a single collection and then sort. Lightroom refers to this sort order as *User Order.* After you either are in a single folder or in a collection, be sure to grab the image itself, not the border, and drag and drop in the order you desire. You can do this from the Grid view of the Library module or from the Filmstrip in any module (see Figure 11-3). Refer to Chapter 5 for more on this sort option.

✔ A connection is formed between the collection and the slideshow template you employ so that each time you bring that collection to the Slideshow module, that template will be active.

✔ You can create an infinite number of collections and sort them independently of each other.

With your photos in hand (so to speak), bring them into the Slideshow module. Press Ctrl+Alt+3 (⌘+Option+3 on a Mac) to jump over to Slideshow (or click Slideshow in the Module Picker). Notice the image grouping you created in the Library module is displayed in the Filmstrip of the Slideshow module.

If needed, you can further refine your image grouping with the filtering options provided in the Filmstrip. For example, you could filter your grouping to only images with a rating of three stars or greater by going to the Filter controls above the thumbnails and clicking the third star shown. The other filtering options (flags, color labels, and copy status) work the same way.

Filters are very helpful, but sometimes you can easily forget that one's been applied. If you find yourself thinking that Lightroom has "lost" some photos you "knew" were there before, press Ctrl+L (⌘+L on a Mac) or click the Filter button at the end of the Filmstrip to toggle the filter on and off, and see if they reappear.

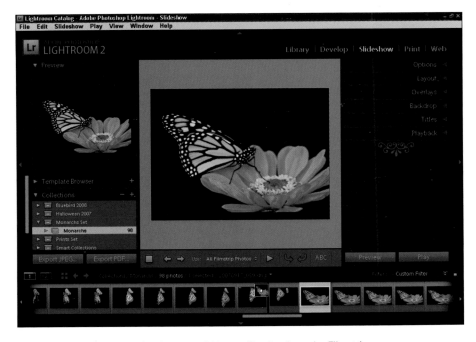

Figure 11-3: Manually sorting images within a collection from the Filmstrip.

Step 2: Select a template for your starting point

A Lightroom template is simply a way of saving unique combinations of settings for reuse. The preinstalled templates are helpful for seeing possibilities but also serve as great jumping off points for creating your own custom slideshows. You can see a thumbnail layout of any template in the Preview panel by moving your cursor over its name. The five preinstalled templates, as shown in Figure 11-4, are listed under the Lightroom Templates heading. Here are the key settings used in each:

- ✓ **Caption and Rating:** Displays the contents of the Caption field from each image's metadata as well as its star rating (if applied).

- ✓ **Crop to Fill:** Layout guides are maximized to fill the screen and the Zoom to Fill Frame option is enabled (I go over this setting in the next section), which results in images displayed full screen.

- ✓ **Default:** Makes use of an identity plate (a personalized graphic or text element) and a text overlay to display the image's filename.

- ✓ **Exif Metadata:** Also includes an identity plate but adds several text overlays, which display creator and capture data pulled from each file's EXIF metadata — the information recorded with each photo by the camera, as in f-stop, shutter speed, etc.

- ✓ **Widescreen:** The layout guides are maximized to fill the screen, but the Zoom to Fill Frame option is disabled, so images are resized to fit within the layout frame without being cropped or distorted.

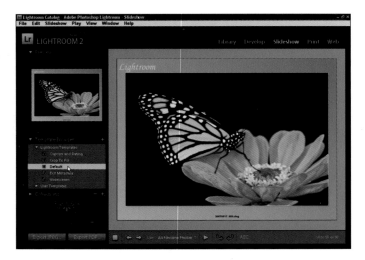

Figure 11-4: The Template Browser and Preview panel displaying the Default template.

After you select a template to start with, you can hide the Left Panel Group to increase the size of the content area by clicking the arrow on the left-most edge of the Left Panel Group or by pressing F7. You can hide the top panel containing the Module Picker for the time being as well by pressing F5.

Step 3: Customize the slideshow as desired

The right side panels are where the rubber meets the road when customizing your slideshow. The panels are arranged with an efficient workflow in mind, so start at the top and work your way down.

I like to reduce workspace clutter by collapsing all the right-side panels except the one I'm using. Lightroom has a Solo Mode option that makes this a snap. Here's how to enable it:

1. **Right-click (Option+click on a Mac) any panel header.**
2. **Choose Solo Mode from the pop-up contextual menu.**

When Solo Mode is enabled, you can only have one panel expanded at a time. As soon as you click another panel header to expand it, the currently opened panel collapses. This reduces the need to keep scrolling down to reach the lower panels. Lightroom provides a visual cue that Solo Mode is enabled by changing the arrow in the panel header from a solid to a dotted pattern. Use the same steps to disable Solo Mode if you want to open more than one panel simultaneously. Alternatively, hold the Alt key (Option on a Mac) and click a panel header to toggle Solo Mode on/off.

In the beginning of this chapter, I give you a brief introduction to all the panels but to get you up to speed on how you actually use them, I need to drill down further. In the sections that follow, I go over all the controls found within each panel.

Options panel

You find three controls in this panel, as shown in Figure 11-5. All three function independently of each other to determine the appearance of the photo on the slide. Here's what they do:

Figure 11-5: The Options panel.

> **Zoom to Fill Frame:** When the Zoom to Fill Frame option is enabled, the aspect ratio of your images is ignored in favor of the *frame* created by the layout guides (see the following "Layout panel" section). In other words, photos appear zoomed in and cropped if they don't have the same aspect ratio as the frame. With this option disabled, the aspect ratio of each image is respected, and the image is sized to fit within the frame accordingly. Figures 11-6 and 11-7 show the difference this setting can have on the same portrait-oriented image.

With Zoom to Fill Frame enabled, all photos are centered in the image area and zoomed until the frame area is filled edge to edge. If a photo appears cropped, you can adjust its position within the frame by clicking and dragging the image to reposition. To aid with repositioning, Lightroom displays a white outline of the photo's edge that falls outside the frame.

Stroke Border: A stroke border can be used to set the image off the background. Check the box to enable the stroke and then click the color swatch to choose a stroke color. The width of the stroke can range from 1–20 pixels. *Note:* The stroke appears inside the layout frame, so increasing the width of the stroke results in decreasing the size of the photo.

Cast Shadow: The ability to add a drop shadow to each image is another way to set it off from the background. You can adjust the shadow's visibility with the Opacity setting, its distance from the photo with the Offset setting, the hardness of its edges with the Radius setting, and its direction with the Angle setting. *Note:* The drop shadow can appear outside the layout frame, so if the layout frame goes to the edge of the slide, a shadow may not be visible.

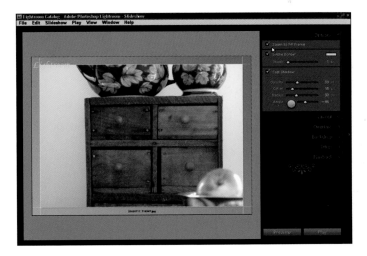

Figure 11-6: Zoom to Fill Frame enabled.

Figure 11-7: Zoom to Fill Frame disabled.

Layout panel

Use the controls in the Layout panel to determine the size and placement of the photos on the slide by adjusting the left, right, top, and bottom guides. The guides create the frame that defines the area within which the photos appear, and are easier to adjust when visible. Click the Show Guides box or press Ctrl+Shift+H (⌘+Shift+H on a Mac) to toggle their visibility on and off. In Figure 11-8, the guides are visible. *Note:* They never appear when the slideshow is playing.

Figure 11-8: The Layout panel.

Guides can be adjusted in tandem or individually, depending upon the configuration of which link boxes (the white square buttons next to each guide) are enabled. For example, you could link just the Top and Bottom guides together and then unlink the Left and Right. This means that any adjustment to the Top guide is mirrored in the Bottom, and the Left and Right are unaffected.

Here are the three different ways to adjust the guides:

- ✔ **Click and drag the guide:** When the cursor is placed over a guide in the content area, it changes to a double-sided arrow. Click the guide and drag to adjust its position.

- ✔ **Use the sliders:** Click and drag the sliders in the Layout panel to move the guides in big increments. Place the cursor over the number field, and it changes to a small, scrubby slider. Click and drag to move the guides in small increments.

✔ **Change the numbers:** Double-click the number field and enter a pixel amount. This number represents the distance in pixels from the edge of the slide. When the number field is active, you can use the up- and down-arrow keys to increase and decrease that number.

Overlays panel

Although photos should definitely take center stage in a slideshow, you still have a lot of room to add supporting cast members, such as an identity plate, rating stars, and text. You can add and modify these supporting elements in the Overlays panel, as shown in Figure 11-9. Here's a closer look at each overlay element:

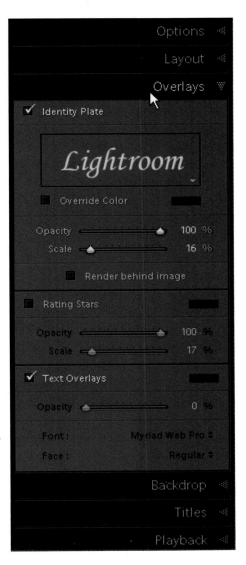

Figure 11-9: The Overlays panel.

✔ **Identity Plate:** Identity plates can be used to brand your slideshows. Checking the Identity Plate box causes the default identity plate to appear on the slide. You can reposition the plate anywhere on the slide by clicking and dragging it into position. *Note:* When you drag the identity plate across the slide, you'll notice anchor points along the slide or guide edges connecting to the nearest Resize handle on the identity plate, as shown in Figure 11-10. These anchor points appear with every overlay element and can be a great help in aligning elements on the slide.

You can choose a saved identity plate or create a new one by clicking the Identity Plate drop-down arrow. (Check out Chapter 5 for more on creating identity plates.) You can override the color of your identity plate — without affecting the saved identity plate — by checking the Override Color box and clicking the color swatch to choose a new color.

Figure 11-10: Anchor points aid in aligning overlay elements on the slide.

You can adjust the visibility of the identity plate with the Opacity slider. This is a great way to turn your identity plate into a low-opacity watermark for exported slideshows.

Identity plates can be resized either by using either the Resize handles on the object or the Scale slider. Checking the Render behind Image box causes your identity plate to become a background element and display behind the photo, stroke, and shadow.

✔ **Rating Stars:** Check the Rating Stars box to display the ratings overlay element on the slide. ***Note:*** If you haven't applied ratings, you won't see the rating element appear on the slide. (Stands to reason, right?) You can apply a rating to the active image while in the Slideshow module by pressing your 1–5 number keys respectively (even while the slideshow is playing).

You can change the color of the rating stars by clicking the color swatch. The Opacity and Scale sliders work the same as for the identity plate, and the element can be repositioned similarly as well.

✔ **Text Overlays:** Although there can be only one identity plate and rating element per slide, you can use any number of text-overlay elements in your presentation. Figure 11-11 shows a filename, a date, and a custom text element in use.

Figure 11-11: Multiple text overlay elements in use.

You can add a new text overlay by clicking the ABC button in the Toolbar or by pressing Ctrl+T (⌘+T on a Mac). After the overlay appears on the slide, you can configure the textual content from the Toolbar by clicking the ABC drop-down menu and selecting an existing text template or choosing Edit from the bottom of the menu to create your own text template with the Text Template Editor. (Refer to Chapter 12 for a step by step example of the Text Template Editor.) If you choose the Custom Text template, an input field appears on the Toolbar. Just enter your text and press Enter.

Any Text Overlay you add is going to appear on every slide. If you want the contents of the Text Overlay to change with each photo, then choose a text template that displays the title, caption, or some other information that is pulled dynamically from each photo's own metadata.

Because multiple text overlays can be used in a slideshow, they each need to be adjusted independently of each other. After you select a text element, the dotted border and Resize handles appear. You can then adjust the text element's color, opacity, and font via the controls in the Overlays panel. Text elements can be resized only via the Resize handles and are repositioned in the same manner as the other overlay elements. To remove any overlay, select it and press Delete.

✔ **Shadow:** Before getting into how this setting works, I need to point out this is one of the few areas where there's a difference between the Mac and Windows versions of Lightroom. If you're a Windows user, you won't see the Shadow section in the Overlays panel (sorry!), but you can look at Figure 11-12 to see what it looks like. I hope the engineers can overcome whatever operating system obstacle stands in the way of including this on Windows in a future version. Windows users can feel free to skip ahead to the next section.

The purpose of this control is to add a drop shadow to an overlay element. You enable the Shadow option by first clicking an overlay element to make it active and then checking the Shadow box. While the overlay element is active, you can adjust the opacity, offset, radius, and angle of the drop shadow in the same manner as the Cast Shadow control in the Options panel. **_Note:_** The opacity setting of the overlay element also affects the opacity of the element's shadow, so if the element itself has a low opacity setting, you'll need a high-shadow opacity setting to see the shadow.

Figure 11-12: Shadow control in Overlays panel on Mac only.

Backdrop panel

A good background supports and frames your photos but doesn't compete with them. The Backdrop panel, as shown in Figure 11-13, offers three ways to adjust the look of the area behind your photos. I don't mind telling you that I wish the controls were arranged differently, and after I show you how to use them, I think you'll agree.

Here's how the controls work in the order I use them:

- **Background Color:** Check the Background Color box to enable it and click the color swatch to choose a color. Keep in mind that your perception of color is influenced by surrounding colors. Because of this, you'll see black or neutral gray as the most common background color choices. Of course, you can use any color you wish if that's what fits with your goals for a particular audience. Know the rules and then break them when it suits you!

- **Background Image:** As an alternative, you can add a background image to the slide. Check the Background Image box to enable it and then drag a photo from the Filmstrip to either the slide background or the Background Image box in the Background panel, as shown in Figure 11-14. After the background image is in place, you can adjust its opacity via the slider. *Note:* When you decrease the opacity of the background image, the background color increasingly shows through. Different background colors affect your background image in different ways.

Figure 11-13: The Backdrop panel.

- **Color Wash:** Each of the earlier options can be further enhanced by applying a color wash, which is why I use this control last. You use it to add an additional color, in the form of a gradient, across the background. You can adjust the opacity and angle of the gradient wash via the respective controls.

As you can see, these controls can be used alone or in tandem to offer an almost unlimited variety of creative background possibilities!

Figure 11-14: Adding a background image to the slide.

Titles panel

A welcome addition to Lightroom 2, the Titles panel, as shown in Figure 11-15, offers a simple bit of polish to your slideshow presentation by providing a means to add a nonphoto beginning and ending screen to your show. The Intro Screen appears before the first photo slide and the Ending Screen appears after the last photo slide. These screens are entirely optional and function independently of each other — meaning you can add an Intro without an Ending and vice versa. The Titles panel is divided into two sections, with the Intro options on top and Ending options on bottom. However, the type of controls for each screen are the same:

- **Enable Screen check box:** Each screen type is enabled by checking the box at the top of each section.

- **Color swatch:** Click the color swatch to set the color of that screen.

- **Add Identity Plate check box:** Check this box to add an identity plate to either screen. This is the only means to add text or a graphic to that screen.

- **Choose/Create Identity Plate:** After you've enabled the identity plate you can choose to use an existing one or create a new one specifically for this purpose.

✔ **Override Color:** This control allows you to override the actual color of a textual identity plate without having to alter the identity plate itself. In other words, if you have a custom identity plate that uses black text, but want to add it to a black Intro screen, you can simply override the original color with this option and change it to white without affecting your custom identity plate. Make sense?

✔ **Scale:** This adjusts the size of the identity plate.

Figure 11-15: The Titles panel.

Playback panel

Okay, one more aspect of the Slideshow module behaves differently on a Mac than on Windows: how a soundtrack is applied. Lightroom on the Mac integrates tightly with iTunes, and Windows doesn't. Mac users can assign any iTunes playlist to a slideshow (music, podcast, even streaming Internet radio!); Windows users can only assign a folder containing MP3 files (yes, MP3 only). Time to take a closer look at each option in the Playback panel:

✔ **Soundtrack:** Check the Soundtrack box to enable it and then

- *On a Mac,* click the drop-down menu and choose an iTunes playlist, as shown in Figure 11-16.

- *On Windows,* click the Click Here to Choose a Music Folder link, as shown in Figure 11-17, and then navigate to a folder containing the MP3 files you want to accompany the slideshow.

Figure 11-16: Selecting an iTunes playlist on a Mac.

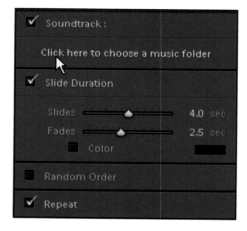

Figure 11-17: Selecting a music folder on Windows.

On either Mac or Windows, if you have more than one song in your playlist or folder (respectively) and the slideshow duration exceeds the length of the first song, the next song begins playing. If the music ends before the slideshow completes, well, you'll have a quiet ending. You can't synchronize the slideshow to the length of the song in Lightroom, so you have to set the duration of the show to match the music you select.

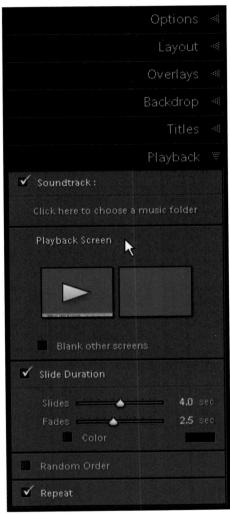

Figure 11-18: Playback Screen for multiple monitor configurations.

- **Playback Screen:** If you don't see Figure 11-18 in your Playback panel, it just means you only have one monitor hooked up to your computer. For those of you with multiple monitors, Lightroom lets you choose which monitor to run the slideshow on. Click the icon representing your monitor choice, and the Play symbol appears on the icon. Check the Blank Other Screens check box to black out the screen not running the show.

- **Slide Duration:** Unless you have a one-photo slideshow (not likely!), check the Slide Duration box to set the slide duration and transition timing. The Slides slider controls how long each photo displays, and the Fades slider controls the duration of the transition from one photo to the next. The Color check box and associated color swatch is a cool feature! When enabled, each slide will fade to that color and then to the next slide, as opposed to simply fading from one slide to the next. I find that adding a color fade keeps the presentation cleaner because it avoids that moment when two photos are partially faded into each other. Try it and you'll see.

✏ **Random Order:** Enabling this option causes your photos to appear randomly in the slideshow.

✏ **Repeat:** Check this box if you want your slideshow to keep repeating in a continuous loop, or leave it unchecked to have it stop on either the last photo slide or the Ending Screen, if enabled.

Step 4: Save your settings as a template for reuse

You don't need to rely solely on the pre-installed templates after you get your feet wet. As you begin to customize slideshows to your liking, I recommend saving your preferred settings as templates. Here's how:

1. **Press Ctrl+Shift+N (⌘+Shift+N on a Mac) to create a new template folder.**

   Alternatively, you can go to Slideshow⇨New Template Folder. Then all you have to do is give the folder a descriptive name and click the Create button.

   Keeping your templates organized can increase your efficiency by providing order to your template collection. The Template Browser displays template folders and individual templates in alphanumeric order, right below the Lightroom Templates heading. To keep my starter template folder at the top of the list, I name it with a number, as shown in Figure 11-19. **Note:** You can't create template folders within folders.

2. **Press Ctrl+N (⌘+N on a Mac) to create a new template from the settings you've specified.**

   Alternatively, you can go to Slideshow⇨New Template. Give the template a descriptive name, assign it to your desired folder, and click the Create button.

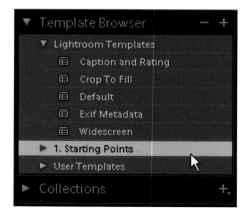

Figure 11-19: Creating a new template folder.

Step 5: Save your photos and settings as a special module collection

I briefly went over collections earlier, but these special collections require a little more explanation. Lightroom 2 brought with it a fundamental change in how collections can be structured, as well as some additional functionality. Let me explain by focusing on what you can do now. Figure 11-20 shows the Collections panel. The Collections panel, designed to put all of your collections within easy reach (almost) everywhere you are, is now a standard feature in all areas of Lightroom except the Develop module.

Figure 11-20: The Collections panel.

When you want to keep a group of collections together, you must put them in a collection set. I am in the practice of creating a new collection set when I am in the process of sorting photos after import (which I cover in Chapter 5), but you can create new sets as you need them using the + symbol in the Collections panel header and choosing Create Collection Set. (Previously you could group collections under existing collections, but this is no longer possible.)

Along with the addition of the Collections panel came a new module-specific type of collection. (There is one for Library, Slideshow, Web, and Print.) You can only create a module collection from inside each respective module. Each collection type has its own icon (refer to Figure 11-20 to see one of each). Here's what makes them special:

> ✔ **The module collection retains all the settings configured in that module from the last time that collection was in use.**

✔ **You can create multiple module collections that each use different settings.**

✔ **Double-clicking the collection icon automatically brings you to that module with that collection of photos with all the settings associated with it.**

So, while module collections are optional, I think you'll find that they can be a great tool for organizing and accessing your photos. Here are the steps for creating a module collection that will be associated with the current module settings:

1. **Click the + symbol in the Collections panel header and choose Create Slideshow.**

   Doing so launches the Create Slideshow dialog box.

2. **Enter a descriptive name in the Name field.**

3. **(Optional) Click the Set drop-down menu to add it to an existing set.**

   I strongly recommend that you use collection sets to keep your collections organized.

Putting it all together

As promised, I close this section by walking you through a practical example. Here's a useful layout for those situations when you want to export the slideshow as a PDF or a collection of JPEG images to hand off to another party. This example is simple and clean, while providing watermark protection and identifying each photo by filename. Here are the steps you need to take to customize your slideshow so it looks like what you see in Figure 11-21:

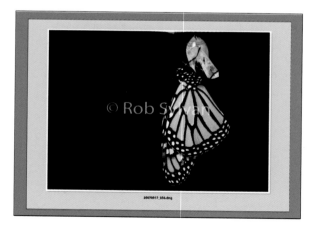

Figure 11-21: Customized slideshow template.

1. **Select the Default template from the Template Browser.**

   I recommend maximizing your workspace and reducing panel clutter as much as possible while you work. To that end, press F to jump to full screen mode, press F5 to hide the Module Picker, and then press F7 to hide the left panel.

2. **Expand the Options panel and use the Stroke Border slider to increase the border to 5 pixels.**

3. **Click the Stroke color swatch and set it to pure white.**

   Leave the other Options panel settings as is.

4. **Expand the Layout panel and click the link boxes for the Top and Bottom guides to unlink them.**

   The default here is to have them linked, so clicking unlinks them. You just want to be able to adjust the bottom guide without affecting the Top. The Left and Right guides can remain as is.

5. **Click and drag the Bottom guide up until its distance from the edge is at least two times greater than the Top guide is from the top edge.**

   You can also eyeball this amount until you think it looks good.

6. **Expand the Overlays panel and then click and drag the Identity Plate element over the center of the photo.**

   As part of the Default template, the default identity plate will already be on-screen. I suggest customizing it to fit your needs. I used the copyright symbol with my name, set to white, to create a simple styled text identity plate. ***Note:*** The keyboard shortcut for the copyright symbol on Windows involves holding the Alt key, using the numeric keypad to type **0169,** and then releasing the Alt key. On a Mac, just hold the Option key and press G.

7. **Scale the identity plate to 40 percent.**

8. **Reduce the opacity of the identity plate to 50–60 percent.**

   The goal is to use the identity plate as a watermark, so use an opacity level that you feel best protects the image without interfering with viewing the image too much.

9. **Click and drag the Filename text overlay right under the photo.**

   The Default template already included this text overlay, so all you need to do is reposition it.

10. **Expand the Backdrop panel and disable the color wash.**

11. **Click the Background color swatch and set it to a light gray.**

    The goal is to have it just gray enough to set off the pure white stroke around the photo.

12. **Press Ctrl+N (⌘+N on a Mac) to save these settings as a new template.**

At this point, your slideshow matches Figure 11-21, and you have a new template in your Template Browser. Well done!

Playing the Slideshow for Your Audience

Showtime! Now, before you head onstage to show your work, do a few dress rehearsals to check your timing and make sure everything flows as it should.

The Slideshow module relies upon the standard-sized previews that Lightroom creates after import. If Lightroom is still in the process of generating previews for the photos in your slideshow, you may experience problems running the show. You can force the generation of standard-sized previews and then wait for the progress meter to complete before running the show. Here's how:

1. **Press G to jump to Grid view in the Library module.**

2. **Press Ctrl+A (⌘+A on a Mac) to select all photos in your show.**

3. **Choose Library⇨Previews⇨Render Standard-Sized Previews.**

4. **Wait for the progress meter to complete and then switch back to the Slideshow module.**

Playback

After you finalize the look and feel of your slideshow, as well as the number of photos you'll show, expand the Playback panel (refer to Figure 11-18) and configure the following:

- ✔ **Slide Duration**
- ✔ **(Optional) Music**
- ✔ **(Optional) Playback Screen**

For that rare instance when you want to randomize the order of the slideshow (hey, it could happen), I'll remind you that that particular option is there, but it isn't likely to see much use.

The real choices here are Music and Slide Duration. You want them to work together. You want people to be able to see each photo, take it in, and be ready to move on when the next transition occurs. You also want the pace of the music to match the pace of the show. The duration of the show should also fit with the duration of the music. Keep in mind that you can adjust the slide duration in tenth-of-a-second increments to help you fine-tune the timing between your show and that perfect music selection.

If you're not adding music — and that's fine — you can just focus on finding that right amount of time for displaying each photo.

To aid you in test-driving your show, Lightroom can play the show right within the content area. Click the Preview button below the Playback panel. You'll hear the music (if enabled) and see the show just as it would play if you had it full screen, but you can also watch the progression of photos in the Filmstrip. Consider this a preflight check to ensure you're ready for prime time. Click the content area or press Esc to stop the preview.

If you have a dual monitor setup, you get to choose which monitor you want to run the show on by selecting its icon in the Playback panel. If you only have a single monitor setup, the choice is made for you.

To start the show, click the Play button, sit back, and enjoy!

There are three keyboard shortcuts worth memorizing for running a slideshow:

- ✓ **Press Enter to start the show.**
- ✓ **Press Spacebar to pause the show.**
- ✓ **Press Esc to quit the show.**

Export

Having options is nice. When you can't bring your computer to your audience or your audience to your computer, you can send your slideshow to your audience. Lightroom's Export function can save your slideshow to either a series of JPEG files or a single multipage PDF file. The good news is that anyone with a simple image viewer can see JPEGs, and the free Adobe Acrobat Reader is in such wide use almost anyone can view a PDF. The bad news is that music isn't included in the export, and the transition times are fixed. Here are the steps to export your show to PDF:

1. **Click the Export PDF button at the bottom of the Left Panel Group.**

   The Export Slideshow to PDF dialog box appears, as shown in Figure 11-22.

2. **In the Save In drop-down menu, navigate to the location on your computer where you want the file saved.**

3. **Enter a name in the File Name field.**

4. **Choose a quality setting for the JPG compression applied to each slide.**

   The higher the quality setting, the less JPG compression, which results in a better-looking image but a larger file size.

5. **Choose the Width and Height of the exported file.**

   This value should be based on the resolution of the monitor the presentation will be viewed on. If you've been working on a widescreen monitor with a 16:9 aspect ratio but are sending this to someone with a 4:3 display, the slide won't fill the entire screen when played. Instead, slide will be *letter boxed,* just like when you try to watch a widescreen movie on your standard TV screen.

6. Check the Automatically Show Full Screen box.

When the PDF file is opened, it displays full screen and begins the slideshow. Warn the people you deliver the file to that this will happen so they know what to expect. Also, tell them to press the Esc key to exit when they're done.

7. Click the Save button.

Figure 11-22: The Export Slideshow to PDF dialog.

When Lightroom's progress meter is complete, the file is ready to test (always test everything). If you're sending via e-mail, check the final output size of the PDF and resave with either higher JPG compression and/or smaller pixel dimensions if the file is too large.

The Export to JPEG functions essentially the exact same way (right down to the dialog box) with one logical difference; there is no Automatically Show Full Screen box. With the Export JPEG function Lightroom simply saves each slide out as a separate JPEG file. How they are viewed depends on what application the viewer opens them with. These files display equally well in the standard Windows Picture and Fax viewer as they do in Mac's standard Preview application or any application that opens JPEGs.

Building a Web Gallery

*I*t's an online world these days. High speed Internet and digital photography go together like peanut butter and chocolate. Lightroom's Web module offers a diverse range of photo gallery styles and configurations for creating professional-looking galleries without touching a bit of HTML code. Seamless integration between your portfolio and Lightroom's built-in FTP (*F*ile *T*ransfer *P*rotocol) software means you can take your photos from import to Web gallery to Web server in a matter of minutes!

Just like a slideshow, you can create a Web gallery from any grouping of images you can pull together in the Library module. You can start from a folder, keyword search, metadata browse, or collection. If you can group them, you can put them on the Web!

Exploring the Web Module

If you've been reading this book from the start, you might be tired of hearing it by now (but at least you won't forget), but each Lightroom module is structured essentially the same way to make your workflow more efficient. Here's the benefit from this consistency: The interface behaves the same way no matter where you are! You can show/hide and collapse/expand panels as needed to maximize your work area, and only display the controls you need. To find out more about the Lightroom interface as a whole, move it on over to Chapter 1.

Getting to know the panels and tools

Figure 12-1 shows the Web module interface. The organizational and preview panels are on the left side of the content area, the right side holds the configuration panels — the Filmstrip (across the bottom) and the Module Picker (across the top) are consistent across all modules. Keep in mind that the only elements that change from module to module are the tools and settings that are specific to that module. Small comfort perhaps when first trying to take it all in, but I'll help guide you through each step of the way!

Figure 12-1: The Web module interface.

Time to take a closer look and see what's here. Here's an overview of all the Web module components:

- ✔ **Menu bar:** Contains applicationwide commands as well as module-specific menu options.
- ✔ **Preview panel:** Displays a preview of each template layout as you move your cursor over the items listed in the Template Browser.
- ✔ **Template Browser:** Provides controls for creating new — and managing existing — templates.

- **Collections panel:** Provides access to all the collections (think of them as virtual folders) you've created in the past as well as the controls to add new ones that retain the slideshow settings. Refer to Chapter 5 for a Collections refresher if needed.

- **Preview in Browser button:** Click this button to display the current Web configuration in your default Web browser.

- **Filmstrip:** Displays thumbnails of the active image grouping. It can be used to reorder the photos if you're working within a collection or single folder.

- **Engine panel:** Lists installed Web galleries and is used to choose the active gallery. The five preinstalled gallery types are

  - *Airtight AutoViewer:* A gallery that displays in a horizontal strip. Scrolls like a filmstrip.

  - *Airtight PostcardViewer:* This gallery resembles a collection of picture postcards spread across a flat surface. Interactive and fun!

  - *Airtight SimpleViewer:* Here you have a pretty simple layout using thumbnails that control what image displays in the large view.

  - *Lightroom Flash Gallery:* The original Flash-based gallery from Adobe. Highly customizable.

  - *Lightroom HTML Gallery:* The original HTML gallery from Adobe that uses a thumbnail grid to link to larger versions.

- **Site Info panel:** Contains input fields for information about the gallery. Options vary with each gallery.

- **Color Palette panel:** Allows for changing the color scheme of certain gallery elements. Options vary with each gallery.

- **Appearance panel:** Configures attributes that affect the structural appearance of each gallery type. Options vary with each gallery.

- **Image Info panel:** Allows you to display information about the images in the gallery. Options vary with each gallery.

- **Output Settings panel:** Most galleries make use of a small thumbnail size photo in combination with a larger version of the same photo. The main option in this panel controls the output size settings of the larger version. Other options vary with each gallery.

- **Upload Settings panel:** Configuration and storage of your FTP settings.

- **Export button:** Click this button to save all your gallery files to a location on your disk.

- **Upload button:** Click this button to begin copying files to the Web server you configured in the Upload Settings panel.

✔ **Content area:** Displays an updated and fully interactive preview of your photos in the active gallery.

✔ **Toolbar:** Displays the name of the active gallery along with navigation controls, the Use menu — for designating which photos to use in the gallery — and the name of the gallery type being used.

As noted above, the contents of the Site Info, Color Palette, Appearance, Image Info, and Output Settings panels change as you change gallery types. None of the Airtight galleries, for example, include the option to add the copyright watermark to the photos. Granted, the copyright watermark feature is rather weak as watermarks go, but don't drive yourself mad looking for it in the galleries that don't include it!

Becoming familiar with the menu options

The File, Edit, View, Window, and Help menus remain largely consistent throughout Lightroom. The one menu option that is unique to the Web module is the aptly named Web menu. It contains commands for creating new templates and template folders, reloading the content area (similar to refreshing your Web browser), exporting the Web gallery, and previewing the gallery in your browser. The Save Web Settings command allows you to save the custom settings temporarily without having to create a template. You can then select a template or change settings to compare, and use the Revert Web Settings command to return to your saved state. The Content command provides the option to choose which photos — within the active image grouping — will display in the gallery. The About menu provides additional functionality details and a Feature list regarding the active gallery type.

What's the Difference between Flash and HTML?

Without getting bogged down in geek-speak, you probably need to have a few things under your belt about the nature of the gallery types found in Lightroom. The galleries fall into one of two flavors:

✔ **HTML:** Think static and linear. They can display in any browser without any special plugins.

✔ **Flash:** Think fluid and interactive. They require the free (and nearly universal) Flash plugin to work.

Okay, those are pretty broad generalizations, but insofar as Lightroom is concerned, the Flash galleries are far more fluid and interactive, while the HTML gallery is kind of a static grid. Yes, I did say *the* HTML gallery; there's only one (it's highly configurable though). The other four are all Flash driven.

While your cursor is over each template in the Template Browser, Lightroom gives you a clue as to which gallery type you're seeing in the Preview panel. HTML galleries, as shown in Figure 12-2, display "HTML" in the lower-left corner, while the Flash galleries, as shown in Figure 12-3, display a stylized "F" in the same location. *Note:* The templates you make from Airtight galleries (as well as other third-party developers) simply show a generic layout preview of that gallery type.

Figure 12-2: HTML template preview.

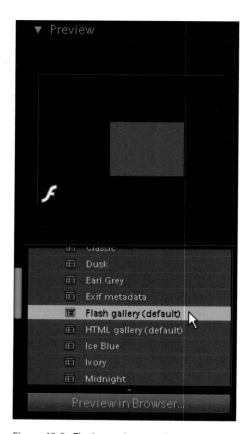

Figure 12-3: Flash template preview.

When Lightroom version 1.0 was released, you only had the Lightroom HTML Gallery and the Lightroom Flash Gallery available to you. With the release of version 1.3, the three galleries made by Airtight Interactive became welcome additions to the program. In Chapter 14, I let you know where you can find some additional galleries you can download and install.

Creating a Web Gallery

The look of your Web gallery is going to be driven by your photos, your intended audience, the reason(s) you're putting these images online, and your own creativity. Some questions you want to think about before you begin are

🖝 Who is my intended audience?

🖝 What image order will make the most sense and impact?

> ✔ Is there any supporting information (such as filenames, titles, camera-generated data like f-stop, etc.) that you want to add to this gallery?

> ✔ Does my audience have any technological limitations (bandwidth, monitor resolution, browser preference, etc.) that would prevent them from enjoying the Web gallery?

> ✔ Is a watermark required to protect my work?

With that in mind, and knowing that new questions will emerge, you can enter into your Web gallery workflow on the right footing.

Employing a Web gallery workflow

Lightroom is all about workflows within workflows! The creation of every Web gallery follows the same basic steps. Here's an overview of the process:

1. **Bring your photos to the Web module.**

2. **Select a template or gallery type for your starting point.**

3. **Customize as desired.**

4. **(Optional) Save your settings as a template for reuse.**

5. **(Optional) Save your settings and photos as a special Web collection.**

   I'll cover this in great detail later in the chapter, but this is a new feature in Lightroom 2 that allows you to bundle photos and settings in a special type of module-specific collection. This is great if you want to save multiple Web gallery versions for a given group of photos with the bonus of having quick access from the Collections panel.

The next few sections take a closer look at each step in the process. I follow up by walking you through the creation of a gallery I find particularly useful.

Step 1: Bring your photos to the Web gallery module

The Library module is your organizational hub. You've already spent time putting photos into a folder structure, embedding them with keywords, and organizing them into collections (refer to Chapter 5 for a refresher on these special virtual folders). You have an array of camera-generated metadata that can also be used to browse your portfolio. All these options are accessible from the Library module, and that is why the first step in Web-gallery creation starts there.

One of the best ways to begin the Web gallery process is to use a collection, because it can contain photos from every corner of your imported portfolio. The other benefits of using a collection are

✔ You can manually control the order the images appear in the Web gallery.

You can only do a manual sort when you're working within either a single folder or a single collection. So, if you want to sort images manually that are across a range of folders (or collections), you first need to put them into a single collection, then sort. Lightroom refers to this sort order as *User Order.* After you're in either a single folder or a collection, then be sure to grab the image itself, not the border, and drag and drop in the order you desire, as shown in Figure 12-4. You can drag and drop images from the Grid view of the Library module or the Filmstrip in any module.

✔ A connection is formed between the collection and the Web gallery settings you employ so that each time you bring that collection to the Slideshow module, those settings will be active.

✔ You can create an infinite number of collections and sort them independently of each other.

Figure 12-4: Manually sorting images within a collection from the Filmstrip.

After you've collected your photos for the gallery, it's time to bring them into the Web module. Press Ctrl+Alt+5 (⌘+Option+5 on a Mac) to jump over to Web module (or click Web in the Module Picker). Notice the image grouping you created in the Library module is still displayed in the Filmstrip.

If needed, you can further refine your image grouping using the filtering options provided in the Filmstrip. For example, you could filter your grouping to only images with a rating of three stars or greater by clicking the third star above the thumbnails. The other filtering options (flags, color labels, and copy status) work the same way.

Filters are very helpful, but sometimes it's easy to forget that a filter has been applied. If you find yourself thinking that Lightroom has "lost" some photos you "knew" were there before, try pressing Ctrl+L (⌘+L on a Mac) or click the Filter button at the end of the Filmstrip to toggle the filter on and off, and see if the photos reappear.

Step 2: Select a template or gallery type for your starting point

A template is simply a way of saving unique combinations of settings for reuse. The preinstalled templates are helpful for seeing possibilities, but also serve as great jumping-off points for creating your own custom Web galleries. You can see a thumbnail layout of any template in the Preview panel by moving your cursor over its name. The preinstalled templates, as shown in Figure 12-5, are listed under the Lightroom Templates heading. These templates are simply variations on either of the two default gallery types:

- ✔ **Lightroom Flash Gallery**
- ✔ **Lightroom HTML Gallery**

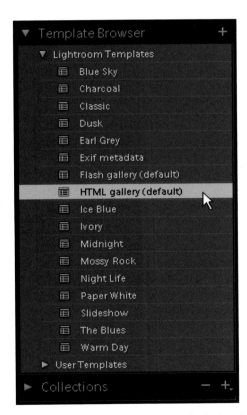

Figure 12-5: The Template Browser displaying the default template.

TIP

When you're finished with the Template Browser, you can hide the left panel to increase the size of the content area by clicking the arrow in the center of the left panel or by pressing F7. To reclaim additional space, you can hide the Module Picker by pressing F5.

No templates are included in the Template Browser for the three Airtight galleries, so to access them you need to expand the Engine panel, as shown in Figure 12-6. Simply selecting the gallery type provides you with default settings to work from and to create your own templates.

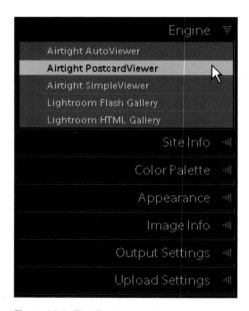

Figure 12-6: The Engine panel.

Step 3: Customize as desired

The controls for customizing your Web gallery are found on the right side of the module. The panels are arranged with an efficient workflow in mind, so start at the top and work your way down.

I like to reduce workspace clutter by collapsing all the right-side panels except the one I'm using. Lightroom has a Solo Mode option that makes this a snap. Here's how to enable it:

1. **Right-click (Option+click on a Mac) any panel header.**
2. **Choose Solo Mode from the pop-up context menu.**

When Solo Mode is enabled, you can have only one panel expanded at a time. This means that as soon as you click another panel header to expand it, the currently open panel will collapse. This reduces the need to keep scrolling to reach the lower panels. Lightroom provides a visual cue that Solo Mode is enabled by changing the arrow in the panel header from a solid to a dotted pattern. Use the same steps to disable Solo Mode if you want to open more than one panel simultaneously. Alternatively, hold the Alt key (Option on a Mac) and click a panel header to toggle Solo Mode on/off.

A nice feature of the Engine panel is that when it's collapsed, a drop-down menu appears in the header, which enables you to switch between gallery types without needing to expand that panel!

Okay, let's roll up our sleeves and go through each panel in greater detail.

Site Info panel

The contents of the Site Info panel will depend on which gallery type you choose. However, all galleries share the Site Title field shown in Figure 12-7. This information is displayed in the title bar of Web browsers visiting your site, and can be displayed within the content area of the gallery depending on the gallery type you choose.

Either you can enter the information into the fields in the panel, or you can click the text you want to edit in the Content area and edit it right in the live gallery preview!

Figure 12-7: The Site Title field.

Only the Lightroom HTML and Lightroom Flash galleries make use of the following fields, as shown in Figure 12-8:

Figure 12-8: Common fields in the Site Info panel.

- ✔ **Collection Title:** Think of this as a subtitle for your site title.

- ✔ **Collection Description:** Enter a description of the contents of your gallery.

- ✔ **Contact Info:** This field works hand in hand with the Web or Mail Link field below it to create a clickable link.

- ✔ **Web or Mail Link:** Enter the link or mailto code to accompany the data you entered for Contact Info.

Although I did say at the start of this chapter that you wouldn't have to touch "a bit of HTML code," here is one place you can. If you want to create a link to another page from your gallery, you use both the Contact Info and the Web or Mail Link fields to make it work. For example, say I want to link this Web gallery to my site's home page, and I want that link to display the following text, "Home." (Home is the text you would click.) To get all that to work, I'd start by entering **Home** into the Contact Info field. I would then enter the complete link to my home page in the Web or Mail Link field, so I'd enter **http://www.myWebsite.com.**

The other option is to create an e-mail link, which when clicked opens that person's e-mail program with a new message already addressed to me. This works the same way. First, enter the text you want visitors to click, like **Email Me,** in the Contact Info field, and then enter the mailto code (this is what tells a Web browser to open the e-mail) followed by your e-mail address. It would look like this:

```
mailto:me@myWebsite.com
```

The default text is formatted that way to remind you to always put `mailto:` before the e-mail address.

Lightroom remembers text you've entered in each field and provides you quick access to previous entries via the drop-down arrow above the field.

Only in the Lightroom HTML Gallery can you add an identity plate in addition to the Site Title at the top of your page, as shown in Figure 12-9. You won't see this in the Site Info panel for any other gallery type. ***Note:*** That said, the Lightroom Flash Gallery gives you the option to swap the Site Title field with an identity plate, but the identity plate control is included in the Appearance panel with that gallery. (I cover that in a bit.)

Figure 12-9: Identity plate added to the Lightroom HTML Gallery.

Check the box to enable the identity plate. You can choose an existing identity plate or create a new one. (Look at Chapter 5 for more about creating identity plates.) The identity plate can be made into a clickable link by completing the Web or Mail Link field that displays below it.

Color Palette panel

As the name suggests, the Color Palette panel holds the controls for changing the color scheme of your gallery. Figure 12-10 shows the Color Palette panel for the HTML Gallery. *Note:* The contents of this panel changes based on the gallery type selected, since each is unique. Although the configurable elements in each gallery type vary, the color controls work the same way in each instance.

Click the color chip corresponding to the element you wish to change to access Lightroom's new-and-improved color picker (it's really cool), as shown in Figure 12-11. You can choose a color a number of ways:

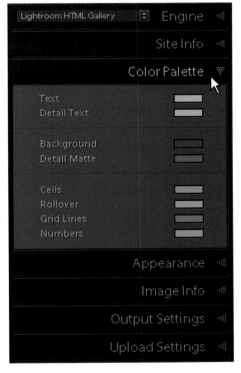

Figure 12-10: The Color Palette panel.

✔ **Enter HSL values:** Uses the HSL (*H*ue, *S*aturation, *L*ightness) color model. You can enter specific values by clicking each H, S, or L field. Right-click (Control+click on a Mac) the color bar to switch between HSL and HSB. (See the next bullet for more on HSB.)

✔ **Enter HSB values:** Uses the HSB (*H*ue, *S*aturation, *B*rightness) color model. You can enter specific values by clicking each H, S, or B field. Right-click (Control+click on a Mac) the color bar to switch between HSL and HSB.

✔ **Enter RGB values:** Uses yet another color model — this time the RGB (*R*ed, *G*reen, *B*lue) color model. You can enter specific values by clicking each R, G, or B field.

✔ **Enter Hexadecimal values:** The numbers that are used in HTML for defining color are commonly referred to as *hex* values. If you know the hex values used on your Web site, click the word Hex; this changes the RGB fields to a Hex field where you can enter the desired values.

✔ **Click a spot on the palette:** You can also simply choose a color by clicking the bar and adjusting the saturation with the ramp slider.

✔ **Eyedropper:** By far the coolest option! Click the color chip, but do not release the mouse button so that you keep the eyedropper active. Move the eyedropper over any (and I mean any) area of your screen to select a color. This is great for pulling colors right from your photos to create the color palette for your gallery. While you move around the screen, you see the color of the element you're working on change. Release the mouse button to select the color.

You can use the swatches along the top of the Color Picker to save colors you like. Placing your cursor over each swatch displays a pop-up ToolTip instructing you how to use that swatch. Close the Color Picker by clicking back on the color chip in the Color Palette you selected to open it.

Figure 12-11: Color Picker.

Appearance panel

The contents of this panel vary the most of any panel among the different gallery types. As you can imagine, each gallery type has a set of controls to alter its appearance. Figure 12-12 shows the Appearance panel for the Lightroom HTML Gallery.

Despite the differences in the controls for each gallery, they're all rather straightforward in their purpose — that you immediately see your adjustment's affects on the active gallery. For example, if you add more cells to the HTML gallery, the live preview automatically updates, or if you increase the

photo borders in the AutoViewer, the gallery rebuilds itself before your eyes.
Note: In the case of the Lightroom HTML Gallery, the controls in the Image
Page section affect the page that displays the large version of the image. Click
a thumbnail in the content area to switch to an Image Page to see the effects
of the controls.

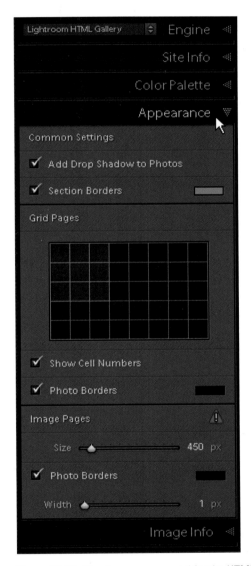

Figure 12-12: The Appearance panel for the HTML gallery.

Image Info panel

This panel is where you find controls for adding a caption and title to go with the large image in your gallery. Figure 12-13 shows the Image Info panel for the Lightroom Flash and HTML gallery types. *Note:* The Airtight galleries only offer the ability to add a caption.

The main difference between Title and Caption is where they're located in each gallery (Title is always higher). You can display any type of textual information in either element. Here's how to add a caption:

1. **Check the Caption box.**

2. **Click the drop-down menu and either choose one of the text templates listed or choose Edit to create a custom text template.**

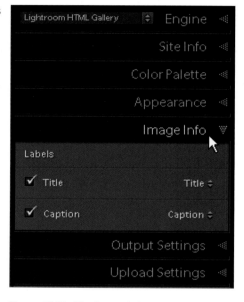

Figure 12-13: The Image Info panel.

After you choose a template, it immediately displays in the gallery. *Note:* Caption and Title only appear when viewing the large version of the photo, so if you're viewing the HTML grid, you won't see them until you click a photo to get to the large version.

While helpful Title and Caption text templates come with Lightroom, I strongly suggest taking a dive into the Text Template Editor to create custom templates that might better suit your needs. Here's how to create a text template that displays the camera model and lens used:

1. **Choose Edit from the Caption drop-down menu.**

   Doing so launches the Text Template Editor, as shown in Figure 12-14.

2. **Select and then delete any text tokens that appear in the Editor window.**

   This allows you to start with a clean slate.

3. **Choose Model from the top drop-down menu in the EXIF Data section.**

   The Model token appears in the Editor window. Notice that the Example preview above the window shows you the contents of the token.

4. **Click in front of the token to insert your cursor there and enter** Camera: **followed by a space.**

   Yes, you can type right in the Editor window! This is great for adding text as part of the template.

5. **Click behind the Model token to insert your cursor there and enter a space followed by** Lens: **and another space.**

6. **Choose Lens from the same drop-down menu as before.**

   The Lens token should appear in the Editor window at the end of the existing text.

7. **Choose the Save Current Settings as New Preset option from the Preset drop-down menu.**

8. **Give your new preset a descriptive name and click Create.**

9. **Click Done to close the editor.**

   You should now see this information display in your gallery.

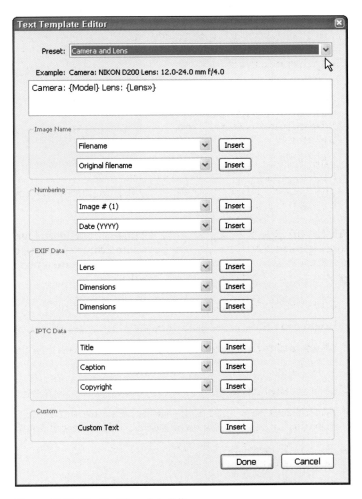

Figure 12-14: The Text Template Editor.

Output Settings panel

The Output Settings panel contains the settings that affect the large image component of the gallery. *Note:* Your options are going to vary with each gallery type. Figure 12-15 shows the Output Settings panel for the Lightroom HTML Gallery. The types of controls that can appear in this panel are

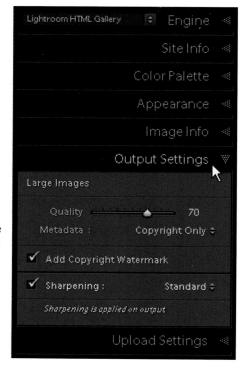

Figure 12-15: The Output Settings panel.

- **Quality:** This control sets the amount of JPG compression applied to the large image. The more compression, the smaller the file size, but the appearance can be degraded with too much compression. I wouldn't go below 50.

- **Size:** This control determines the width of the large image in pixels. Only available in the Airtight galleries. A large image is easy to see, but also easy to steal (and use). For most uses I can't see going larger than 800 pixels.

- **Metadata:** Gives you the option to leave all metadata intact in the large JPGs (by selecting All from the drop-down menu), or stripping everything but your copyright (by choosing Copyright Only). Only available in the Lightroom Flash and HTML galleries.

- **Add Copyright Watermark:** Pulls the copyright data you entered into the Copyright field of the Metadata panel in the Library module and displays it as a watermark on the photo. Only available in the Lightroom Flash and HTML galleries.

- **Sharpening:** This is a new addition to Lightroom 2, which applies one of three levels of sharpening (low, standard, or high) when the gallery leaves Lightroom. Standard is a good default amount. (Sharpening is only available in the Lightroom Flash and HTML galleries.)

- **Photo Borders:** Controls the width of the border around the large image. Only available in the SimpleViewer.

✔ **Padding:** Controls the amount of space between the large image and thumbnails. Only available in the SimpleViewer.

✔ **Allow Right-Click to Open Photos:** When checked, a viewer of your gallery can right-click the large photo and choose to have that image open by itself in a new window. Enable this option if you want people to be able to download a copy of the large image. Only available in the SimpleViewer.

Step 4: Save your settings as a template for reuse

You don't want to have to re-create the wheel each time you upload a Web gallery, so this is where templates come into play. In fact, I keep the Lightroom Templates collapsed, and only use my templates these days. Here's an overview of how to manage and save yours:

1. **(Optional) Create a new template folder.**

   Press Ctrl+Shift+N (⌘+Shift+N on a Mac), or go to Web⇨New Template Folder. Give the folder a descriptive name and click the Create button.

Keeping your templates organized can increase your efficiency by providing order to your template collection. The Template Browser only displays template folders and individual templates in alphanumeric order below the Lightroom Templates folder. To keep my starter template folder at the top of the list, I name it with a number, as shown in Figure 12-16. **Note:** It isn't possible to create folders within folders.

Figure 12-16: Creating a new template folder.

2. **Create a new template.**

   Press Ctrl+N (⌘+N on a Mac), or click the + symbol in the Template Browser header, or go to Web⇨New Template. Give it a descriptive name, assign it to your desired folder, and then click the Create button.

Step 5: Save your photos and settings as a special module collection

I briefly went over collections earlier, but these special collections require a little more explanation. Lightroom 2 brought with it a fundamental change in how collections can be structured as well as some additional functionality. Let me explain by focusing on what you can do now. Figure 12-17 shows the Collections panel. The Collections panel is now a standard feature in all areas of Lightroom except the Develop module, which puts all of your collections within easy reach (almost) everywhere you are.

The best way to keep a group of collections together is to put them in a collection set (as in a set of collections). I am now in the practice of creating a new collection set when I am in the midst of sorting photos after import (which I cover in Chapter 5), but you can create new sets as you need them via the + symbol in the Collections panel header and choosing Create Collection Set.

Figure 12-17: The Collections panel.

Along with the addition of the Collections panel to other modules came a new module-specific type of collection (there is one for Library, Slideshow, Web, and Print). You can only create a module collection from inside each respective module. Each collection type has its own icon (refer to Figure 12-17 to see the Web icon highlighted). Here's what makes them special:

- ✐ **The module collection retains all the settings configured in that module from the last time that collection was in use.**
- ✐ **You can create multiple module collections that each use different settings.**
- ✐ **They can contain any grouping of photos you wish.**
- ✐ **Double-clicking the collection icon will automatically bring you to that module with that collection of photos with all the settings associated with it.**

So, while these are optional I think you will find that they can be a great tool for organizing and accessing your photos. Here are the steps for creating a module collection that will become associated with the current module settings:

1. **Click the + symbol in the Collections panel header and choose Create Slideshow.**

   This will launch the Create Slideshow dialog box.

2. **Enter a descriptive name in the Name field.**

3. **(Optional) Click the Set drop-down menu to add it to an existing collection set.**

   I strongly recommend that you use Sets to keep your collections organized. If you don't already have a set created you can create a set later and drag drop individual collections into the set.

4. **Click Create to add the collection to the Collections panel.**

If you change your mind about any collections you've created you can delete them (just the collection, not the photos inside them) by selecting the collection and clicking the - symbol in the Collection panel header.

Putting it all together

As promised, I'm going to close this section by walking you through a practical example. I recommend maximizing your workspace and reducing panel clutter as much as possible while you work. To that end, press F to jump to full screen mode, press F5 to hide the Module Picker, and then press F7 to hide the left panel. Here are the steps to customize the AutoViewer gallery so it looks like what you see in Figure 12-18:

Figure 12-18: Customized Web gallery.

1. **Select the Airtight AutoViewer from the Gallery panel.**

   I love this gallery! It's just a fun and simple way to create a slick gallery that can double as a slideshow. For the sake of creating a template, I'm going to skip the Site Info panel, as there's nothing to configure there until you're actually creating a working gallery, in which case you enter the name of your gallery and move on.

2. **Expand the Color Palette panel.**

3. **Click the Background color swatch and set it to a light gray.**

   You're certainly free to choose a different color, but keep in mind that a neutral gray doesn't compete or influence the colors in your photos.

4. **Click the Border color swatch and set it to black.**

   In case it wasn't clear from Figure 12-18, I'm going for a "filmstrip look" here.

5. **Expand the Appearance panel.**

6. **Set Photo Borders to 10 pixels.**

7. **Set Padding to 0.**

   This brings all the images into a single contiguous strip. The width of the border is what sets them apart.

8. **Set the Slide Duration to 4 seconds.**

   I find that 4 seconds is often just the right amount of time for a slideshow. This setting only comes into "play" if the user activates the slideshow by clicking the Play button.

9. **Expand the Image Info panel.**

10. **Choose Edit from the Caption drop-down menu.**

    This launches the Text Template Editor so you can create a custom text template (refer to Figure 12-14).

11. **In the Text Template Editor, delete any text tokens in the Editor window.**

    Deleting all tokens means you start with a clean slate.

12. **Select Copyright from the last drop-down menu in the IPTC Data section of the Text Template Editor. (Refer again to Figure 12-14.)**

    Doing so puts the Copyright token in the Editor window, which pulls the data entered into the copyright field of each photo into the gallery image. Because this gallery type doesn't include a copyright watermark function, but does display caption data across the photo, you now have a means to apply a copyright watermark to your photos!

13. **Choose the Save Current Settings as New Preset option from the Preset drop-down menu.**

    You now have a copyright text template.

14. **Click Done to close the editor and use that text template.**

    The Text Template Editor closes, and you return to the Web module. You see your copyright information displayed on the active photo. (If you don't, go back and enter your copyright via the Metadata panel in the Library module.)

15. **Expand the Output Settings panel.**

16. **Set Size to 600 pixels and leave Quality at 90.**

    When you put photos on the Web, you need to think about a file's dimensions in pixels and its size in kilobytes. You always want it just large enough to get the job done, but no larger.

17. **Click the Preview in Browser button below the Collections panel.**

    Although it's great to get a live preview inside Lightroom, a truism in Web development is that what really counts is how an image displays in a browser, so always check in your Web browser before you decide it's done. Click everything that is clickable and make sure everything works as expected.

18. **Press Ctrl+N (⌘+N on a Mac) to save these settings as a new template.**

At this point, your gallery should match Figure 12-18. You now have a new template in your template browser. Well done!

Web Gallery Output Options

Testing your Web gallery locally (meaning on your computer) is standard operating procedure in Web development, but the next phase is testing on a Web server. Lightroom has a built-in FTP (*File Transfer Protocol*) utility that enables you to upload your gallery directly to your Web server without ever leaving Lightroom! However, you also have the option to export all the Web gallery files directly to your hard drive if you either don't have FTP access to your Web server, or prefer to use your own FTP application.

Uploading your gallery with Lightroom

To test your images on a Web server, you need access to a Web server. A Web server is just a computer that "serves" files over the Internet. If you're just sharing your gallery with friends or family, you should check your Internet Service Provider (ISP). ISPs commonly include Web server space as part of your package. Just keep in mind that the link to this type of gallery will probably look something like this:

```
http://internetserviceprovider.net/~yourusername
```

Although people might look at you funny when you say, "tilde," (which is how you pronounce that symbol in front of `yourusername`), you're already paying for that Web server space, so don't worry about the funny looks and learn to live with the tilde in order to save yourself some money.

Clearly, the professional solution is to get your own Web site. It doesn't cost as much as you might think (sometimes as little as a few dollars per month). Web-hosting companies are a dime a dozen, so ask your Web-savvy friends who they recommend.

I'm going to assume, then, that you've somehow secured access to a server. Nicely done. Now, you need to come up with three critical pieces of information to configure Lightroom so that it can upload your files to your Web host:

- **Server address:** This is the FTP address needed to access the Web server.

- **Username:** The username for your FTP account

- **Password:** The password for your FTP account

The following Steps list walks you through the steps involved in setting up Lightroom's FTP configuration dialog:

1. **Choose the Web module from the Module Picker and expand the Upload Settings panel, as shown in Figure 12-19.**

2. **Choose Edit from the FTP Server drop-down menu.**

   The Configure FTP File Transfer dialog box appears, as shown in Figure 12-20.

3. **Enter your FTP server information in the Server field, along with the username and password you were given for that server.**

   Check the Store Password in Preset check box if you're the only person using that computer.

4. **Configure the Server Path field.**

   What you enter here will vary based on the Web server. *Server path* refers to the folder on the Web server where Lightroom

Figure 12-19: The Upload Settings panel.

stores the files you upload. In some cases, you leave this field blank; in others, it might be something like `public_html/`. Ask your Web hosting provider if you're not sure what to enter. Unless you're instructed otherwise, leave the Protocol drop-down menu set to FTP, the Port menu set to 21, and the Passive Mode for Data Transfers drop-down menu set to Passive.

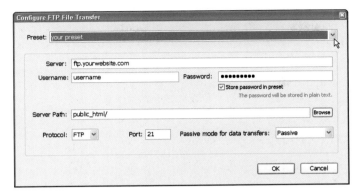

Figure 12-20: The Configure FTP File Transfer dialog box.

5. **Choose the Save Current Settings as New Preset option from the Preset drop-down menu.**

6. **In the new dialog box that appears, give the Preset a name and then click Create.**

   You return to the Configure FTP File Transfer dialog box.

7. **Click OK in the Configure FTP File Transfer dialog box to close it.**

   In the Upload Settings panel, you now see the name of your preset listed as the FTP Server. Now, all you need to do is decide where on your Web server you want to store your gallery.

8. **In the Upload Settings panel, check the Put in Subfolder check box, enter a name in the field below (refer to Figure 12-19), and then press Enter.**

   The "Full Path" that displays at the bottom of the panel shows where your folder sits in relation to the Server Path field you configured in Step 4. *Note:* Do not use spaces in your folder names because spaces in links can be problematic.

   This subfolder becomes part of the path or URL (Uniform Resource Locator) to your gallery. Therefore, if you're uploading a gallery of flower photos (and who doesn't have a gallery of flower photos?), you might name the subfolder "flowers," which would result in the following path to your gallery:

   ```
   http://www.yourdomain.com/flowers/
   ```

9. **Click the Upload button in the bottom right of the panel.**

After the progress meter has done its thing, navigate to your new gallery in your Web browser and give it a test drive! If you make any changes to the gallery in Lightroom be sure to reupload it.

Exporting your gallery

If you have preferred FTP software, or if you don't have FTP access to your hosting environment, you can click the Export button and save your Web gallery to your hard drive and then upload the files outside of Lightroom. Here are the steps:

1. **Click the Export button.**

   It's in the bottom left of the panel, next to the Upload button.

2. **In the dialog box that appears, navigate to the location on your hard drive where you want to save the gallery files.**

3. **Enter a name for the folder containing the gallery and click Save.**

Wait for Lightroom's progress meter to complete before attempting to upload the gallery to your Web host. Be sure to upload the entire contents of the folder. You can change the name of the folder holding all the files, but do not change the name of any files within the folder unless you update the HTML code within the files to reflect that change. At this point, Lightroom's job is finished and it's up to you to complete the job. If you make any changes to the Web gallery in Lightroom, you need to re-export the entire gallery.

13

Making Your Own Prints

*T*he goal of Lightroom's Print module is to facilitate getting your digital work to paper in a color-managed environment with a high-quality output. (Say *that* three times fast.) While originally geared toward sending data to a local inkjet printer, Lightroom now also makes it possible to save your print layouts as a JPG file that you can deliver to a print service.

Inkjet printing has come a long way. The technology behind today's printers, inks, and papers offer photographers an incredible array of choice (combined with high quality) for creating dazzling prints of all sizes. At the same time, more online print services are appearing on the scene, offering both high quality and a competitive price. No matter which output path you choose, this is really an exciting time to be printing!

Can I tell you what I think is one of the greatest things about printing from Lightroom? It's that you can create a print right from your raw image data without first having to save a TIFF, PSD, or JPG copy of the original (most printing applications are unable to print raw files). Gone are the days of having to create and manage multiple versions of each file cropped, optimized, and prepared for each print size! The disk space savings alone can recoup the cost of purchasing Lightroom. Of course, you might need to render TIFF, PSD, or JPG versions of your raw files at times, and that's fine, but it sure is great when you don't have to bother!

Exploring the Print module

I'd like to take a moment to reinforce that each Lightroom module is structured essentially the same way, which means the interface behaves the same no matter where you are! You can show/hide and collapse/expand panels as needed to maximize your work area, and only display the controls you need. For a look at the Lightroom interface as a whole, flip back to Chapter 1.

Getting to know the panels and tools

As is typical for all Lightroom modules, the organizational and preview panels are on the left side of the content area, while the right side holds the configuration panels. The Filmstrip is across the bottom and the Module Picker is across the top. Specific to each module are the tools provided for completing the task.

A unique aspect of the Print module is that it contains two different layout possibilities (Contact Sheet/Grid and Picture Package), and although I will go into each layout in great detail, I want to point out that your choice of layout controls what configuration panels are available on the right side. To illustrate the difference, Figure 13-1 shows the Print module interface with the Contact Sheet/Grid layout selected (which I'll refer to only as *Grid* from here on), and Figure 13-2 shows the Picture Package layout. It's like having two Print modules for the price of one!

Figure 13-1: The Print module interface showing the Grid layout.

Figure 13-2: The Print module interface showing the Picture Package layout.

An embarrassment of riches? Wait until you see the plethora of tools and panels Lightroom lays at your feet. Admittedly, you never see all these panels at the same time, but I thought it would be a good idea to list all of them for easier reference:

- **Menu bar:** Contains both the applicationwide commands, as well as module-specific menu options.

- **Preview panel:** Displays a preview of each template layout as you move your cursor over the items listed in the Template Browser.

- **Template Browser:** Provides controls for creating new — and managing existing — templates.

- **Collections panel:** Provides access to all the collections (think of them as virtual folders) you've created, as well as the controls to add new ones that retain all the print settings. Refer to Chapter 5 for a Collections refresher if needed.

- **Page Setup button:** Launches the Printer Driver dialog box for choosing your printer and paper size. The *printer driver* is the software that installs with your printer for the purpose of configuring printer settings and running printer maintenance. It's a very important part of the printing pipeline.

- **Print Settings button:** Launches the Printer Driver dialog box for configuring your printer settings. The appearance of this dialog box varies based on your operating system and printer model. It's not a Lightroom dialog box. You might need to pull out your printer manual if you're not familiar with configuring its settings.

- **Filmstrip:** Displays thumbnails of the active image grouping. It can be used to reorder the photos if you're working within a collection or single folder.

- **Layout Engine panel:** Provides access to the two types of layout options:

  - *Contact Sheet/Grid:* Create print layouts using a grid model where each cell in the grid has the same dimensions. You can print different photos on a single layout (meaning a different photo in each cell, but the cells are all the same size).

  - *Picture Package:* Create print layouts using cells of various dimensions, but only one photo can appear on a single layout (meaning the same photo in each cell, but the cells can be various sizes).

- **Image Settings panel:** Contains settings that affect the look of the photos appearing in the layout.

- **Rulers, Grid & Guides panel:** Specific to Picture Package, this panel provides options for the configuration of these particular layout aids.

- **Cells panel:** Specific to Picture Package, this panel controls the addition and configuration of new cells to a print package layout.

- **Layout panel:** Specific to Grid, this panel provides options for creating the desired grid layout to be used.

- **Guides panel:** Specific to Grid, this panel provides options for the configuration of these particular layout aids.

- **Overlays panel:** Allows for an identity plate and supporting text to be added to the print layout for output. *Note:* Textual photo information can't be added to a print package.

- **Print Job panel:** Controls output settings for sending data to a printer or saved to JPG.

- **Content area:** Displays an updating and fully interactive preview of your print layout.

- **Toolbar:** Provides controls for navigating between print jobs containing multiple pages, an indicator for how many pages will be printed, and the Use controls for designating which photos will be used in the print layouts.

The choice of layout engine affects which panels display and the available options within panels shared by both engines. I'll continue to reinforce the differences as we move through the workflow.

Becoming familiar with the menu options

The File, Edit, View, Window, and Help menus remain largely consistent throughout Lightroom. You soon discover, though, that a couple of print options are located in the File menu, as shown in Figure 13-3. The Print One Copy command sends the current layout directly to the printer using the existing settings without opening the printer driver — a great command to have when you're set up and just want to print. You also have a new submenu — Print Settings — that opens the printer driver. Take note of the keyboard shortcuts!

The Print menu contains commands for creating new templates and template folders, navigating between pages in a multiple page print job, and rotating the photos. The Save Print Module Settings command allows you to save the custom settings temporarily without having to create a template. You can then select a template or change settings to compare layouts and then use the Revert Print Module Settings command to return to your saved state.

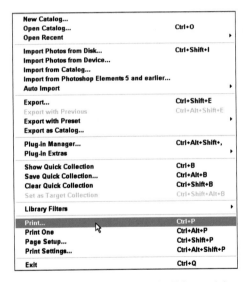

Figure 13-3: The File menu in the Print module.

Setting Up a Print Job

Waiting to see a print for the first time can be a little bit like opening a birthday present. A mixture of hope and anticipation that it will be just what you want while bracing for disappointment if it isn't. Unless you're buying your birthday presents, you can't do much about that, but you can ensure the best-possible print emerges from your printer. To see what I mean, check out the next sections where I provide you the process of setting up Lightroom to get consistently good results.

Employing a print workflow

Although the layout engines — Grid and Picture Package — have some distinct differences and options, they still fit within the same place in the larger print workflow. I do my best to address their individual quirks and foibles, but for now, I just want to give you the big picture:

1. **Bring your photos to the Print module.**

2. **Configure the page setup.**

3. **Select a layout engine for your starting point.**

4. **Customize the layout as desired.**

5. **Configure the output settings.**

6. **(Optional) Save your settings for reuse.**

7. **(Optional) Save your settings and photos as a special print collection.**

    I cover this in detail later in the chapter, but this new feature in Lightroom allows you to bundle photos and settings in a special module-specific collection. This is great if you want to save multiple print layout versions for a given group of photos with the bonus of having quick access from the Collections panel.

8. **Print the layout.**

In the next few sections, you get to take a closer look at each of the steps in the process. I follow up by walking through the creation of both a Grid layout and a Picture Package.

Step 1: Bring your photos to the Print module

The Library module is the most likely place you'll begin to gather your photos before moving to the Print module because it provides the greatest access to your portfolio and contains tools for finding, organizing, and grouping. Whether you select a folder, a collection, or create a grouping based on keywords or metadata, you need to identify and select the photos you want to print before you can print them.

One of the best ways to begin the process is to use a collection because it can contain photos from every corner of your imported portfolio. The other benefits of using a collection are

- ✔ **You can manually control the order the images appear in the print layout.**

- ✔ **You can create an infinite number of collections and sort them independently of each other.**

You can only do a manual sort when you're working within either a single folder or a single collection. So, if you want to sort manually images that are across a range of folders (or collections), you first need to put them into a single collection and then sort. Lightroom refers to this sort order as *User Order*. After you're in either a single folder or a collection, then be sure to grab the image, not the border, and drag and drop in the order you desire, as shown in Figure 13-4. You can do this from the Grid view of the Library module, the Filmstrip in any module, or in the Grid view of the Secondary Display when enabled.

Figure 13-4: Manually sorting images within a collection from the Filmstrip.

After you've collected your photos for printing, it's time to bring them into the Print module. Press Ctrl+Alt+4 (⌘+Option+4 on a Mac) to jump over to Print (or click Print in the Module Picker). Notice the image grouping you created in the Library module is still displayed in the Filmstrip. If you're using the Secondary Display window — Window⇨Secondary Display — you can set it to Grid and access your photos from there as well.

If needed, you can further refine your image grouping with the Refine and Custom Filtering options provided in the Filmstrip. For example, you could filter your grouping to only images with a rating of three stars or greater by clicking the third star above the thumbnails. The other filtering options (flags, color labels, copy status, file type, metadata, and so on) work the same way.

Step 2: Configure your page setup

Before you dive into creating your layout, you need to tell Lightroom a few things about the page you want to create. Click the Page Setup button below the Collections panel, or press Shift+Ctrl+P (Shift+⌘+P on a Mac) to launch the Print Setup (Page Setup on a Mac) dialog box, as shown in Figure 13-5.

The three things you want to do here are

1. **Select your printer.**
2. **Select your paper size.**
3. **Select your paper orientation.**

Figure 13-5: The Print Setup dialog box.

Click OK to close the dialog box. Lightroom uses this information to determine how the page displays in the content area as well as the document size and the minimum margins. Choose View⇨Show Info Overlay (if it is not already showing) to enable the display of a nonprinting indicator that shows you key information about your setup. You can also press the I key to toggle this overlay on and off. Keep Info Overlay on while you get familiar with Lightroom to serve as a reminder of what you've configured.

Step 3: Select a layout engine for your starting point

Expand the Layout Engine panel (refer to Figures 13-1 and 13-2) and choose either Grid or Picture Package. Many of the panel options stem from this choice. Before I get into the details, I want to clarify the differences between these two layout engines so that you know which will best suit any given job.

If you've used Lightroom 1.0 for printing, then you've already used the Grid layout engine. You already know that the Grid divides the paper into equally sized cells and that it's not possible to span a single photo across multiple cells. You also know that the more cells you add, the smaller each cell becomes (because the paper size remains constant). The Grid is for when you want to print several different photos on a single page, although it's possible to fill every cell on a page with a single photo. To print a single photo requires just a single cell; to print a contact sheet you add more cells.

Picture Package is new to Lightroom 2. The essential distinction is that when you create a Picture Package, you're creating a layout for printing a single photo in a range of sizes on one or more pages. Think school portraits, where a single pose can be purchased in a package that includes prints from 8 x 10 down to wallet size, and in various quantities. This is a great feature for anyone needing to produce a set package of prints quickly. Just keep in mind that you can't create a single-page Picture Package that includes more than one photo. You can apply the same Picture Package layout to multiple photos, but each photo requires its own page.

Step 4: Customize the layout as desired

This is the fun part! The rest of the right-hand panels are arranged with an efficient workflow in mind, so keep working your way down. As I've said, you're going to see some differences in the options available depending upon the layout engine you choose.

With Grid you have

- ✔ **Layout panel**
- ✔ **Guides panel**

With Picture Package you have

- ✔ **Rulers, Grid & Guides panel**
- ✔ **Cells panel**

The rest of the panels appear in both engines, aside from a few minor differences in the Image Settings and the Overlays panels. The next few sections allow you to get up close and personal with each configuration panel.

Image Settings

The controls in the Image Settings panel, shown in Figure 13-6, affect what happens inside each photo cell, regardless of the layout engine used. Here's what the various controls do:

- ✔ **Zoom to Fill:** When this option is unchecked, your entire photo fits within each cell. If the aspect ratio of the cell is different from the aspect ratio of the photo, the photo won't fill the entire cell. When Zoom to Fill is checked, the photo is sized to fill the entire cell. If the aspect ratio of the cell is different from the aspect ratio of the photo, the photo appears cropped. **Note:** If your photo *does* appear cropped, you can reposition it within the cell by clicking and dragging while in Grid layout or by holding the Ctrl key (⌘ on a

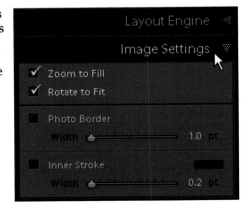

Figure 13-6: The Image Settings panel.

Mac) and clicking and dragging while in Picture Package.

✓ **Rotate to Fit:** Check this box to have Lightroom automatically rotate each photo to best fit the orientation of the cell. This is handy when printing a sheet of both portrait- and landscape-oriented photos and you want each photo to fill as much of the cell as possible.

✓ **Repeat One Photo per Page:** This pretty much does what it says — fills every cell on a single sheet with the same photo. This option doesn't appear in Picture Package because you can only include one photo in a given package anyway.

✓ **Stroke Border:** Adds a stroke around each photo. Click the color swatch to choose your color. Keep in mind that the stroke remains inside the cell, so increasing the stroke decreases the size of the actual photo. In Picture Package, this option is called Inner Stroke.

✓ **Photo Border:** Controls the width of the border around each photo in a Picture Package

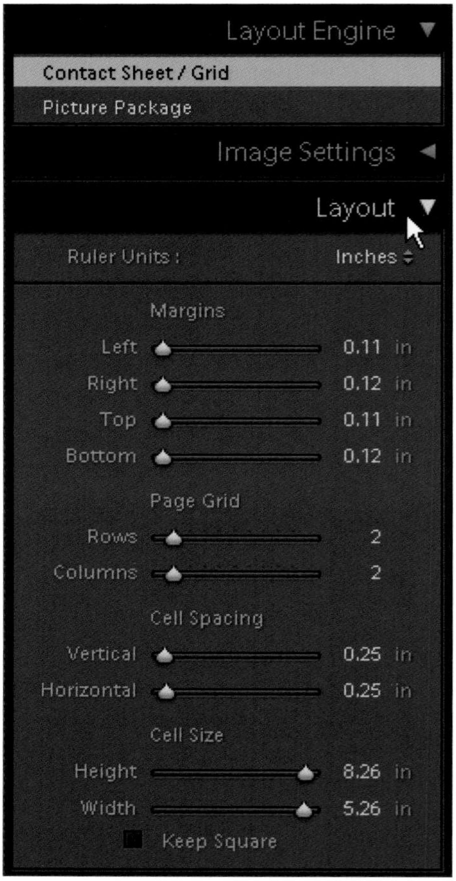

Figure 13-7: The Layout panel.

layout. The color of this border can't be changed and is always white. The option doesn't exist in the Grid engine.

✓ **Inner Stroke:** Adds a stroke around each photo in Picture Package. Click the color swatch to choose your color. Keep in mind that the stroke remains inside the cell, so increasing the stroke decreases the size of the actual photo. In Grid, this option is named Stroke Border.

Layout

The Layout panel, shown in Figure 13-7, appears only when the Grid engine is active because all the controls affect the layout of the grid on the page. The Layout panel has four sets of controls:

✓ **Margins:** The Margins sliders function independently of each other and control the edge of the printable area on the page. The smallest margin amount is determined by your printer driver settings, so if you want to print borderless, be sure to enable borderless printing in your printer driver (via the Page Setup button) before trying to zero out the margins. (Borderless isn't an option for every paper size and printer.) Set all margins to the same value to create centered prints.

- ✔ **Page Grid:** Controls the number of cells in the layout. Rows are horizontal and columns are vertical.

- ✔ **Cell Spacing:** Adjusts the amount of spacing between cells. This option is grayed out when the grid consists of a single cell.

- ✔ **Cell Size:** This determines the size of the actual printed photo. Maximum cell dimensions are determined by the size of the paper and the number of cells being used. Keep in mind that all cells in the grid are the same size. If you're interested in creating square cells, check the Keep Square check box and the Height and Width sliders will be set to the same value and linked to each other when moved.

Guides

The Guides panel, as shown in Figure 13-8, is also unique to the Grid engine. It contains a set of layout guide tools (under Show Guides) that can be enabled by checking their respective boxes. When the guides are enabled, you see them display in the content area. Placing your cursor over any one of the guides and clicking and dragging allows another means to make layout adjustments. You can modify margins, cell size, and spacing this way. Checking the Dimensions check box displays the cell size dimensions as an overlay in each of the cells.

Figure 13-8: The Guides panel.

Rulers, Grid & Guides

The Rulers, Grid & Guides panel, shown in Figure 13-9, is specific to Picture Package. It provides the following layout aids for creating your package layout:

- **Ruler:** The check box toggles the ruler on or off, and the drop-down menu allows you to choose the unit of measurement.

- **Grid:** The check box toggles the Grid overlay on or off, and the Snap drop-down menu allows you to choose to have each photo cell "snap" to either other cells or the layout grid when moving cells around, and to turn snapping off. I find that snapping to cells helps prevent cells from overlapping each other when aligning them tightly.

- **Bleed:** This check box toggles the shaded area showing the unprintable margin on or off.

- **Dimensions:** This check box toggles the display of the cell dimensions within each cell on or off.

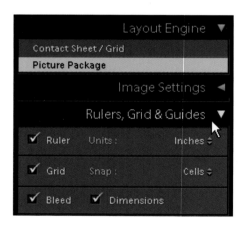

Figure 13-9: The Rulers, Grid & Guides panel.

The problem with cells overlapping is that one photo will print on top of the other and cost you money in wasted paper and ink. Lightroom does try to warn you if two or more cells overlap by displaying an exclamation point inside a yellow triangle in the upper-right corner of the layout, as shown in Figure 13-10. Click the Auto Layout button in the Cells panel (see next section) to have Lightroom rearrange the cells correctly.

Figure 13-10: Cell overlap warning.

Cells

The Cells panel, shown in Figure 13-11, is also specific to Picture Package. As the name of the panel indicates, all the controls contained here are for the creation and modification of Picture Package cells. In the Add to Package section, you find the following:

- **Cell buttons:** You use the cell buttons to add new cells to your layout — just click the button representing the size you want to add. The six buttons represent the default cell sizes, but you can click the drop-down arrow next to any button and choose a different cell size — or click Edit to enter a custom cell size. Every button click adds a new cell. Additional pages are added to the package as needed to accommodate new cells.

- **New Page button:** As you might expect, clicking this button adds a new page to the package. You can create multiple new, blank pages before adding cells, and then drag and drop cells between pages to create your layouts.

As soon as you have more than one page in a package, Lightroom displays a red Delete Page button in the upper-left corner of each page, as shown in Figure 13-12. Click that button to delete that page (and any cells it contains) from the package.

🖝 **Auto Layout button:** Click this button to have Lightroom attempt to arrange the cells to make the most efficient use of paper by rearranging cells in the layout across all available pages.

🖝 **Clear Layout button:** Removes all the cells from the layout. Good for starting over.

After you've added a cell to the layout, you can click and drag a resize handle to change the dimensions of the cell, or you can make height and width adjustments using the Adjust Selected Cell sliders. You can reposition a cell in the layout by clicking and dragging the cell to a new location, or even move cells between pages if you so desire. To delete a cell, just select it and press Backspace (Delete on a Mac). To duplicate a cell, hold the Alt key (Option key on a Mac) while clicking and dragging a cell.

Figure 13-11: The Cells panel.

Keep in mind that each cell is simply a frame in which to place a photo. Your photo has a particular aspect ratio, but you could potentially create multiple cells with a range of aspect ratios. For example, a typical aspect ratio of an uncropped photo is 2:3 (also known as *1:1.5*). A 4-x-6 print has an aspect ratio of 2:3. Therefore, if you place a photo with a 2:3 aspect ratio in a 4-x-6 cell, it should fill the entire cell without being cropped. Now, if you also want to include a 5-x-7 print in that package, you need to do some cropping because the 5 x 7 would have a 1:1.4 aspect ratio. However, you don't want to crop the source photo itself because then it wouldn't fit the 4-x-6 cell!

Figure 13-12: Delete page button.

Here's where that Zoom to Fill check box comes in handy. After you check that box, you see the photo in the 5-x-7 cell appear to get larger and fill the available space in that cell; the 4 x 6 remains the same because it was already filling the cell. Now you can print a full 4 x 6 and a full 5 x 7 from the same source photo, and yes, the 5-x-7 print will be cropped, but the source photo will remain unchanged. Additionally, you can move your photo within that 5-x-7 cell to improve the default placement. Hold the Ctrl key (⌘ on a Mac) and click and drag the photo within the cell for better placement. (You have to hold the modifier key because otherwise you are moving the cell itself.)

Overlays

The Overlays panel contains the controls for the Identity plate in both layout engines, as well as a few additional layout engine-specific overlay elements. Figure 13-13 shows how the panel looks in each layout engine.

Look at the identity plate section first because it functions the same way in both Grid and Picture Package. The purpose of the identity plate is to provide a means to add either a textual or a graphical element to your printed page. This could be your graphical logo or simply a textual copyright notice and your name. You could apply it as a watermark on each image or place it on a blank area of the page.

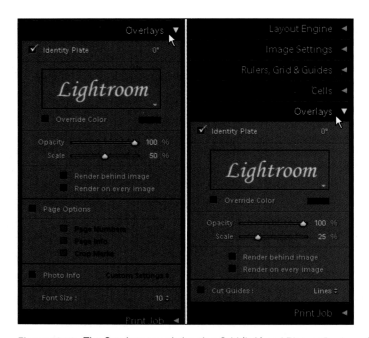

Figure 13-13: The Overlays panel showing Grid (left) and Picture Package (right).

The identity plate appears in many places throughout Lightroom. (I provide more in-depth coverage of it in Chapter 5.) Here are the basic steps for using identity plate in the Print module:

1. **Click the Identity Plate check box to toggle it on.**

2. **Choose Edit from the Identity Plate drop-down menu.**

   Choosing Edit launches the Identity Plate Editor.

   If you previously created a custom identity plate, you'll see it listed in the menu and you can (obviously) choose it. I'm going to assume for the sake of argument, though, that one hasn't been created.

3. **In the Identity Plate Editor, select either a styled text or graphical identity plate.**

4. **Customize as desired.**

   Chapter 5 has bunches more on customizing your identity plate.

5. **Choose Save As from the Custom drop-down menu if you want to save your customized identity plate for future use.**

   Doing so launches the Save Identity Plate As dialog box, where you can name this identity plate and click Save.

6. **Click OK.**

The identity plate appears in the content area. Click and drag the identity plate to reposition it. You can adjust opacity and size as desired with the provided sliders. The Override Color option allows you to change the color of a textual identity plate temporarily without permanently altering your saved identity plate. You can rotate the identity plate by clicking the rotation amount indicator (starts at 0 degrees) in the top-right corner of the panel. Choose the amount and direction of rotation you require.

Check the Render on Every Image check box if you want to use the identity plate as a watermark for all images in the layout. Just keep in mind that when this option is enabled, the identity plate will be "rendered" to the center of each photo. You can still adjust its rotation, scale, and opacity, but it cannot be repositioned off the center.

Render behind Image is a little-used option that places the identity plate behind your photos. This can be used when you want your identity plate and photos to overlap, but don't want the identity plate to print on top of the photos.

From here, the remaining options are unique to each layout engine. In the Grid engine you have

- **Page Options:** Allows for the addition of page numbers, page information, and crop marks to be printed on the page with your photos. Page information includes

  - *Sharpening setting:* The amount of sharpening you choose in the Print Job panel.

  - *Profile used:* The color-management setting you choose in the Print Job panel.

  - *Name of printer:* The name of the printer you use.

- **Photo Info:** Provides the ability to include a limited amount of textual information about the photos being printed. Click the check box to enable, and then click the drop-down menu to choose a text template to apply or click Edit to create a new text template. You can adjust the size of the font via the Font Size drop-down menu. The font face and positioning cannot be changed.

In Picture Package, Cut Guides provide a printed visual to aid in cutting the photos after printing. Choose either Lines or Crop Marks.

Step 5: Configure the output settings

After you finalize your layout, as outlined in the previous sections, it's time to prepare the data for output. This is the phase where you prepare Lightroom to hand off the image data to the printer (or a JPG file to a print service). The prep work here involves configuring a few settings in the Print Job panel and/or tweaking settings in the printer driver — if you're printing locally. (To access your printer driver, click the Print Settings button at the bottom of the right panel.) The most critical component of this hand-off process is the color management of the image data. The next few sections take a closer look at each setting involved.

Print Job

The Print Job panel, as shown in Figure 13-14, is where you configure your Lightroom output image data so that it meets the specifications for the job at hand. The options are the same for both Grid and Picture Package layout engines:

- **Print To:** The Print To drop-down menu is where you choose whether you want to send your output to a printer or save it as a JPG file.

- **Draft Mode Printing:** When checked, Lightroom uses the image data from its preview cache instead of rerendering image data from your source files. The benefit of this is purely speed. The tradeoff is quality. The quality of the image data in the preview cache (controlled by the File Handling tab of the Catalog Settings dialog box) is usually good enough for thumbnails on contact sheets, which is when *I* am most likely to use Draft Mode printing. Believe me; if you're printing contact sheets for hundreds of images, you'll appreciate the speed boost! When in Draft Mode print resolution, Print Sharpening and Color Management configuration options are disabled. The Color Management setting is set to Managed by Printer.

- **Print Resolution:** When checked, you can set the resolution value for Lightroom to use when it renders the image data you want delivered at output. Here's why I tend to leave it unchecked: If enough pixels exist in my source photo so that the native resolution is between 180–480 ppi, then I don't worry about it. Here's an easy way to see the native resolution at a given print size:

1. **Select your photo.**

2. **Choose the Grid layout engine from the Layout Engine panel.**

3. **Create a cell that matches your desired print size.**

   The "Layout" section, earlier in the chapter, has everything you need to know about creating cells for the Grid engine.

4. **Check the Dimensions box in the Guides panel.**

5. **Uncheck Print Resolution in the Print Job panel.**

6. **Look at the Print Size overlay in the cell.**

   This little trick works in both layout engines, but I just picked Grid for this example. The key is to have Dimensions checked and Print Resolution unchecked. Lightroom displays the print size in the selected units as well as the native resolution for that size of print (refer to Figure 13-12).

If you're in the 180–480 ppi window, then you're good to go. However, if that makes you the least bit uneasy, then go with the default setting of 240.

If you're printing to a JPG and you're not sure what your print service requires, your safest setting is going to be 300 ppi.

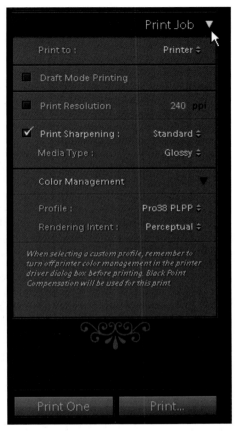

Figure 13-14: The Print Job panel.

✔ **Print Sharpening:** This function received a substantial upgrade in Lightroom 2 and I'm pleased to say that the upgrade produces some excellent results. Adobe worked with the group of folks who wrote the book on print sharpening to create the sharpening algorithms that are applied to your image data. Now, you won't see any change in the content area because this sharpening is applied only after you click the Print button, when Lightroom renders the image data from the source file and applies all your Lightroom adjustments. The proof is going to be in the print, so I highly suggest you perform a set of test prints on each type of media you use with each sharpening setting to get a sense of which you prefer. Here's how you do that:

1. **Check the Print Sharpening box.**

2. **Choose the desired amount (Low, Standard, or High) from the Print Sharpening drop-down menu.**

3. **Choose either Matte or Glossy (depending on the paper type you're using) from the Media Type drop down menu.**

You can also apply sharpening when saving your output in JPG format — you determine your settings the same way as when you're printing to your attached printer. Don't be surprised by how the image looks if you open it in Photoshop; the proof is still going to be in the print.

✔ **Color Management:** Possibly the most important setting in this module, simply because a bad Color Management setting can single-handedly ruin your output (and possibly your day). The goal of color management is to literally manage the conversion of colors between Lightroom's working color space and the color space of the output device. The method for achieving the best output is to let Lightroom manage the conversion. The alternative is to let the printer manage the colors.

When the print job is configured to let the printer manage colors — by selecting Managed by Printer from the Profile drop-down menu — Lightroom sends the image data using its ProPhoto RGB color space and leaves it up to the printer driver to convert those colors to the output color space correctly. The problem is that not all printers know how to handle ProPhoto RGB data and, therefore, are unable to convert the colors correctly. Feel free to test the Managed by Printer option, but I don't really recommend it. That said, if you want to try it, here are the steps:

1. **Choose Managed by Printer from the Profile drop-down menu.**

2. **Configure the other Print Job settings as desired.**

   Things like unchecking Draft Mode Printing, setting your resolution (or not), and applying sharpening.

3. **Click the Print Settings button and do the necessary Print Settings stuff in the Print Settings dialog box.**

   Stuff like going into Advanced Settings and turning on the printer driver's color adjustment setting, setting paper type and print quality, and then clicking OK to return to Lightroom.

If the colors look good, then your printer can handle the data Lightroom is sending. If you see a color cast, or the colors look washed out, then your printer can't handle the data Lightroom is sending and you need to have Lightroom manage the color.

You may be wondering why Managed by Printer is the default setting for Draft Mode printing. The reason is that, with Draft Mode printing, the image data is sent from the preview cache in Adobe RGB space, which most printers can handle.

To let Lightroom manage the colors, you need to have installed the ICC profiles for the paper and printer combination you're using. (ICC stands for International Color Consortium, a group of major players in the digital-imaging industry that define the format for color profiles with the goal of improving color management across systems.) The manufacturer of the paper (which can also be the same company that makes the printer) typically provides these profiles. Go to the paper manufacturer's Web site and download the latest profile available for the specific paper and printer model you're using. After installing the profile with the directions provided by the supplier, do the following to set up Lightroom correctly:

1. **Choose Other from the Profile drop-down menu.**

   The Choose Profiles dialog box opens, as shown in Figure 13-15.

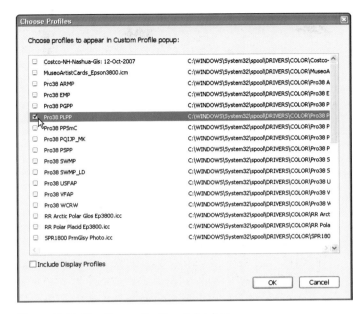

Figure 13-15: The Choose Profiles dialog box.

2. **Check the box next to the profile for the paper you're going to use and then click OK.**

   You're brought back to the Print module.

3. **Click the Print Settings button at the bottom of the left panel, go into the properties or advanced settings of the printer driver, and turn off color adjustment.**

   This is absolutely critical or else the printer driver will attempt to manage the colors, which typically results in light prints with a magenta cast. Access to these settings varies with each operating system and printer. Depending on your printer driver, look for a color management setting that reads "off," "no color adjustment," or "no ICM." Consult your printer manual if you're not sure where this setting is on your system. Figure 13-16 shows the location of this setting for an Epson 3800 on Windows.

4. **In the print driver, select paper type and quality settings and then click OK.**

   You're brought back to the Print module.

Figure 13-16: Color adjustment setting on an Epson 3800 on Windows.

After you return to Lightroom, you still need to choose a rendering intent. "What's that?" you ask. Well, when Lightroom is set to convert colors to the output space by using the ICC profile you choose, it needs you to tell it how to handle colors that are beyond what the printer is capable of printing. In other words, it needs you to tell it what your "rendering intent" is. It gives you two choices:

- *Relative:* This option keeps all the colors that are within the gamut of the output color space and chops off those outside it.

- *Perceptual:* This option remaps all colors in the source space to fit within the destination space. The downside is that colors that are within the gamut can appear desaturated, but the upside is better gradation between colors and overall better color detail when many out-of-gamut colors are present.

I don't blame you if you're thinking that neither of these choices sound that great, but keep in mind that the goal of both Rendering Intent options is to preserve the original color appearance. Therefore, you probably wouldn't notice a difference with either choice for many photos. The safest general-purpose choice is Perceptual, but I would encourage you to make a few test prints with both to get a feel for any differences.

If you're a Mac user running Leopard and you're printing to a printer that supports 16-bit data, you can now print in 16-bit from Lightroom. The benefit is improved gradations, but it might take a keen eye to spot the difference between an 8-bit and 16-bit print. If you fit the above criteria, you can enable this feature by first checking the 16-bit Output box in the Print Job panel, and then enabling 16-bit printing in the printer driver.

After you have a layout and your print settings are configured, it might be in your best interest to save them for reuse. Read on to find out how to do that.

Step 6: Save your settings for reuse

This optional step in the workflow has the potential of combining all the steps to this point into a single click. You just invested all that time creating the layout and configuring all your output settings, so if there's any chance that you'd repeat those steps with the same or different photos, then I highly suggest you save your work. Here's how:

1. **Press Ctrl+Shift+N (⌘+Shift+N on a Mac) to create a new template folder.**

   Alternatively, you can go to Print⇨New Template Folder. Then all you have to do is give the folder a descriptive name and click the Create button.

Keeping your templates organized can increase your efficiency by providing order to your template collection. The Template Browser displays template folders and individual templates in alphanumeric order, right below the Lightroom Templates heading. To keep my starter template folder at the top of the list, I name it with a number, as shown in Figure 13-17. *Note:* You can't create template folders within folders.

Figure 13-17: Creating a new template folder.

2. **Press Ctrl+N (⌘+N on a Mac) to create a new template from the settings you've specified.**

   Alternatively, you can go to Print⇨New Template. Give the template a descriptive name, assign it to your desired folder, and click the Create button.

Step 7: Save your photos and settings as a special module collection

I briefly cover collections earlier, but these special collections require a little more explanation. Lightroom brought with it a fundamental change in how collections can be structured as well as some additional functionality. Let me explain by focusing on what you can do now. Figure 13-18 shows the Collections panel. The Collections panel is now a standard feature in all areas of Lightroom except the Develop module, which puts all of your collections within easy reach (almost) everywhere you are.

The best way to keep a group of collections together is to put them in a collection set (as in a set of collections). I'm now in the practice of creating a new collection set when I am in the midst of sorting photos after import (which I cover in Chapter 5), but you can create new sets as you need them by clicking the + symbol in the Collections panel header and then choosing Create Collection Set.

Along with the addition of the Collections panel to other modules came a new module-specific collection (there's one for Library, Slideshow, Web, and Print). You can only create a module collection from inside each respective module. Each collection type has its own icon (refer to Figure 13-18 to see the print icon highlighted). Here's what makes them special:

- ✔ **Module collections retain all the settings configured in that module from the last time that collection was in use.**

- ✔ **You can create multiple module collections that each use different settings.**

- ✔ **Module collections can contain any grouping of photos you wish.**

- ✔ **Double-clicking the collection icon will automatically bring you to that module with that collection of photos and all the settings associated with it.**

Figure 13-18: The Collections panel.

So, although these are optional, I think you'll find that they can be a great tool for organizing and accessing your photos. Here are the steps for creating a module collection that will become associated with the current module settings:

1. **Click the + symbol in the Collections panel header and choose Create Print.**

   The Create Print dialog box launches.

2. **Enter a descriptive name in the Name field.**

3. **(Optional) Click the Set drop-down menu to add it to an existing collection set.**

   I strongly recommend that you use Sets to keep your collections organized. If you don't already have a set created, you can create a set later and then drag and drop individual collections into the set.

4. **Click Create to add the collection to the Collections panel.**

If you change your mind about any collections you've created, you can delete them (just the collection, not the photos inside them) by selecting the collection and clicking the - symbol in the Collection panel header.

Step 8: Printing the layout

It took a bit of work to get here, but this is the moment you've been waiting for . . . clicking the Print button. Doing so launches the printer driver and gives you one last chance for a preflight check of your settings. Until you feel confident in your setup and configuration of Lightroom (as well as the setup and configuration of the printer driver), I strongly recommend that you double-check the printer driver settings after clicking the Print button. It just takes a few seconds, and it can save you both time and money. When you feel like you have it down and you consistently get the expected results from the printer, click the Print One button to bypass the Print Driver dialog box and simply send the data directly to the printer.

Putting it all together

I'd like to walk through a couple of examples to demonstrate how you'd set up both a Grid layout and a Picture Package layout. I'll save the Grid layout as a JPEG file and send the Picture Package to my inkjet printer, just to highlight the key differences in output as well.

Scenario One: Create a layout for four different photos, as shown in Figure 13-19, that are saved as a JPEG and uploaded to a print service where the layout is printed on 8-x-24 luster paper:

1. **Select your photos in Library module and then switch to Print module.**

2. **Click the Page Setup button, located at the bottom right of the content area.**

   Doing so launches the Print Setup (Page Setup on a Mac) dialog box.

3. **Select the printer, paper size, and paper orientation, and then click OK.**

   Even though this layout is being saved to JPG, you still need to set the layout parameters. In this case, I choose an Epson 3800 printer, create a custom 8-x-24 paper size, and choose landscape orientation. ***Note:*** The Info Overlay in Figure 13-19 reflects this configuration. The paper size is the key factor in this step.

4. **Click Contact Sheet/Grid in the Layout Engine panel.**

5. **Expand the Image Settings panel, check the Zoom to Fill check box, and leave the other options unchecked.**

   I typically crop my photos in Develop to match the desired output aspect ratio because it provides greater control over the cropped composition, but I want to demonstrate that it isn't required.

6. **Expand the Layout panel, and set the number of rows to 1 and the number of columns to 4.**

   This creates four cells.

7. **Check the Keep Square check box, and set the Cell Size height to 5 inches.**

   The width snaps to 5 inches because the Keep Square check box is checked, which creates four 5-x-5 cells.

8. **Set all margins to 0.80 inches.**

   This amount varies with each layout, but in this case, the 0.80 setting creates an equal amount of horizontal spacing between each photo from edge to edge. Because my top and bottom margins are equal, the photos are also centered vertically.

9. **Click and drag each photo within each cell for best composition.**

   These four photos were not previously cropped to a 1:1 aspect ratio, but by choosing Zoom to Fill, they appear correctly cropped in the print layout. However, this autocropping might not be the best composition, so a little tweaking to center each subject is required.

10. **Leave everything in the Overlays panel unchecked.**

11. **Expand the Print Job panel and make sure the Print To drop-down menu is set to JPEG File.**

12. **Uncheck Draft Mode Printing.**

13. **Leave File Resolution set to 300 ppi.**

    300 ppi is what most print services will expect, so leave it there unless instructed to do otherwise by the print service.

14. **Choose Standard from the Print Sharpening drop-down menu and Glossy from the Media Type drop-down menu.**

    I'm using luster paper, which is a soft gloss.

15. **Set the JPEG Quality slider.**

    The default is 100, but if you're concerned about file size (because you're uploading this file), you can dial it back to 90 without any visible loss of quality.

16. **Leave the Custom File Dimensions check box unchecked.**

    Lightroom has already calculated the pixel dimensions of the JPEG file based on the page dimensions and the file-resolution setting.

17. **Choose the correct profile from the Profile drop-down menu.**

    What is correct is determined by the print service you use. Asking them will give you the best answer, so always ask. Lightroom will embed the profile in the resulting JPG. I know the print service I use prefers sRGB, so that's what I choose.

18. **Choose a rendering intent.**

    Perceptual is usually the safest choice.

19. **Click the Print to File button.**

20. **In the new dialog box that appears, choose a Save location on your hard drive, name the file, and then click Save.**

    The JPEG file is saved to that location and is ready for you to deliver to your print service.

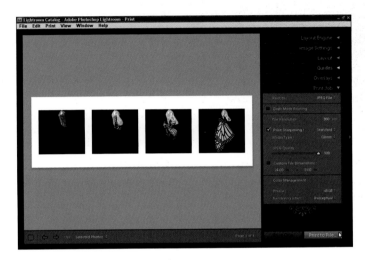

Figure 13-19: Grid layout example.

Scenario Two: Create a Picture Package made up of 3 5-x-7 prints and 24 3½-x-2½ prints to be printed with an attached inkjet printer on 11-x-17-inch Epson's Ultra Premium Photo Paper Luster.

1. **Select a photo in Library module and switch to Print module.**

    I'm only going to demonstrate a single photo in landscape orientation. Additional photos can use the same package, but they'll be printed on additional pages.

2. **Click the Page Setup button, located at the bottom right of the content area.**

    Doing so launches the Print Setup (Page Setup on a Mac) dialog box.

3. **Select the printer, paper size, and paper orientation, and then click OK.**

    In this case, I choose an Epson 3800, 11-x-17 paper in portrait orientation. *Note:* The Info Overlay in Figure 13-20 reflects this configuration.

4. **Expand the Layout Engine panel and select Picture Package.**

5. **Expand the Image Settings panel, check the Zoom to Fill check box, and leave the other options unchecked.**

   I typically crop my photos in Develop to match the desired output aspect ratio because it provides greater control over the cropped composition, but I want to demonstrate that it isn't required.

6. **Expand the Rulers, Grid & Guides panel, check all boxes, and choose Cells from the Snap drop-down menu.**

   I find the guides helpful, but feel free to leave them off if you don't.

7. **Expand the Cells panel, click the Clear Layout button, and then click the 5 x 7 button in the Add to Package section three times.**

   Lightroom positions each new cell tightly against the previous cell.

8. **Click the 2.5 x 3.5 button 24 times.**

   With each click, a new cell appears in the layout. After the first page is full, a second page is created automatically. The result is a two-page layout, as shown in Figure 13-20.

9. **Leave everything in the Overlays panel unchecked.**

10. **Expand the Print Job panel and make sure the Print To drop-down menu is set to Printer.**

11. **Uncheck Draft Mode Printing.**

12. **Uncheck Print Resolution.**

13. **Choose Standard from the Print Sharpening drop-down menu and Glossy from the Media Type drop-down menu.**

    I'm using luster paper, which is a soft gloss.

14. **Choose Other from the Profile drop-down menu.**

15. **In the Choose Profiles dialog box that appears, check the box next to the profile for the paper printer being used, and then click OK.**

    In this case, I select Pro38 PLPP, which is the profile for the premium luster paper on the 3800. Profile names are notoriously cryptic, so I suggest writing the name of the profile on the paper's box as a reminder. The paper manufacturer should indicate which is which when you download the profiles, but if not, a Google search will likely yield the correct name. The selected profile shows in the Print Job panel.

16. **Choose a rendering intent.**

17. **Click the Print Settings button and choose your paper type, quality setting, and most importantly, turn off Color Management, and then click OK.**

18. **Choose Print⇨New Template from the main menu.**

19. **Enter a descriptive name in the New Template dialog box that appears and then click Create.**

    Doing so stores all the settings that you just made in that template.

20. **Click the Print button, confirm all printer driver settings in the Print dialog box that appears, and then click Print.**

    In the beginning, I urge you to confirm your printer driver settings before committing the print to paper. Paper and ink is just too expensive to waste.

21. **Eagerly await the print at the output tray!**

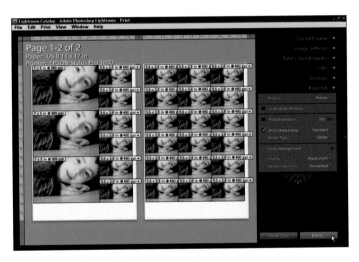

Figure 13-20: Picture Package example.

Working With Your Printer

Although Lightroom is an integral component in the process of producing a printed photo, it can't do it alone. Whether you're printing to a local printer or saving your print job as a JPG you want to send to a print service, the role of the actual printing device (and its software) is crucial to your success.

If you're printing locally, take some time to do the following:

- ✔ **Locate your printer's manual and find out how to care for your printer. They need love too.**

- ✔ **Perform a nozzle check and clean and align the print heads if needed.**

- ✔ **Check the printer manufacturer's Web site to see whether there's a newer version of your model's printer driver.**

✔ **Keep at least one spare set of ink cartridges on hand.**

✔ **Go to the paper manufacturer's Web site and download the latest ICC profiles for the paper type you're using.**

If you're planning to send your JPG layout to a print service, take some time to do the following:

✔ **Go to the print service's Web site and read its file submission requirements. Take special note of pixel dimensions, resolution, and ICC profile suggestions.**

If you can't find the information, call Customer Service and ask it to send you that info.

✔ **Look through its frequently asked question (FAQ) section. You might find an answer to a question you didn't know you had.**

✔ **If it provides a custom ICC profile for its paper/printer, then download and install it.**

✔ **Send a test file prior to relying on it for an important job.**

The great thing about a print service is that it's staffed with people who make prints for a living, and they want you to have a good experience! If you have any questions about them or the process of preparing a file for delivery, shoot them an e-mail or give them a call before you send that first test file.

The time you spend maintaining your printer, preparing for its use, and checking in with your print service can save you countless hours of frustration and headache by preventing problems before they occur.

Part V
The Part of Tens

In this part . . .

1 truly believe Lightroom is the future of digital photo processing and management, and I want you to get the most from it. Lightroom is still a young application, and I expect it to grow and mature with time. The contents of the first four parts of this book enable you to use Lightroom from import to output, but I'm grateful for this last opportunity to help you take your Lightroom experience to the next level.

In Chapter 14, I introduce you to a whole world of Lightroom resources that might prove to be just as important as anything I tell you about how Lightroom works. There's an international community of Lightroom users out there just waiting for you to join them!

I close things out in Chapter 15 by training you to become your own help desk, helping you avoid a few gray hairs in the process.

Ten Resources All Lightroom Users Need To Know

In This Chapter

▶ Adobe's Lightroom Support Center

▶ Lightroom Community Help

▶ Lightroom Journal

▶ George Jardine on Lightroom

▶ Lightroom-News.com

▶ The National Association of Photoshop Professionals

▶ Lightroom Killer Tips

▶ Lightroom Forums

▶ Lightroom Galleries

▶ Lightroomers!

Clearly, you are someone who wants to increase your understanding of how Lightroom works, and how to get the most from it. Lightroom is a dynamic and evolving product. Over the life cycle of the first version of Lightroom, six free updates were released. These updates not only kept Lightroom up-to-date with the latest cameras on the market, but each release included some bug fixes, some enhancements, and even some new features. Some updates were must-haves and some were not, but in every case, it's in your best interest to stay informed of Lightroom's evolution.

In addition to keeping Lightroom up-to-date, a growing community of Lightroom users and third-party developers offer product support, templates, tutorials, and plugins that can significantly improve your Lightroom experience. When I pulled together this top ten list, I realized these are resources I rely on and use multiple times every day, and the great thing about them is that they're all open 24/7 and most of them are free.

Making the Most of Adobe's Online Support Center

www.adobe.com/support/photoshoplightroom

Make the Adobe Photoshop Lightroom Support Center your first stop if you run into a Lightroom problem that you need help solving. (Don't forget to see if I cover it in Chapter 15 first.) If you like to get information straight from the horse's mouth, then this resource fits the bill. In addition to Adobe's fee-based support service (a last resort), the Support Center has a stunning array of free resources available. Everything from technical support to video and text-based tutorials can be found here.

Adobe has separated the content into four options:

- The first option is a search of its vast Knowledgebase, which includes the Lightroom Help file as well as tutorials and "TechNotes" (short articles providing solutions to common problems).

- TechNotes for the most common questions are found listed under Option 2.

- If the Knowledgebase doesn't provide the answer you're looking for, then head to Option 3 (my favorite) and click the Discuss It in the Forums link. Adobe hosts User-to-User forums for each of its products. These are Web sites where users can post questions to other users and get answers free. The Lightroom User to User forum is populated by a wealth of experienced users who go out of their way to answer questions and help troubleshoot problems. Here's a quick look at how you can use it to find help:

  1. If this is your first time visiting the forums, you need to create a free user account first.

  2. Check whether an answer already exists by doing a search. A quick forum search might reveal that your question has already been answered!

  3. If not, start your own topic and be sure to provide key information, such as your operating system, version of Lightroom, type of files being used, and any other relevant information to help other members help you.

  4. If you're still coming up empty, or you simply need to speak to an Adobe representative, the links to Product Support and Customer Service are also listed in Option 3. Be advised: Depending on the nature of your issue and the contact you need to make, there might be a fee involved (which is why I suggest this as a last resort).

Lightroom Community Help

`http://learn.adobe.com/wiki/display/LR`

In keeping with the community feeling that has grown up around Lightroom's development and evolution, Adobe is testing a community help system. What Adobe did was take its standard Help file (the same one bundled with Lightroom) and tie in relevant external resources to specific topics, and then put a bunch of industry experts (referred to as *Lightroom Learning Advisors*) in charge of adding new content.

Blogging, RSS, and Podcasts

So many blogs these days are pouring out so much content at all hours that it can be nearly impossible to visit all your favorites in your Web browser just to see if new content has been released. The answer to this problem is RSS, which is a TLA (three-letter acronym) for Really Simple Syndication. How it works is that each blog has an RSS *feed,* which is a means to send blog content directly to an RSS *reader* (which is an application that can display the code in an RSS feed). So, instead of visiting your favorite blog multiple times a day, you subscribe to its RSS feed and new content will be delivered directly to your RSS reader when it comes online!

To subscribe, you need a blog's RSS feed and an RSS reader. Many of the resources I provide in this chapter are blogs so that should get you started.

- ✔ **RSS feed:** To find a blog's feed, look for a link labeled something like "RSS Feed" or keep an eye out for the (near) universal orange and white RSS icon.

- ✔ **RSS reader:** After you locate the feed, you need to get it into your RSS reader. RSS readers come in many flavors (and most are free). I use Mozilla Thunderbird as my e-mail client of choice (on both Windows and Mac) and it has a built-in RSS reader (go to `http://mozilla.com/thunderbird`). This way, I have all my e-mail and feeds in one always-open application. Check your current e-mail client or Web browser; odds are you'll find they have built-in RSS reading capability as well. You might also check out the Web-based Google Reader (go to `http://reader.google.com`), or the Mac only NetNewsWire (go to `http://newsgator.com`), which are both good, free options. After you enter the feed into the RSS reader, you can just sit back and watch the content roll in!

Bloggers not satisfied with delivering text-based content to their audiences have moved into providing audio and video as well; and so the *podcast* is born. A *podcast* (think broadcast for your iPod) is either an audio or a video file that's delivered via an RSS feed and then played in a compatible player. Tutorials on using software are well-suited to this video format, and there's no shortage of quality video tutorials for Lightroom. I find iTunes (free for both Windows and Mac) to be well-suited for subscribing to and playing video and audio podcasts. You can download iTunes from `http://apple.com/itunes`.

One of the greatest aspects, in my view, is that it's a living document. It continues to expand as new content comes online. It's fully searchable, and topics are cross-linked to other related topics. If you find the Help content leaves you wanting more, then click the Learn More link on each page to see if additional educational content has been added. You can even log in (after creating a free user account) to add links to content, ask questions, and leave your comments. Because of the cross-referenced nature of the content, your search for one answer can lead you to many interrelated topics.

Lightroom Journal

http://blogs.adobe.com/lightroomjournal

Lightroom Journal is the official blog for the Lightroom team. What it lacks in quantity is made up in quality. Essential information about Lightroom issues, releases, and more can be found here. Visitors are able to leave comments and more often than not receive a timely response from someone on the team.

You can also subscribe to this blog's RSS feed to get new content delivered right to you automatically when it comes online. See the sidebar on RSS feeds and blogs for more information.

George Jardine on Lightroom and Digital Photography

www.mulita.com/blog

George Jardine is Adobe's pro photography evangelist, and he really knows Lightroom! He's been involved with Lightroom's development from the start and is creating the single best archive of Lightroom's history and development on his blog. It takes the form of a series of audio and video podcasts going back to 2006. When you have the spare time, go back to the beginning and keep listening (and watching) until you're caught up. You'll gain an appreciation for the thoughtfulness that has gone into Lightroom's development.

History is fine, but you find some real tutorial gold interspersed throughout the interviews and discussions with photographers and engineers. I sincerely believe the complete podcast archive should be included on the Lightroom installation disk, but I guess this is as close as it will get.

Lightroom-News.com

http://lightroom-news.com

When you want all Lightroom news, all the time, Lightroom-News.com, is the place to go. A staff of industry experts on an ongoing basis adds new content covering Lightroom releases, plugins, tutorials, and other relevant news. ThisWeb site is delivered in blog format, complete with a link to add to your RSS reader.

A cool aspect of the site's design is that it takes a page from Lightroom's ability to reduce and simplify the interface. You can click any of the arrows in the headers of the left and right columns to show or hide the contents. Nice!

The National Association of Photoshop Professionals

www.photoshopuser.com

I admit my bias for this one right off the bat, but even if I didn't work for them, it would be a mistake not to include the National Association of Photoshop Professionals (NAPP) as a top-ten resource. Becoming an NAPP member isn't free, but it pays for itself many times each year. Although Photoshop remains the focus of NAPP, the organization has fully embraced Lightroom. I think an NAPP membership is a great value to Lightroom users because it includes the following:

- **Subscription to *Photoshop User* magazine:** Eight issues per year devoted to Photoshop, industry news, product reviews, and a special Lightroom section.

- **NAPP member Web site:** Here you find a wealth of tutorials, news, reviews, and discounts, along with a dedicated member forum full of knowledgeable and helpful folks.

- **Awesome discounts:** I mentioned discounts already, but they're so good they deserve to be mentioned again! If you buy any photography gear or related training, you'll easily recoup your membership cost in no time at all.

- **Member-only Help Desk, Gear Desk, and Advice Desk:** If you have any question about what camera gear to buy, what monitor will fit your needs, or how to solve a Photoshop or Lightroom problem, real live people are standing by to provide you with an answer. If you send in a Lightroom question, there's a good chance I will be the one who answers!

I could go on, but even if I stop here, it's the best $99 you can invest in supporting your photography this year.

Lightroom Killer Tips

www.lightroomkillertips.com

Before opening your wallet, if you want to get a taste of the quality material NAPP offers, head to Lightroom Killer Tips and see what Matt Kloskowski (NAPP's education and curriculum developer) is sharing.

I don't know where he finds the time, but every week Matt adds new content in the form of presets, tips, and video tutorials that are driven in large part by the comments left by visitors to the site. Matt really knows his stuff and has such an accessible personality; I think you'll find this one of your favorite places to get your Lightroom fix.

As a testament to how popular Matt's presets have become, some 600+ (and growing) Flickr users created a group dedicated to showcasing photos developed with his presets. If you're a Flickr member, too, go to www.flickr.com/groups/647354@N23 and show off what you have!

Lightroom Forums

www.lightroomforums.net

When you want to rub virtual elbows with fellow Lightroom users from around the world, Lightroom Forums is the place you can hang your virtual hat. This resource is a labor of love populated by new and experienced users alike. In fact, I've never found an Internet forum more welcoming to new users than this place. So don't be shy!

Discussions range from problem-solving to Lightroom news to sharing tips and techniques. You need to set up a user account, but it's completely free (and mildly addicting). One thing the portal asks of all members is to indicate your operating system and Lightroom version when you ask for help (not to be nosy; it's critical information for diagnosing any problem). This is a frequent stop in my Web surfing, so I'll be sure to say hello when you introduce yourself.

Lightroom Galleries

`www.lightroomgalleries.com`

The Web galleries that come with Lightroom are great and quite versatile, but there comes a point in every Lightroom user's life when he or she starts wanting more. The Lightroom Galleries site was the first resource to start offering additional Lightroom Web galleries and one that still contains the most comprehensive offering. Before downloading new galleries, you can take the sample versions for a test drive, leave comments, and ask questions.

As a bonus, there's a dedicated forum for discussing the galleries as well as tutorials for diving under Lightroom's hood and creating your own custom galleries (although I don't recommend that for the inexperienced Web developer).

Lightroomers!

`http://lightroomers.com`

I'd like to say I saved the best for last, but not only am I too modest it just isn't true. What I will say is that this is my blog dedicated to helping Lightroom users. I regularly share news, tips, reviews, and tutorials. Subscribe to the RSS feed, leave me a comment, or shoot me a question. I'm always happy to help folks get the most out of their Lightroom experience.

...

15

Ten Common Lightroom Problems and Their Solutions

In This Chapter

▸ Troubleshooting Lightroom

▸ Restoring from a backup

▸ Uninstalling and reinstalling Lightroom

▸ Fixing a black or blank slideshow

▸ Figuring out why a slideshow isn't finishing

▸ Vanishing buttons and missing photos

▸ Knowing what to expect with preview display

▸ Improving performance

*E*veryone has off days, and computers do too. Even worse is when those days coincide! A time may come when you're working along, and Lightroom behaves in an unexpected manner. This isn't cause for panic (that comes much later); it just means you have a problem to solve. Luckily, a number of resources and people can help.

Between my work on the National Association of Photoshop Professionals (NAPP) Help Desk and my time spent on various Lightroom-centric forums, I've found that if one person's had a particular problem, someone else has probably already gone through the same thing — a completely unique problem is rare. Sometimes problems are a result of user error, some are a result of a conflict with other applications on your system, and some are the result of limitations in the application.

Here are some of the most-frequently reported issues I've encountered (and their solutions) to hopefully save you a few gray hairs and lost hours. I've also included some guidelines on how to be your own Help Desk!

Lightroom Troubleshooting 101

The essential goal of troubleshooting is to find the exact location where a known good input results in a bad output. At that point, you've isolated the "bad" component and can then focus on fixing, replacing, or sometimes working around it. Tracking down the problem component among your computers, monitors, printers, and software is often easier said than done! Unless plumes of smoke are pouring from the back of the computer, just knowing where to start looking can be a challenge. The following steps can help you diagnose where things went wrong and perhaps even solve the problem:

1. **Take a step back and triple-check that the settings you're using are configured correctly for the task you're trying to accomplish.**

   I often rely on what I think is happening instead of what is actually happening. Sometimes I just have other things on my mind and sometimes I just can't see what's right there in front of me. Even if you're sure you've configured Lightroom correctly, take a moment to double-check those settings one more time before moving to Step 2.

2. **Close and reopen Lightroom.**

   Sometimes turning Lightroom off and then back on is just the ticket. If Lightroom is still acting quirky, proceed to Step 3.

3. **Reboot your computer.**

   The problems you see in Lightroom may be a symptom of a larger system issue. Rebooting gives every application a chance for a do-over, and it gives you a chance to get up and get more coffee. Start Lightroom back up and attempt to repeat the behavior. If the problem persists, move to Step 4.

4. **Replace Lightroom's preference file.**

   Lightroom stores all your applicationwide preferences in a single file. If Lightroom or the computer shuts down unexpectedly (whether a system crash, an electrical storm, or someone tripped over the power cord), the preference file can become corrupted and cause all kinds of quirky problems (as most corrupted things tend to do).

   If you replace the preference file, Lightroom re-creates a brand new one and reverts to its default settings. I've seen this cure all kinds of strange problems! The basic steps are the same (with some slight differences) for both Windows and Mac OS X operating systems, so I separate the steps for Windows and Mac.

On Windows:

> **a. Choose Edit⇨Preferences, and then click through each tab and note your settings.**
>
> This is so you can reconfigure them the same way later, if needed.
>
> **b. Click the Preset tab and then click the Show Lightroom Presets Folder button.**
>
> This launches a Windows Explorer window showing the Lightroom preset folder.
>
> **c. In Lightroom, on the Preferences dialog box, click OK to close the dialog box and then close Lightroom.**
>
> **d. In Windows Explorer, double-click the Lightroom folder to open it and then double-click the Preferences folder to open it.**
>
> **e. Rename the** `Lightroom Preferences.agprefs` **file to** `Lightroom Preferencesagprefs.old`.
>
> The purpose of this is to hide the old preference file from Lightroom and trick it into creating a brand new one. You could just delete the old one, but renaming it allows you to go back to it later if the preference file isn't to blame.
>
> **f. Restart Lightroom.**

If the problem goes away (great!), the old preference file was the cause. You can go back into the Preferences folder, delete the "old" one, and then reconfigure your new preference settings (Edit⇨Preferences) the way you had them before.

If the problem continues (not so great!), the preference file wasn't the cause, so you can delete the "new" preference file Lightroom created and then change the name of the "old" preference file back to `Lightroom Preferences.agprefs`. You can then move to Step 5.

On a Mac:

> **a. Choose Lightroom⇨Preferences, click through each tab, take note of your settings, click OK, and then close Lightroom.**
>
> **b. In Finder, go to the** `[User]\Library\Preferences` **folder.**
>
> **c. Drag the** `com.adobe.Lightroom.plist` **file to the trash and then restart Lightroom.**

If the problem goes away (great!), the old preference file was the cause. You can now reconfigure your new preference settings (Edit⇨Preferences) the way you had them before.

If the problem continues (not so great!), the preference file wasn't the cause, and you can move the `com.adobe.Lightroom.plist` file from the Trash to restore your original settings. Lightroom gives you the following warning: *A Newer Item Named* `com.adobe.Lightroom.plist` *Already Exists in This Location. Do You Want to Replace It with the Older One You Are Moving?* Click Replace. You can then move to Step 5.

5. **Choose File⇨New Catalog, enter a filename, and click Save.**

   The problem may be in your catalog file, and you need to rule that out. Import some test images and attempt to re-create the problem. If everything works as it should, the problem was likely in your working catalog file. This is where those catalog backups can pay off. See the next section for more information about restoring from a backup. If the problem persists in the new catalog as well, you know your original catalog isn't the problem. Choose File⇨Open Recent and then choose your real catalog file and delete the test catalog.

   If you're still facing a problem after Step 5, seek help from one of the great resources I cover in Chapter 14. People really are standing by!

 In case you're wondering why I don't include uninstalling and reinstalling Lightroom as a troubleshooting step, it's because I've never seen that fix a problem that popped up after you've been using Lightroom for a while. I include the steps a little later in this chapter in case you ever need to know how.

Restoring a Catalog from a Backup

Storing catalog backups is just like keeping a fire extinguisher in your kitchen: You kind of forget about it and hope you never have to use it, but if you need it, you're sure glad you had it on hand! You pull a catalog backup off the bench and send it into the game for two main reasons:

- ✔ You had a disk failure and lost the working catalog.

- ✔ The working catalog became corrupted and wasn't functioning correctly (or at all).

The backup catalog created by Lightroom is an exact copy of your working catalog (at that moment in time) and has the same name and file extension of the working catalog. Here are the steps to replace a bad catalog file with a good backup copy:

1. **Close Lightroom.**

2. **Navigate to and open the Lightroom folder.**

   The default location of the Lightroom folder is in the My Pictures folder (Pictures folder on a Mac). If you're not sure where your folder is, choose Edit➪Catalog Settings (Lightroom➪Catalog Settings on a Mac), click the General tab and select the Show button to have Lightroom open the folder for you.

3. **Remove the existing catalog (.lrcat) file from the Lightroom folder.**

   If you know this is a bad catalog, you can delete it, but if you're unsure, just put it on your desktop (or some other folder) for safekeeping until you're certain it can be deleted.

4. **Place the most recent backup copy of the catalog in the Lightroom folder.**

   When you ran the backup function, you chose where catalogs are saved. The default location is within the Lightroom folder in a Backups subfolder.

5. **Restart Lightroom.**

Lightroom opens at the same point it was at when the backup was run. Any work performed in the working catalog after that backup was created is lost (which is why the frequency in which you create backups is so important). If Lightroom is functioning normally, you can safely delete the old catalog file (if you haven't already).

How to Uninstall and Reinstall Lightroom

If you notice a problem with Lightroom the first time you start it, something may have gone wrong during the installation process. Uninstalling and then reinstalling may be all that's required to correct the problem. The process is different for each operating system, so I separated the steps for each.

On Windows:

1. **Close all running applications.**

2. **Choose Start➪Control Panel➪Add or Remove Programs.**

3. **Select Lightroom from the applications list and click Remove.**

4. **Close the Add or Remove Programs dialog box.**

On a Mac:

1. **Open the Applications folder and drag the Lightroom application to the Trash.**

2. **(Optional) Open the OS X Library folder (not the Library folder under the User account), open the Receipts folder, and send the** `Adobe Photoshop Lightroom.pkg` **file to the Trash.**

This optional Step 2 should be used only if you're downgrading to an earlier version of Lightroom or you're having trouble installing a new version. Otherwise, you can skip this step.

Uninstalling Lightroom doesn't touch the catalog file, the preference file, your presets, or your photos. Uninstalling Lightroom removes only the application. When you reinstall, you find all those other files just as you left them. To reinstall on either platform, just double-click the installation file and follow the installation instructions.

The Black/Blank Slideshow Problem

This one seems to affect Windows users and is the cause of some frustration because the solution isn't readily apparent. The problem can present itself the first time you try to run a slideshow, or it can present itself after you've used the slideshow successfully for some time. What happens is that you trigger a slideshow to play, and all you see is a black screen. You may see the slides advance in the Filmstrip if you're playing the slideshow in the content area, but the content area is black and stays that way.

The solution in all the cases I've dealt with is to update your video card driver. Go to the Web site of your video card manufacturer and download the latest video card driver for your specific card. The file you download is most likely just like an application you install — double-click it and follow the prompts. Restart your system after the installation is complete. Then recalibrate your monitor, launch Lightroom, and attempt another slideshow.

My Slideshow Stops after a Few Photos and Jumps Back to the Beginning

Another common slideshow-related issue is a slideshow that doesn't play to the end. Instead, the slideshow goes some number of photos in, and then automatically jumps to the beginning and starts over. Subsequent attempts may get a little farther into the show, but then the slideshow still jumps back to the beginning before getting to the end.

Before you get to the end of your rope

1. **Press the G key and jump to Grid view.**

2. **Press Ctrl+A (⌘+A on a Mac) to select all the photos in that grouping.**

3. **Choose Library⇨Previews⇨Render Standard-Sized Previews.**

4. **Wait for the progress meter to complete.**

5. **Switch to the Slideshow module and play the slideshow.**

The most likely cause for this behavior is that Lightroom hasn't finished rendering the standard-sized previews for that group of photos, so your slideshow displays all the images it has previews for and then jumps back to the start. After all the previews are rendered, the slideshow plays all the way through.

The Minimize, Maximize, and Close Buttons Have Vanished

Sometimes as a new user, you enable features without realizing you have and then you're stymied trying to figure out how to get back to the way things were before. I'm the first to admit it's happened to me, and judging by the number of times I see this issue raised, I know I'm in good company.

Lightroom has three screen modes:

- ✔ **Standard Screen Mode**
- ✔ **Full Screen with Menu**
- ✔ **Full Screen**

You can move through each screen mode by pressing F. Sometimes people inadvertently hit the F key and then find themselves in Full Screen mode and don't know how to get out! You can either continue pressing F to cycle back to Standard Screen Mode or press Ctrl+Alt+F (⌘+Option+F on a Mac) to jump right to Standard Screen Mode.

Lightroom Shows Photos Are Missing, but I Know They're There

The person who coined the phrase *no good deed goes unpunished* may have done so after having just reorganized her photo library with her file browser of choice (Windows Explorer, Adobe Bridge, or Finder on a Mac) only to open

Lightroom and find that all the folders and the thumbnails are all sporting question mark icons.

I don't think a day goes by where someone somewhere doesn't run smack into his own good intentions in this manner. These stories all seem to start the same way . . . "I finally decided to organize all my photos" or "I needed to move all my photos to a new drive," and they all end with a new problem to solve.

The nature of the problem is that if you move folders and photos outside Lightroom, Lightroom doesn't know where to find them. All Lightroom knows is what's in its database. If the path in its database doesn't lead to a photo, Lightroom just considers the photo missing until you reconnect it to the photo's new location. The reconnection process isn't difficult but does require that you know where the file or folder is located. Here are the steps to reconnect a folder that's been moved:

1. **Right-click (Control+click on a Mac) the folder showing a question mark.**

2. **Choose Find Missing Folder from the contextual menu.**

3. **Navigate to the actual location of that folder, select it, and click OK (Choose on a Mac).**

   Lightroom then reconnects to that folder and all its contents (including any subfolders).

If only a few files show question marks, which indicates they're missing, you can reconnect them with a similar process:

1. **Click the question mark icon.**

2. **Click the Locate button in the Confirm dialog box.**

3. **Navigate to the actual location of that photo, select it, and click Select.**

Another reason files and folders appear to be missing is that a network or external drive is disconnected. In the case of disconnected media, the solution is to reconnect the drive, and after your computer recognizes the drive, Lightroom finds it, too.

Previews Are Gray or Show a Color Cast

After import, Lightroom goes through the process of rendering preview files of all your imported images. When everything is functioning correctly, you may not notice anything is happening or you may notice that the embedded camera-generated preview file is being replaced by the Lightroom-rendered preview.

When things aren't functioning correctly, you notice that either the previews aren't rendering at all (they just appear as gray or black rectangles) or all the previews have a strange color cast (typically magenta). I've only seen this problem occur on Windows, and both issues are caused by a bad monitor profile.

If you're using a hardware-calibration device, the first thing to do is recalibrate your monitor. This results in a new profile being created and should solve the problem. If you're not using a hardware-calibration device, this might be a sign that it's time to invest in one. In the interim, you can try removing the current default profile to see if that makes a difference. The process is slightly different between Windows XP and Vista.

On Windows XP:

1. **Close Lightroom.**

2. **Right-click an empty area of your desktop and choose Properties.**

   The Display Properties dialog box appears.

3. **In the Display Properties dialog box, choose the Settings tab, and click the Advanced button.**

   This opens the dialog box for controlling the advanced display properties.

4. **Choose the Color Management tab, select the profile in the Color Profiles Currently Associated with This Device field, and click the Remove button.**

   This removes it only from being associated with the monitor and doesn't delete the file. Repeat this step if more than one profile is listed.

5. **Click OK to close the advanced display properties dialog box and then click OK again to close the Display Properties dialog box.**

6. **Relaunch Lightroom.**

On Vista:

1. **Close Lightroom.**

2. **Choose Start⇨Control Panel⇨Color Management.**

3. **Select the default profile listed in the Color Profiles Currently Associated with This Device field and click the Remove button.**

4. **Click OK and then relaunch Lightroom.**

Remember that removing the current default profile is a temporary solution. Ideally, calibrate and profile your monitor with a hardware device.

Previews Change After Import

This is an often-asked question that stems from a misunderstanding more than a problem. When you shoot in raw mode, your camera saves that raw data to your memory card without processing it. However, your camera embeds a JPG preview in each raw file — the same JPG preview that you see on the back of your LCD screen. However, Lightroom has to render its previews for every raw file. The result is that while you watch the imported files appear on-screen, you first see the JPG preview you saw on the back of the camera, and then it's replaced by Lightroom's version of the default processing of that raw file. It's very likely that the two versions won't match, and the new Lightroom user's first thought is, "Why is Lightroom destroying my raw files!?"

When the camera renders its JPG preview, it relies on the in-camera settings you applied for color mode, saturation, sharpness, and so on. Your camera may even have some special picture styles or black-and-white mode. Lightroom doesn't have access to any of those in-camera settings. All Lightroom has is the raw capture data and its default rendering instructions for each camera model it supports, which is kind of a recipe for disappointment if you don't know what to expect.

To get around this situation, you can apply a develop preset during import, and Lightroom uses that preset setting to inform its default rendering. Some users shoot in Raw+JPG mode and then import both as individual files. With both versions in Lightroom, they attempt to match the rendering of the JPG and then save those settings as a new Develop preset to be applied at import to raw files. Most of the time, just knowing what to expect can make all the difference. You can find more about the Import process in Chapter 4.

Lightroom Seems Sluggish

Over time, you may notice that Lightroom isn't as snappy as it used to be (hey, who is?). A decrease in speed as your catalog grows larger and larger is normal, but you can do a few things for your disk and for Lightroom's catalog to keep them both running as smoothly as possible.

Here are some things you can do for your hard disk:

✔ **Maximize your free space.** It's an inescapable fact that hard drives fill up fast. Keep an eye on the amount of free space left on your startup drive and don't let it drop below 20 percent free. Some applications require free space to function correctly. You don't want your applications fighting each other over space. Uninstall unused applications, delete unused files, empty your recycle bin (Trash on a Mac), or move important files off to a different internal or external drive.

✏ **Perform basic disk maintenance.** Hard drives get a lot of use and can often benefit from a little tender loving care. On Windows, you can run the Error-checking utility, and after that's complete, run the Defragmentation utility. On Mac, periodically repair permissions with the Disk utility. Mac users typically don't benefit from running a Defragmentation utility because the operating system does a better job of managing the disk during normal operation.

After you do your housekeeping on the startup disk, you can turn your attention to Lightroom:

✏ **Render standard-sized previews.** Lightroom runs on previews. When needed, Lightroom renders previews in the background while you're working. You can take control of this process by setting Initial Previews on the Import dialog to Standard, which tells Lightroom to start rendering standard-sized previews as soon as the import process is complete. You can also force the rendering process from within the Library module by selecting all photos and choosing Library⇨Previews⇨Render Standard-Sized Previews menu.

✏ **Render 1:1 previews.** If you view images at 1:1 (meaning 100 percent or actual size view) in the Library module, Lightroom needs to render a 1:1 preview. If you're trying to skip quickly between photos at 1:1, notice the time it takes Lightroom to render each 1:1 preview while you work. After the preview is rendered, switching between photos is much faster. Just like with standard-sized previews, you can set Initial Previews on the Import dialog to 1:1, which instructs Lightroom to begin rendering when the import is complete, or you can force the rendering of 1:1 previews by selecting all photos and choosing Library⇨Previews⇨Render 1:1 Previews menu.

✏ **Turn off Automatically Write Changes into XMP.** This feature has been greatly improved since Lightroom's initial release, but this background process could be causing the performance lag you're experiencing. Choose File⇨Catalog Settings, and then click the Metadata tab. Deselect the Auto Write setting and then click OK. Run Lightroom normally and see whether you notice any change in performance. You can still manually write to XMP by selecting files and pressing Ctrl+S (⌘+S on a Mac). Check out Chapter 2 for more about what this setting offers.

✏ **Optimize the catalog.** If your catalog has gotten large and could use a little housekeeping, choose File⇨Catalog Settings and click the General tab. Click the Relaunch and Optimize button. Lightroom closes, and the catalog file is reorganized internally to operate more efficiently. This also removes any unused space from inside the catalog file, which can reduce its file size. The result is a smaller and more-efficient catalog, although gains are only likely to be noticed by very large catalogs.

I hope you see some gains after following these suggestions. If Lightroom is otherwise functioning normally and your system is getting a little long in the tooth, you may want to consider a hardware upgrade in your future.

Index